Rubbing Shoulders

in Yemen

Peter Twele

.

Many names of individuals mentioned in this book have been changed.

ISBN-13: 978-1480145016
ISBN-10: 1480145017

Dedication

I dedicate this book to the average Yemeni who really wants nothing more than to live a meaningful life in an environment of peace ... and I pray that true peace will soon come your way.

Contents

Acknowledgments

I want to thank the many friends (Yemeni, Egyptian, Somali, Sudanese, Dutch, American, etc) who hosted and helped me during my time spent in Yemen ... even though the majority of them will most likely never get the chance to read this. And a special thanks to Sian who helped me extensively with the grueling research, and who was therefore part of many of my adventurous trips.

Thanks to the American Institute for Yemeni Studies and the Yemeni Centre for Research and Studies, both of which helped me get the necessary permission to carry out my research, without which none of what I write in this book would have happened.

A big thank you to my wife, Hazel, for dedicating many many hours to reading through drafts of what I wrote, and for giving invaluable feedback and direction.

I also want to thank my three children, Anita, Heather and Andrew, who are the ones who initially encouraged me to start the writing process, and who have also given me very useful feedback and encouragement along the way.

Reasons for Writing

I've traveled extensively throughout the Middle East ... at times studying, at times working, and sometimes carrying out research. Even before I first set foot in Jordan in 1984, I had been fascinated with the Middle East in general, and with the Arabic language in particular. And then, not long after getting married in 1988, I took my wife there (*not* with my father-in-law's approval ... but Hazel did come willingly). Eventually our three children were born in Amman, the capital of Jordan (they did *not* have a choice in the matter). And even when we returned to live in Canada in 1998 (to which my son would say a hearty *hurray*, since otherwise he would never have had the chance to be an ice hockey playing Canadian), much of my focus and part of my heart remained in the Middle East ... but since 1998 I've been limited to only periodic trips rather than residing there.

I've been to Yemen a number of times over the past 25 years, but in this book I'll just be focusing on my most memorable time spent in that rustic country ... namely, a period of four months in 1987 doing sociolinguistic[1] research.

For those of you who may not know the lay of the land, Yemen (officially known as the *Republic of Yemen* since 1990) is a country located in the southern half of the Arabian Peninsula. It's bordered by Saudi Arabia to the north, the Arabian Sea to the south, the Red Sea to the west, and Oman to the east.

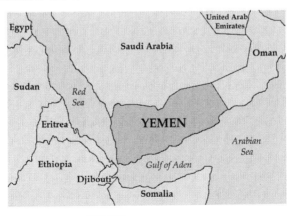

---

[1] Sociolinguistics has to do with the study of the effect of society on the way language is used.

Back in 1987, Yemen was still divided into North Yemen (known as the *Yemen Arab Republic*) and South Yemen (known as the *People's Democratic Republic of Yemen*). I carried out my research within the borders of North Yemen.

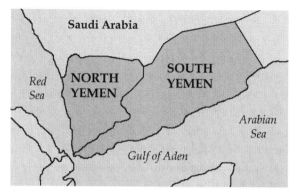

As you may have noticed in the second map, showing the divided Yemen of 1987, South Yemen actually reached further north than North Yemen ... and it would have been geographically more accurate to refer to North Yemen as *West Yemen* and to refer to South Yemen as *East Yemen*, don't you agree? Well there's some history I won't take the time to get into, but I'll just point out that the capital of North Yemen, Sana'a, was located directly north of the capital of South Yemen, Aden, and that's enough about that topic.

I wrote above that my time in North Yemen was *memorable*. But what I really should have said was my time spent there was *unforgettable* ... often finding myself in the midst of gun wielding Yemenis out in some of the remotest parts of the country ... areas that were not under government control at the time ... and in fact, still aren't to this day. I often traveled all alone, and it wouldn't have taken much for me to disappear without a trace.

And yet, as I think back on those experiences, I have plenty of good memories. It wasn't always easy ... in fact, it was *never* easy ... most often traveling as one of many passengers crammed into a 4-wheel drive vehicle, all of us shaking, sliding and bouncing around together as we maneuvered along unpaved roads with a seemingly infinite number of potholes and bumps. In some of the areas where I traveled, the roads were usually no more than one lane wide ... actually, at times not much wider than the vehicle itself, cut out of the sides of towering mountains ... some of which reach over 3,000 meters above sea level! One wrong move would have sent the vehicle (and more problematically, all its passengers ... none of whom wore seatbelts ... not that the seatbelts would have made any difference) plunging thousands of meters down the side of some mountain with not the slightest chance of survival.

Sometimes, after the seasonal rains, the roads were washed out. That meant we were forced to cross over raging rivers ... rivers which had formed overnight. This would create detours and delays that at times forced the drivers to carry on driving us to our destination in total darkness ... and I mean it was pitch black, with the headlights barely even making a dent in the all encompassing gloom.

Now I really want to point out that, in general, Yemenis are a great bunch of people. I want to emphasize that to balance out all the bad publicity the media constantly feeds us about Yemen. We are very rarely, if ever, told anything positive about the country. Personally, I was always treated well by the Yemenis I interacted with ... and believe me, I had numerous opportunities to rub shoulders with them ... at times quite literally in those 4-wheelers. Most of them were patient, and many of them put up with my endless questions, and showed me wonderful hospitality.

Now not everyone opened up to me by any means, but there were always those who did ... and I really can't blame those who didn't. I mean, it was rather strange for them to encounter this person from Canada (wherever that was) who unexpectedly showed up in their villages ... often in small remote villages where no Westerner had ever set foot before. I interrupted their schedules, and they usually didn't appear to mind. Many of them actually seemed to enjoy my company, even if it was often nothing more than mere curiosity on their part ... and maybe it was also a means of providing them with a new form of entertainment, or an opportunity to meet a *real* Westerner.

Of course, all those adventures I'm going to relate to you took place before I got married. I'm not so sure I would have done any of it had I already been married and had kids.

As my three kids were growing up, from time to time I would tell them stories about some of the adventures I had back in *the old days* when I was single and doing my research in North Yemen. Well, a few years ago our whole family was watching the hilarious film *Secondhand Lions* for the first time (I've watched it many times since) which relates the fictitious adventures of two elderly men who, in their younger days, had lived adventure-packed lives in North Africa. After watching the film, I found myself once again reminiscing and relating to my kids, who were at the time 15, 13 and 10 years old, some of my *real* adventures I had had in North Yemen. They were fascinated at some of the things I told them ... things I myself would find hard to believe if I hadn't actually experienced them first hand, and if I hadn't taken copious notes and numerous photos at the time (some of which I include in this book).

My kids encouraged me to write down those experiences of my encounters with Yemenis. And so that's what I'm doing in this book ... I'm writing down my experiences for my kids, and for future generations. And you are more than welcome to read about those experiences too.

1

The Wild Wild North

I felt worn out. I hadn't slept well during the night. I usually didn't sleep all that well when traveling and staying in unfamiliar places. The heavy breathing and periodic snoring of the two bodies slumbering on the nearby mattresses didn't exactly help. And neither did the well-worn mattress which just barely kept me separated from the concrete floor.

As the morning light started to penetrate through the gap conveniently provided at the bottom of the door, I decided it was time to get up. I tried to move about quietly so as not to disturb my hosts. I slipped on my shoes (I had slept in my clothes), grabbed my notebook and pen, and snuck out the door. The creaking hinges didn't seem to bother them.

"It's time to jot down a few notes," I mumbled to myself as I sat down just outside the building on a concrete step.

But my gaze was automatically drawn to the heart of the tiny village, namely, to the downtown core which was situated a short distance below me in elevation, an area covering the equivalent of one short city block.

It was lying in complete silence at this hour of the day ... a silence which was only broken from time to time by a couple of distant roosters, and by the braying of a hungry donkey, located somewhere closer by but also out of sight.

I forced my eyes to return to my notebook. Only after completing the task of jotting down my observations and thoughts from the previous day, did I allow myself the luxury of some more down time, taking in the spectacular view of the endless rugged mountains ... mountains as far as the eye could see in every direction.

"Sabaah el-kheir Butros," (translated, *Good morning Butros*) Hassan greeted me from behind in his very distinct Cairene[2] accent, interrupting that tranquil moment. "How did you sleep?"

"Good morning Hassan. I slept very well thank you," I lied.

"Al hamdu lilah" (meaning, *Praise be to God*), he replied.

I repeated a "Praise be to God" automatically, since it was the appropriate response.

Ibrahim was right behind him, and the two of us went through a slight variation of the greeting routine as well.

I had been in that remote mountainous region of North Yemen, known as *Munabbih*, for three days. Did I say *remote*? I probably should have said *pretty near inaccessible*! I was staying in the most central village of Munabbih known as *Suq al-Munabbih* (translated, *the market of Munabbih*). My first night was spent sleeping in a prison. Then the next two nights I was offered accommodation in the local elementary school, sharing the sleeping quarters (in one of the school's classrooms) with my two hosts, Hassan and Ibrahim, Egyptians who worked in the village as teachers.

"Are you sure you need to leave today?" inquired Hassan with a look of sadness on his face.

"Yes," I answered, "I need to get back to Sa'da."

"Well if you really have to leave, then today should be a good day to catch a ride," said Ibrahim.

"Why's that?" I asked.

"Because today is the market day, and people will come from all over to buy and sell goods," he clarified.

That was news to me ... *good* news in fact. He went on to explain that even though the village was named *the market of Munabbih*, the full-blown *market* only happened one day a week. So today, being the actual market day, would be the best day to depart because more vehicles than usual would be making their way in and out of the village, providing me

---

[2] The variety of Arabic spoken in Cairo, Egypt.

with more possibilities for catching a ride in one of the departing trucks. And I was ready to move on ... I was definitely and undeniably exhausted.

In case you're wondering, I should clarify that no regular bus or taxi system operated in those mountainous areas. Well, maybe that's not quite true, because men with privately owned 4-wheel drives did make runs in and out of those regions, carrying goods and passengers ... but I'm not so sure I'd refer to them as being a *regular* form of transportation, but rather more accurately *irregular* according to my observation. It kind of all seemed to depend on the whim of the driver ... like, "Hey, I think I'll make a trip to Sa'da today." Then word would get around, and once he had gathered enough passengers to make the trip profitable, he'd start driving. The reason 4-wheelers were needed was because paved roads were non-existent in that region.

So, if you were looking for a ride, like I was, you'd need to make your desire to travel known. Then when a 4-wheel drive was available and ready to go, you'd get a seat.

From what I had observed thus far, the most common and most reliable 4-wheel drive vehicles in the country were the Toyota Landcruisers. Toyota had definitely done some very good business within North Yemen.

Well, even though it would be a good day to catch a ride, I was quite sure any departure on market day wasn't going to happen during the early morning hours, since that was when most people would be arriving to do their buying and selling. And so, as fatigued as I was, I still had a portion of the day ahead of me before I could catch a ride.

After a rather leisurely breakfast provided by my hosts, I asked, "Hassan, do you mind if I leave my backpack here at the school while I have a look through the market?"

"No problem, Butros. Enjoy yourself," was his reply.

I walked slowly through the village, which by then had vendors lining both sides of the main street ... a wide dirt road littered with numerous flattened plastic water bottles, along with various other debris.

It could be compared to one of our North American flea markets. All the usual products were easy to find on market day ... things like blankets, clothes, baskets, a variety of fresh, dried or canned foods, curved knives, etc.

As I was meandering along the road, having an unhurried look around, out of the corner of my eye, I noticed someone selling their goods *behind* one of the buildings. It wasn't a huge market, and I had plenty of time on my hands, and I didn't want to miss anything, and so, out of curiosity, I wandered over to have a quick look.

Well, as I rounded the corner, my adrenalin suddenly kicked in. Trying not to show my surprise, or make my staring too obvious, I observed before me a blanket neatly spread out on the ground. Laid out in a nice display on the blanket were a variety of rifles, hand guns and ammunition ... including a number of Kalashnikovs (AK-47s ... assault rifles)! This was obviously some of the *etcetera* that was being sold in the market.

When the seller caught sight of me, he stared in disbelief. "What's he doing here?" I heard him ask another man who was standing nearby having a look at the vendor's goods.

"I've seen the foreigner wandering around the market," the man replied. And they said a couple of other things back and forth that I couldn't understand.

The seller's reaction really wasn't all that different from the reactions I had observed over and over again ever since the very first moment I had arrived in the village. As far as I knew, no other non-Yemeni had ever set foot in that region ... the only exception being the few Egyptian elementary school teachers (like Hassan and Ibrahim) who were assigned to these out-of-the-way parts of the country by the North Yemen Ministry of Education.

I sure wish I could have taken a photo of the firearms exhibit, but I usually wasn't brave enough to ask to take photos of such sensitive things ... and I certainly wasn't going to sneak a photo, since I didn't know what the reaction would be if I was caught doing so. On second thought, I think I do know what the vendor's reaction would have been. He definitely wouldn't have liked it since he was selling contraband. I knew for a fact that that region of the country was not under the government's control, and easy access to sophisticated weapons was one of the main reasons why.

Well, it just so happened that, at a later date, a Munabbih resident actually asked me to take a photo of him while he posed for me holding his Kalashnikov. So how could I refuse.

You know, I really shouldn't have been surprised to see weapons being sold in that market. I mean, nearly every man I saw in those remote parts carried a rifle of some sort ... myself and the Egyptians (all of us non-Yemenis) being the exceptions. My experience in the market that day merely demonstrated for me how easy it was to acquire one. And no, I was not tempted to ask how much they cost.

After my very quick look (more like a glance) at the weapons, I casually moved back to the main street, leaving the vendor and his current customers to wonder about who I was and why I was there. I hadn't taken the time to interact with any of them.

I nonchalantly headed toward the local supermarket, which was nothing more than a room about three meters by three meters filled with various items stacked high on its shelves. I asked the store merchant for a bottle of *Canada* ... it was actually *Canada Dry* cola,[3] but everyone throughout North Yemen called it *Canada* for short. Sometimes it was a little confusing when I told Yemenis I was from Canada ... a country that was not well known, especially not in such remote parts of Yemen.

The man pulled a bottle of *Canada* out of the fridge and handed it to me. Now, even though the bottle came out of a fridge, the drink was cool, not cold ... and that's because the generator that provided electricity only came on for a few hours each evening ... one generator

---

[3] In the country of Canada today people equate *Canada Dry* with *Gingerale*, but Canada Dry used to make a variety of drinks, including a cola, and that's what was most popular in Yemen. Yemenis would often refer to it as "Canada black".

for the entire village to bring light and operate the few existing appliances. Not enough to keep things like drinks consistently cold.

Okay, back to my departure from Suq al-Munabbih. Having finished my *Canada*, it was time to get serious about finding a ride. Actually, I had already let a few people know I needed a ride, but to be on the safe side, decided I better get to a spot alongside the one and only road heading east towards the city of Sa'da, my destination.

So I returned to the school to pick up my possessions, and then spent an appropriate amount of time thanking my new Egyptian friends over and over again for their helpfulness and hospitality, and wishing them all the best and every success in their work and future. Then I shouldered my small backpack and headed the very short distance down the hill to start my more serious waiting and asking for a ride to Sa'da, hoping I would soon be on my way.

So there I was, hanging around just below the school, waiting and observing the goings on. The market was still buzzing with activity ... someone haggling over the price of a blanket, a couple of men heading into a restaurant to have something to eat, men in small huddles chatting away about who knows what. From time to time I could see women tagging along behind their husbands.

Traffic was sparse, and what 4-wheelers did pass my way were either going just a short distance or were already full up, and so weren't able to take on another passenger. And believe me when I tell you that the drivers weren't afraid to pack those vehicles as full as possible ... and so, when I say a vehicle was full, it was *full*.

The general hum of voices was everywhere, when suddenly, "What was that?" I asked myself. A strange and, yet somehow, not unfamiliar sound caught my attention. I couldn't quite figure out what it was. But a few seconds later I started to comprehend the potential danger that was looming just a few meters (far too few meters!) from where I was standing.

First it was only a couple of *clicks*. Those clicks were followed by a few more clicks. The chatter suddenly died down. Then dozens of clicks echoed throughout the village ... clicks made by rifles, all getting ready to discharge if the need arose ... a very eerie unsettling sound, standing out loud and clear in the otherwise silence that had overtaken the entire village.

Yes, silence ruled ... except for the sound of the argument ... the argument which was responsible for this whole incident, and which was still going on full force a little ways up the hill, just off to the right of the school.

All eyes were fixed on that argument ... two men having it out with words, with a few other men cautiously yet forcefully coming between them. Still others held each of the aggressors back, which indicated to me that a physical fight had already started or had almost started ... I really didn't know which was the case.

Rifles all over the village were cocked and raised ... every man armed and prepared for battle. It was tense (talk about an understatement!).

I had no idea who was who ... or who would be shooting at who. I felt like I was watching an action movie, waiting for the inevitable to happen. But wait a minute, something was wrong ... very very wrong! Why was I in this crazy scene? And I was quite sure, unlike in the movies, that not one of those rifles had blanks in them. Someone could really get hurt ... or worse yet, killed! And didn't anyone even care that an innocent foreign bystander was in their midst who could end up getting seriously injured?

Nope, nobody was staring at the foreigner any more ... something new was drawing everyone's attention.

This was so unexpected. And at that moment all I knew was I had to be prepared to take cover as soon as I heard the first shot go off ... or maybe better yet, *before* the first shot went off. And I was fully expecting a shot (most likely more than one shot) would be going off very soon.

And yet I still hesitated, not wanting to overreact ... not wanting to look like a total fool, giving the whole village something new to laugh at and talk about. Okay, so I'd rather be shot than look like a fool?!

There just so happened to be a metal water tank situated only a couple of steps to my left. I was getting prepared to jump for cover behind it. I slowly moved over the couple of steps so I could casually lean against it. But my eyes remained focused on every movement close to the on-going argument ... hands poised near knives, fingers eagerly paused on triggers.

To be continued in chapter 17, entitled *The argument*. But please don't do like I know my oldest daughter will do and turn to chapter 17 just yet!

2

City of Wonders

I arrived in Sana'a, the capital of North Yemen, on the 21st of January 1987. It was a Wednesday ... and I'm quite sure it was late in the evening ... or maybe it was very early in the morning. Anyway, as I recall, most flights usually arrived or departed either just before or not too long after midnight.

I made my way to *The American Institute for Yemeni Studies* (AIYS[4]) and rang the bell at the gate. Jeff, the resident director, came out to open the small metal door (made for people) which was set inside a large metal gate (made for vehicles) and let me in to the courtyard which, along with the AIYS building, was completely surrounded by a high wall.

The presence of a wall was pretty typical for houses in Sana'a. Not only did many houses have a high wall, but if you looked up, then you'd notice either barbed wire running along the top of the wall, or broken glass protruding out of a layer of concrete ... their way of preventing any unwanted visitors from attempting to scale the wall and invade their privacy.

AIYS occupied a large traditional house that contained the resident director's office and residence, a library consisting of scholarly works about Yemen (I'm assuming at a later date my thesis, which was based on my research, started gracing one of the shelves as well), a meeting room, and a hostel for resident researchers like me.

Jeff showed me to my room, which I had reserved prior to my arrival. As I entered the room, I thought, "I've made it." I was in North Yemen and ready for action.

I already had two and a half years of experience living and traveling around the Middle East prior to my arrival in Yemen. Most of that time was spent in Jordan. But I had also been to Palestine, Syria, Kuwait,

---

[4] AIYS was established in 1978 to facilitate, coordinate, and encourage academic research dealing with Yemen in all disciplines through its offices in the U.S. and in Yemen. (http://www.caorc.org/centers/aiys.htm).
I explain my connection to AIYS in Appendix 3.

Bahrain, the United Arab Emirates, and Egypt, and so I figured I was prepared for some differences when I arrived in North Yemen. I mean, how different could North Yemen be?

Well, let me tell you, when I arrived in North Yemen, it was far more *unique* than I had expected. I was captivated by it from the very first time I set foot on its soil during my exploratory trip six months earlier ... and even more so once I settled there for this longer stretch of time to do research. And, of course, my North Yemen experience started in the capital, Sana'a.

Sana'a is one of the oldest continually inhabited cities in the world. According to the UNESCO World Heritage site,[5] Sana'a has been inhabited for more than 2,500 years. But according to a popular legend, Sana'a was actually founded by Shem, one of Noah's three sons (you can read the story of Noah in the Torah [the Old Testament], in Genesis chapters 6-10), and so it was common to hear it referred to as *the city of Shem*. Who knows. Anyway, it's name today, Sana'a, means *well-fortified*.

Sana'a is situated on the narrowest point of a major mountain plateau, about 2,200 meters above sea level ... located at the intersection of two major ancient trade routes, one of which linked the historic city of Marib[6] in the east to the Red Sea in the west. So Sana'a has always been a natural commercial center.

Talk about a pleasant place to live. In general, there are no extreme weather conditions in Sana'a to speak of, so there's really no need for central heating in the winter or air conditioning in the summer ... just a sweater or light jacket would suffice during the cooler rainy season.

Now the reference to year round pleasant weather has to do with Sana'a. As for other parts of the country, some regions can get extremely hot, like the harsh dry desert in the east, or the sweltering humid west coast ... I experienced both firsthand.

I really never tired of wandering along the streets of Sana'a. What really drew my attention right from the start was the unique way the buildings were constructed ... and I don't say that just because in my younger years I had hoped to become an architect. From one end of this sprawling city to the other I found the buildings, old and new alike,

---

[5] http://whc.unesco.org/en/list/385

[6] Marib is an ancient city located about 120 kilometers east of Sana'a. Modern Marib is located about 3.5 km north of the ancient site.

fascinating ... the bricks and stones artistically placed so as to create some very pleasant patterns. I think it's time for a photo ...

or two ...

Notice the small half-circular windows in the above photos, which are set above every rectangular window. It's a distinctive style that, in my opinion, gives a very special effect, so even the oldest and most decrepit looking buildings still have a certain appeal to them.

What you can't make out in those two photos (but is clear in the following photo) is the fact that each of those little half-round windows is stained glass.

From the inside, the multi-colored glass, enhanced by the natural daylight, brightens up any room. And in the evening, as the sun starts to set and the darkness slowly envelops the city, the man-made lights carry those colors out to the street for all passers-by to enjoy ... turning the city into an enormous rainbow.

One of my favorite places to hang out in Sana'a (not to imply that I had a lot of time to hang out there) was the Old City located in the midst of the expansive metropolis ... an attraction well worth seeing ... having been declared a World Heritage Site by the United Nations in 1986, the same year I visited Yemen for the first time.

"Please take me to the gate of Yemen," I instructed the taxi driver as I attempted to get comfortable in the well-worn passenger seat of his well-worn car.

And off we went, winding through some of the narrow streets of the city, one of which eventually emptied out onto Az Zubayri Street, a main road running in an east-west direction ... we were heading east. Suddenly I noticed a massive clay wall off to my left. We followed that wall until we reached our destination, *the gate of Yemen*, the main gate of the old city ... in Arabic, *Baab al-Yemen*.

"There's Baab al-Yemen," the driver informed me, stating the obvious, as we drew near.

"Thank you, I'll get out here," I instructed him.

He pulled the cab over to the side of the street.

Then it was time to start the negotiation process with the driver. Taxis in Sana'a did not have meters. I must confess I found that a little frustrating (and stressful) because I was used to riding taxis in Amman, Jordan which did (usually) have meters. It was nice to know that you paid only what you should have paid at the end of the ride.

But on the other hand, in Sana'a there actually were understood fares, and typically the passenger merely handed the driver the correct amount when the ride ended. But being new to the city, and being a foreigner, and having ridden in taxis where the driver has charged me an inflated rate for the *rich foreigner*, I tended to be a bit nervous when it came time to pay because I didn't like confrontation, but I also didn't like being taken advantage of.

On this occasion I wasn't really sure how much it should be, and so I had to ask "How much?"

I was pleasantly surprised when the driver asked for what I considered to be a reasonable amount ... most likely the going rate. That encouraged me to give him a generous tip.

"Thank you very much!" the driver said after noticing the amount I had placed in his hand.

"God be with you," I replied as I moved away from the cab just as two new passengers quickly hopped in.

I was standing on the opposite side of the street from Baab al-Yemen, which gave me a great view of the oft talked about gate. I was impressed by the spectacular site before me ... and my camera naturally slipped into my hand to snap a quick photo.

It was then time to cross (or more realistically stated, *attempt to cross*) the street to reach the towering gate, which required some adept maneuvering through the never-ending flow of traffic. I had plenty of experience doing the same on a regular basis in Jordan where the drivers always had the right of way, much to the frustration of the huge number of pedestrians who were constantly overflowing onto the busy streets.

With that accomplished, I next took on weaving in and out between the parked cars and endless human traffic on the other side of the street.

Vendors were out in full force at that time of day, some squatting with a few goods laid out before them, while others paced back and forth shouting out to the crowds, hoping for a sale. One man was holding an array of prayer beads, another, half a dozen suit jackets on hangers.

A man selling a curved dagger, gravitated towards me, knowing that foreigners were always on the lookout for such souvenirs, and were more likely to pay the over-inflated price he would be asking.

"Please meester, you like? You buy?" he almost pleaded in his broken English.

"No thank you," I said in Arabic as I walked past him.

But the fact that I even took notice of him and had reacted, encouraged him to try all the harder. "Sir, a good price for you," he said, again using English.

He followed in my footsteps and then quickly came up beside me and eventually got right in front of me with his knife held high for me to see (held up in a non-threatening way I should point out), forcing me to either stop and deal with him or to try and maneuver around him.

Usually it's better to do as the locals do and walk right past the vendors without making any indication that you even noticed them. My problem was that I was indeed interested in looking at such things. But I also knew it would be better to wait and have a look in the market area where there'd be a much larger selection, and most likely a much better price.

After my fourth "no thank you," he realized he wasn't going to change my mind, so he gave up on me and started calling out (reverting back to Arabic) "knife for sale" to no one in particular in the passing crowds.

But I wasn't free yet, because the vendor was replaced by someone else who started tailing me ... a small beggar girl. Beggars abounded in Sana'a ... and throughout the country for that matter. I always made sure some small change was in my pocket for just such occasions. How could I resist a cute little girl looking up at me with her big brown eyes? My hand went into my pocket, while the little girl kept reciting what seemed to be set phrases used by all beggars, said in her whining pitiful voice.

"God bless you," I said as I handed her the equivalence of a few pennies.

"May God repay you," she said as her small form quickly disappeared into the crowd long before her voice faded, as she continued with her recitation which she hoped would bring her more good fortune. I then refocused on my goal, and started heading towards the open gate where the endless crowds were funneling in and out of the old city.

The Gate of Yemen was more than a thousand years old. What remained of the ancient clay walls which once surrounded the old city, stood 9–14 meters high. As I said above, the name *Sana'a* means *well-fortified,* and seeing that gate and the wall made me realize it was definitely an appropriate name.

I managed to make it through the gate, even though I felt like I was often going against the flow, and then suddenly found myself standing in a large open courtyard with yet more vendors to try and avoid, and still more milling and roaming crowds to contend with. I'm not much for crowds, and yet being in the middle of it all exhilarated me.

Looking above the crowds, I got my first glimpse of some of the several-story-high gingerbread-like buildings ... ancient buildings that have been standing for hundreds of years.

I decided to move off to one side, out of the way of the ever-shifting crowds, and out of sight of the vendors, so I could stand undisturbed for a few moments to take a good long look at the sight before me. I had read that over six thousand such buildings were located within the old city, many of them six or more stories high. Over a hundred mosques and twelve hammaams (traditional steam baths) were also to be found there.

Straight ahead I could see the beginning of the narrow streets that would lead me into the famous market area, the labyrinth known as *Suq al-Milh* (translated, *the Salt Market*) ... an outdoor colorful bustling shopping bazaar lining both sides of long narrow alleys where shoppers were able to buy almost anything they needed or wanted. Definitely not limited to selling *salt* as you may have been deceived into thinking by its name.

Vendors (some of them very zealous, and others much more passive) were selling clothes, spices, dried goods, fruits and vegetables, and a variety of handcrafted items ... many intended for practical use, like baskets and pots, and many specifically made for tourists.

My favorite items in the market were the janbiyas. A janbiya is a curved dagger which is carried in a pouch attached to a thick ornate belt.

Men (usually above the age of 14) wear them around their waists. I rarely saw a Yemeni man without one. The janbiyas typically are not used as weapons. For the most part they are merely decorative.

The most significant part of a janbiya is its handle. It's the handle that determines its value. Most janbiya handles are made of different kinds of horns or wood. But the most valuable handles are made from African rhinoceros horns ... worth thousands of dollars.

If you're wondering, I do own a janbiya, but only a cheap one with a handle made of bone ... information which I offer to those of you who may be rightfully concerned about poaching and endangered species.

While I'm at it, let me tell you more about what Yemeni men customarily wear in addition to the janbiya. Most wear a multi-colored wrap-around of varying lengths, reaching down somewhere between the ankles and the knees, along with a button up shirt worn untucked. Many Yemenis prefer to wear full robes, like the man on the right in the following photo. On top of the shirt or robe, men usually wear a suit jacket.

As for the women's apparel, coming from Amman to Sana'a, the contrast was quite dramatic. In Amman it was rare indeed to see a woman with her face fully veiled, whereas the opposite was true in Sana'a ... and in most of North Yemen for that matter. In most cities, towns and villages of North Yemen, women were usually covered from head to toe, wearing long black loose robes.[7]

Some women actually allowed their eyes to show, but the majority wore a fine thin mesh veil which covered their eyes. They could see out, but no one could see in.

---

[7] Photo taken by Sian.

Once my venture into the old city was over, I returned to the Gate of Yemen and passed through the funnel once more with the intent of catching a ride back to AIYS. But this time, rather than look for a private taxi, I decided to catch a ride in a *dubaab*. Dubaabs are very mini mini-vans.

The word *dubaab* comes from an Arabic word meaning *to crawl or creep along*, and that's just what they did ... definitely made for put-put-putting along rather than for beauty or speed.

I typically preferred riding in dubaabs. They were abundant ... thousands of dubaabs crept along the streets here and there all over the city. Dubaabs were also efficient, and had a very reasonable predictable fare. Each driver had a specific route which he followed. As he drove along, passengers would be standing anywhere along the side of the road (there were no specific dubaab stops) hoping to get a ride. The driver would slow down while the potential passenger yelled out where he wanted to go. At that point in time (unlike today) the mini-vans were unmarked as to their destination. If the driver was going their way, he'd pull the van over to allow the passenger to get in. I was able to get from one end of the city to the other (and anywhere in between) quite easily by riding in these local tiny passenger vans.

Let me describe the interior of a dubaab for you. Every dubaab has three bench seats ... one bench seat in the front for the driver and a passenger (or often two passengers ... a rather tight fit I can tell you from experience), and two bench seats in the back facing each other (front to back), where six passengers are supposed to squeeze in.

The very first time I got up the nerve to wave down a dubaab, I looked inside and was rather shocked to see what I thought was a full vehicle stopping to let me in. But it wasn't full. Someone quickly scooted over and, low and behold, there was still one seat empty. It was a squeeze, but I managed to fit in.

The mini-vans were not built for comfort ... and they were definitely not built for tall people. I'm not all that tall (even though most Yemenis thought I was), but I always had to remember to duck as I entered. I should also point out that most Yemenis had slight builds, and so they seemed to manage quite well in those microscopic interiors.

Yup, I was in a city of many wonders.

3

Whatchu say?

Having learned Arabic in Jordan, it was a challenge having to learn a whole new dialect when I arrived in North Yemen. For the most part I could make myself understood. The bigger struggle was my lack of understanding of what was coming at me. I did my best to pick up the new vocabulary, but it would take some time for my tongue and ears to make the adjustment.

Soon after my arrival at AIYS, I headed to the nearest grocery store, which was conveniently located right across the street, so I could pick up a few provisions. It was a small store with no door, only a long counter running the entire width of the store, from one side wall to the other. Part of the counter had a hinge which allowed the proprietor to flip it up and enter or exit as need be. Not all stores were set up like this one was.

I walked up to the counter and, looking inside, noted floor to ceiling shelving completely covering the two side and back walls which were stocked with a large assortment of canned and boxed goods, as well as a few fresh fruits and veggies. The store also boasted a fridge which, unlike the fridges I would soon be encountering in the villages, had a variety of drinks that were actually *cold*. And yes, they sold *Canada* (aka Canada Dry) there too.

Anyway, using a mixture of my Jordanian and Modern Standard Arabic,[8] along with some pointing and the use of a "pardon me" or a "how do you say" from time to time, I managed to communicate adequately with the store keeper stationed on the other side of the counter so that he grasped what I wanted. He fetched each requested item off a shelf and placed the product in front of me on the counter.

When I was done ordering, I used a phrase that I had always used in Jordan when I was done with my order ... I said, "maashii" ... a single word which literally means "it walks" in Jordanian Arabic ... the

---

[8] Modern Standard Arabic (MSA) serves as the literary standard throughout the Middle East and all across North Africa. MSA is the variety I learned at the University. More is explained in Appendix 1, *A Linguist's Nightmare*.

equivalent of "okay" in English. Namely, I was trying to inform him I was done with my order and was ready to pay for it.

Well, much to my surprise, the store keeper suddenly gave me a strange look. It was quite obvious he was frustrated with this foreigner standing across from him. Without any explanation whatsoever, he started removing the products he and I had just worked so hard to gather ... he took them off the counter one at a time and returned them to their appropriate places on the shelves ... at which point I must have looked extremely confused.

It took me a moment to realize just what he was doing. My mind started whizzing, "What did I say wrong?" I asked myself. So I quickly got his attention and said to him, as politely as possible, "Excuse me. Wait a second. I'd like to buy those things."

His look of frustration turned to one of confusion. "Do you or do you not want to buy something?" he inquired.

To which I replied, "Yes sir, I'd like to buy all those things that you had on the counter."

After a short pause, while his brain churned away, realizing there must have been an unintended blunder on my part, he willingly replaced all the items on the counter.

"How much do I owe you?" I inquired.

He told me, and I handed him a couple of bills, got my change, and after a very sincere "thank you very much," I walked back across the street with a bag of groceries ... albeit still rather confused over what had just transpired.

I had to find out what had happened so I wouldn't be making the same mistake again. And so the first chance I got, I explained the strange encounter to a non-Yemeni friend of mine who had also spent time in Jordan and therefore would surely know what I had done to miscommunicate so badly.

He laughed.

"Why are you laughing?" I asked. "Please don't tell me I said something rude!"

"No, don't worry," he assured me, "you didn't say anything offensive. You just confused the poor store keeper. The phrase *maashii* here in Yemen doesn't mean *okay*. It means *no thing*. In other words you were telling him you didn't want any of those things on the counter." And my friend started laughing again at my expense.

So, those *two words* in Yemen came together and sounded exactly like the Jordanian *single word*, but conveyed the exact opposite meaning.

I could tell I was going to have a challenging time communicating in North Yemen if there were many more words or phrases that had totally different meanings.

That incident inspired me to start weaning myself from Jordanian Arabic and start learning some Sana'ani Arabic as quickly as possible. In the meantime, I consciously kept adjusting to using something a little closer to my University-learned Modern Standard Arabic to try and make myself better understood. Well, at least better understood by those who were educated ... although many Yemenis were not.

4

Base Two

As I peered out of the Boeing 727's window the very first time I flew into North Yemen (which thankfully happened to be a daytime flight), I was utterly amazed as I caught my initial glimpse of the majestic mountains. Nobody had prepared me for that spectacular and unforgettable sight. What surprised me the most was that perched close to the peaks of many of those rugged mountains, reaching up thousands of meters above sea level, I could very clearly make out a village here, and a village there ... dozens of villages! I wondered, "Who would be living way up in those mountains?"

Based on what I could only observe from a distance, I very much doubted that many of those villages were easily accessible. And my first trip into those mountains, traveling over land, proved just how right I was. Those mountains were what had kept (and today still keep) so much of the North Yemen population in isolation, century after century, and what made travel, even relatively short distances as the crow flies, so extremely difficult. And so, the very thing that was so intriguing from the plane window that day, became one of the greatest obstacles to reaching the areas where I was hoping to carry out my research.

After much reading, map gazing, discussing and thinking, I eventually picked two provinces where I hoped to concentrate my research. Details about what my research was all about can be found in Appendices 1 and 2 (entitled *The Linguist's Nightmare* and *The Test*).

One of the chosen provinces was Sa'da. Sa'da was actually the name of both the province and the capital city of that province ... a province situated in the northeast of North Yemen, sharing a border with Saudi Arabia. The following map shows North and South Yemen with the Sa'da province highlighted.

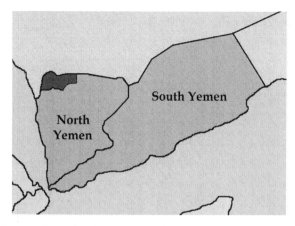

When I was there back in 1987, the Sa'da province was definitely known to contain some of the most inaccessible regions of North Yemen. And from an economic viewpoint, it was ranked among the poorest in the country.

More recently, on and off since June 2004, a violent conflict has been going on in Sa'da.[9] The majority of Yemenis are Sunni Muslims, but in Sa'da most of the population belongs to the Zaydi[10] branch of Shi'a Islam, a branch which is unique to Yemen. The 2004 conflict started as a result of an uprising against the government of Yemen, initiated by a rebel Zaydi religious leader. The Zaydis claimed the government was aggressively discriminating against them. The regime, of course, didn't agree, and made counter claims that the Zaydi group was trying to overthrow the government. The fighting has resulted in hundreds of deaths. It has also caused a huge displacement of much of the local population.

I'm informing you about this current conflict because even when I was hanging out in Sa'da in the latter half of the 1980's major tensions already existed. In fact, those tensions were already present long before that.

For over a thousand years prior to 1962, the Zaydi Imams[11] ruled North Yemen. For the majority of that time, Sa'da city served as their

---

[9] Some of the historical information given in the next few paragraphs of this chapter were taken from Wikipedia articles "Shia insurgency in Yemen" and "Houthis" (2012) (http://en.wikipedia.org).

[10] A Muslim religious minority close to Shi'a Islam (from which they separated at the end of the 8th century after a dispute about the identity of the fifth Shi'a Imam).

[11] An Imam is a Muslim religious leader.

capital. Then in the 17th century the Zaydi capital was moved south to Sana'a. And from that point on, Sa'da declined in national importance ... although it did continue to serve as an administrative center for the north of the country.

Then in 1962 a revolution resulted in the overthrow of the Zaydi rule. An additional consequence was that the north region was from then on ignored economically so it remained underdeveloped. But the new government never actually had much authority in Sa'da ... and definitely didn't while I was there in 1987. Sounds like a fun place to be, right? You've already read a little about what it was like in chapter 1 (*The Wild Wild North*), and you'll find out a great deal more in the following chapters.

The second province in focus was Jawf, located to the east of Sa'da (highlighted on the following map).

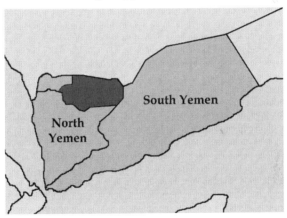

Jawf was another province that preferred to do its own thing. In other words, the local population was not totally under the control of the North Yemen government.

In light of the fact that my focus would be on two provinces located in the far north of the country, it made a lot of sense to try and establish a second base in Sa'da city. I would then make my research forays out to the remote unsuspecting populations from there.

One of my contacts in Sana'a had good friends living up in Sa'da city who worked at a foreign run hospital. An introduction by phone resulted in an invitation to head up that way for a visit, and I readily accepted.

I wasted no time planning my first road trip. I was relieved to hear that a good quality paved road existed connecting Sana'a and Sa'da ... a

240 kilometer stretch. Not much prior to 1987 a large section of the road was still only gravel.

As for choice of transportation, I could ride in a modern comfortable, dependable and inexpensive bus (operated by the *General Transport Corp.*) driven by a very capable driver ... or, I could get a cramped seat in a shared taxi with a driver who (from reports I had heard) would most likely take unnecessary chances on blind corners and drive like a maniac to make good time and increase his profits. Hard choice, eh? I decided to take the bus.

"This is definitely a nice comfortable bus," I thought as we pulled away from the station. I even had a front row seat ... a great place from which to watch the scenery coming at me through the large windshield.

But after a while more than just scenery was coming at me. "Good grief, that car is in our lane, and it's heading straight for us!" I wanted to shout. But our driver had obviously observed that fact. My comment wouldn't have made any difference. He slowed the bus way down while the oncoming car, passing another vehicle on a blind corner, kept right on coming, and then quickly tucked itself safely back into its own lane again just in time to miss hitting us. That was a little too close for my liking.

"I'm not sure I want to be sitting in the front row anymore," I mumbled to myself. I was told I'd be traveling through mountainous areas, but had no idea how windy some stretches of the road would get, and how treacherous it could be. Thankfully most corners didn't have *surprises*, and the ones that did, never again resulted in such close calls. The driver was clearly experienced, and for that I was thankful. He'd probably driven this road dozens and dozens of times, and was obviously still alive to drive it yet once again.

Talking to people afterwards, I found out that numerous fatalities occur on the road between Sana'a and Sa'da due to the careless fatalistic driving habits of many Yemenis. I'm glad I didn't end up a statistic that day.

We stopped in the city of Huth, the half-way mark, so anyone who wanted to could have some lunch. I assumed a few passengers wouldn't be eating lunch since they'd probably just lose it again like they lost their breakfast during the first half of the trip on those mountain roads. It was common practice for the bus driver to walk through the bus before the start of the drive and hand out plastic bags for you know what purpose. I must admit I was glad I wasn't sitting next to someone who had used one of those bags. I preferred the view out the front window.

I didn't plan to eat in the restaurant. I even hesitated to get off the bus, because I could see a crowd of beggars forming. I had experienced the same thing during my exploratory trip months earlier while traveling by bus to other parts of the country. At every stop beggars were waiting to confront *the rich* who could afford such luxurious travel, hoping they would find it in their hearts to share some of their wealth with the less fortunate.

Many citizens of North Yemen were not well to do at the time (and apparently far more are struggling today in 2012). I really felt sorry for beggars, especially young children, because many children were forced to beg by their guardians, some having been purposefully maimed to draw in more money. And so I never knew how to respond, because whatever was given to a beggar was going to end up in the pockets of their guardian or *employer*, meaning the beggar himself (or herself) would not benefit.

I did disembark to stretch my legs, but I merely walked close to the bus for a few moments before being surrounded by the beggars. After handing out a few coins, I got back on the bus. But being on board the bus wasn't necessarily a way to avoid them. They just climbed boldly onto the bus, walking up and down the aisle begging until the driver, who had allowed them that privilege, eventually kicked them all off (not literally) so we could start on our way again.

Actually, it wasn't even necessary to exit the bus to buy food, since even the vendors came onto the bus selling their goods. Needless to say, a lot of activity took place whenever a bus stopped.

After arriving in Sa'da, I headed straight to the hospital where I met Herb, the director, and his wife, Trudy. I was also introduced to the fix-it man ... a kind Dutch fellow named Harry, whose home became my second base. From then on, whenever I happened to be up in Sa'da, which was typically never for more than a day or two at a time, I stayed in the comfort of Harry's mud house.

Yes, you read correctly ... Harry lived in a mud house ... just like the rest of the Sa'da population. I had never seen mud houses before arriving in the north of North Yemen. In Sana'a everything was made from some sort of stone, brick or concrete. So my arrival in Sa'da offered me another one of those unique unforgettable architectural experiences. Although later on, I found out that mud house construction was used in many parts of both North and South Yemen. All the buildings in the following photo, taken in Sa'da, are built of mud.

I'm sure you must be curious about how a mud house is constructed, right? Well, I'll give you a brief description. In fact, that's all I can give you, because I have no first hand mud house construction experience.

A mud house is built one layer at a time. Each layer is allowed to dry completely before adding the next layer on top of it. What I'm describing is quite clear in the following photo which shows a new house nearing completion. Notice how the corners are raised, which I'm told gives the house greater stability.

The walls are quite thick, and when dry, these houses are very solid ... no problem with hammering in nails to install door frames or hang items on the walls. And the mud keeps the internal temperature of the house warm during the cooler winter months and cool during the hot summer months.

You may have noticed and wondered about the straw piled up in front of the house in the above photo. After the initial structure is finished, the straw is mixed with mud, and then a thin outer layer of mud and straw is spread over the entire house. The outer layer protects the rest of the structure and is replaced yearly (if I recall correctly). It was also important to have good drainage to keep any water from building up on the roof during the rainy season, otherwise the water would soak in and the dry mud would turn back into wet mud and the roof would collapse. I saw a few deserted structures that had suffered such a heartbreaking fate.

Now what really amazed me was that some of the mud houses were built four, five or even six stories high. Wooden beams and planks placed between floors made that possible.

Remember my mentioning the large clay wall surrounding the old city of Sana'a? Well Sa'da also had an old city with a wall around it ... but Sa'da's wall was made entirely of dried mud!

I talked earlier about armed conflict, and my experience in Munabbih (see chapter 1, *The Wild Wild North*) demonstrated how well armed the residents of this northern region of the country were, and how easy it was to acquire weapons. Pretty well every man up in the north carried a rifle hung over his shoulder at all times.

Hey, I noticed plenty of rifles in Sana'a too, but they were only ever carried by the abundant soldiers and police officers stationed throughout the city. And as expected, the men posted at military stops were always armed. So I was used to the idea of crossing paths with rifle-toting Yemenis. But it wasn't quite like what I was experiencing in the province of Sa'da.

So it was easy to believe that the north was not very well controlled by the government. It wasn't that the government didn't try to control this part of the country. They always had their government representatives up in Sa'da city as an attempt to keep a foothold and some control in the area, but those government workers walked a very fine line. It wasn't wise to try and push the locals around too much.

Not long after my arrival, I heard about how the locals didn't like how things were being handled and so they had recently run the government representative right out of town ... and he wasn't the first one to suffer such humiliation.

As far as getting around was concerned, Sa'da province consisted of rough terrain and a lack of paved roads, but at least at the time I was doing my research there were dirt roads heading up into the mountains making travel to remote areas in a 4-wheel drive possible.

And so, having met and spent time with Harry, and having his open invitation to come and stay with him whenever I needed a place to stay, I boarded the southbound bus for a *relaxing* trip back to base one in Sana'a.

5

The Elusive Ride

The two men who were slowly approaching Dave and me obviously had an agenda. I could tell we were their target because, as they interacted with one another, they were constantly looking our way. They both seemed somewhat uneasy, and I suspected that was due to their wondering if either of us could speak any Arabic.

"Asalaam 'aleikum" (meaning, *peace be with you*), one of them greeted us.

"Wa 'aleikum asalaam" (*and with you be peace*), I responded.

I noticed a slight glimmer of relief in his eyes after having heard me use Arabic. And so he bravely continued, "The Police Chief would like to see you."

That didn't surprise me in the least. Within two minutes after our arrival in Marran, I'm sure we were the talk of the small town. So, of course, the Police Chief would have heard about us.

"Okay," I responded, "we would be happy to see him." But deep down inside I was wondering how the Police Chief would react to our being there.

I did have in my possession a government approved travel document which granted me the freedom (at least on paper) to travel around within North Yemen nearly unrestricted, but this was the first time I would try out the document in such an out-of-the-way location. I knew for a fact, as I'm sure the Police Chief did, that at the time, North Yemen put very heavy restrictions on any foreigner's movement within its borders, especially up in the northern provinces.

Throughout this book I will often be referring to my above mentioned travel document as my *to whom it may concern* document. If you want more details about why I deserved such a document, then I would recommend you take the time to read appendix 3. I was hoping my document would do the trick in our current situation.

But even if the Police Chief did accept my presence, what about Dave? I was the only one who had an official paper. Dave merely had a basic travel document, and places like this were definitely off limits to him. (Sorry Dave!)

And so Dave and I set out to meet the Police Chief, escorted by his two messengers, neither of whom spoke another word to us. We only had to walk a relatively short distance, and yet it felt much longer as I went over and over in my mind potential directions my interaction with the Police Chief could take.

Let me explain how Dave and I managed to get ourselves into that predicament ...

I had been in Yemen for just over two weeks when my good friend Dave came to pay me a visit. That was a very special treat for me! And it was only fair that I give him a treat as well ... and my treat for him was the privilege of accompanying me on my first trip out into the unknown.

In the previous chapter, I mentioned the selection of two provinces where I would concentrate my research, namely, Sa'da and Jawf. But I had yet to pick the specific areas within those provinces. I decided the selection should be made up in Sa'da city after discussing possibilities with people who were very knowledgeable with the Sa'da province.

Of course, Dave and I commenced our trip on a comfortable intercity bus from Sana'a up to *base two* in Sa'da. ... with front row seats, blind corners and all! Upon our arrival, Harry was kind enough to host both me and my guest in his mud house.

"So what are the main areas of Sa'da province that would be beneficial for me to include in my research?" I asked Dr. Herb during our meeting with him and his wife Trudy over a nice dinner at their residence.

"You say you want to focus on some of the more remote uneducated areas," Dr. Herb recapped based on what he had gathered from our interaction thus far. "Well there certainly are plenty of areas to choose from."

"Yeah, that's what I thought," I responded.

Our fruitful discussions resulted in a number of possibilities. In the end, I decided Dave and I should head to a region lying to the southwest of Sa'da city known as *Khawlaan*.

The next day, after making a few inquiries, I found out we should be able to find a ride to Khawlaan from Suq Arubua (meaning, *the Wednesday market*). Apparently every Wednesday (hence the name) trucks came from many of the surrounding villages to sell their goods in that market.

Since it was only Tuesday, we were able to dedicate the rest of the day to tourism in Sa'da city ... hence the following photo of Dave standing on the old city's deteriorating mud wall that I referred to in the previous chapter.

Then on Wednesday morning we got right to work. "Excuse me," I started a conversation with a man standing outside a store next to what I assumed to be his truck, "Can you tell me where I can catch a ride to Suq Arubua?"

"You want to go to Suq Arubua? I'll take you there," he offered.

"Thank you," I said. "How much?" The price he quoted me seemed quite reasonable.

Muhamad (which I learned was his name) drove us about ten kilometers to the south along the main road heading back in the direction of Sana'a, and then turned off the paved road onto a sand path that took us west for about another kilometer or so, at which point he announced, "Suq Arubua is just up ahead."

But as we approached the so-called *market,* all I could make out was dozens of trucks ... no, it was hundreds of trucks, all of them seemingly parked in a random fashion (from my perspective) on a large section of the most desert-looking land I had yet seen ... all of them parked somewhere in the vicinity of one large distinct and rather strangely-shaped tree.

"Excuse me Muhamad, but where's the market?" I asked the driver as I scanned our surroundings. Not a single building was in sight. I had just assumed there'd be at least a few buildings based on my preconceived ideas of what a market should consist of.

"That's it, right in front of you," he clarified for me ... not that it really clarified much.

Muhamad drove part way into the market, pulled up beside a row of parked trucks, and turned off the engine. The whole scene suddenly became much clearer. Whoever had something to sell, merely parked their truck, laid out a blanket on the ground close to their truck, and then spread out their goods on the blanket for any potential buyers to see.

Add to the mix all the customers who showed up at the market to haggle over and buy the goods, and it resulted in quite a crowd gathered there that day. And this was clearly a market for Yemenis, probably not a place where foreigners would typically show up. So Dave and I definitely made an impression on anyone who spotted us ... we certainly didn't blend in with the crowd very well.

As I mentioned earlier, people would travel quite a distance to get to the market, and that's why it was such a good place to try and find rides to places like Khawlaan.

Small Toyota pickup trucks definitely dominated the market. In the flatter regions of the country, or where decent roads existed, a Toyota pickup was a great vehicle for getting around and very practical for transporting goods. But if anyone wanted to head off into any of the mountainous regions, like Khawlaan, only 4-wheelers could even attempt such a trip. So we were obviously on the lookout for 4-wheel drive Toyota Landcruisers.

I had already done my homework by asking Muhamad what the going fare should be. That way I'd know right away if a driver was quoting me an inflated price or not. Many trips later, I realized it was only the odd driver who might try to take advantage of me and rake in some extra money. Most drivers would go by what was known to be the acceptable fare.

The only way to find a ride was by asking around, and Dave and I were very thankful that Muhamad offered to help us find our next ride. I made it a habit early on never to refuse help when it was offered. I liked and trusted Muhamad.

"Butros, I'm sorry but I haven't found anyone who's going to Khawlaan," Muhamad apologized as he approached us. Dave and I had been hanging around his truck waiting for him ... letting him do all the work.

"So what do you suggest we do?" I asked, concluding that if he couldn't find anyone then what hope would I have of doing so.

I could tell he was feeling bad about his lack of success. He finally said, "Listen, I'm going to try and round up some more passengers, and then I'll drive you to Khawlaan myself."

"Are you sure? You don't have to do that for our sake," I started to argue.

"But I want to," he insisted as he turned and walked off again, not giving me the chance to continue the argument. And to tell you the truth, I was relieved to hear those words coming out of his mouth. "Not only would he be helping us out, but he'd make a little extra money at the same time," I reasoned, to make myself feel less guilty for letting him do all the work.

I filled Dave in on what was happening. The extent of Dave's ability in Arabic was merely a few courtesy words I had taught him, and so he was oblivious unless I translated for him. "I think we still have some time on our hands," I said to him. "So why don't we have a look around."

"You lead the way," he responded.

We didn't wander far from Muhamad's truck so he'd be able to spot us easily in case he suddenly returned from his search. Well, in fact, it would be hard for him not to spot us even from a distance. I really felt like we were on display in the market, even more so than the various goods being sold. And I know for a fact that Muhamad had been asked about our presence in the market numerous times.

When Muhamad showed up half an hour later all by himself, I already guessed what he was going to tell us. "I couldn't find a single person needing a ride to Khawlaan," he said with disappointment in his voice.

"Not even one?" I inquired.

"No, not one," he confirmed.

It just seemed like Khawlaan wasn't a popular destination on that particular day. So I said to him, "Muhamad, thank you very much for all your help. I think we should return to Sa'da with you, and then we'll try a new approach to find a ride tomorrow."

"You don't have to return to Sa'da," he said. "I'm going to take you and your friend to Sagayn." Sagayn was a small town situated at the beginning of the Khawlaan district.

I had a feeling that Muhamad's honor was at stake. He had confidently declared he would help us find transportation to Khawlaan, and now he couldn't let us down. I could tell that he had made up his mind, and yet the culturally appropriate thing for me to do was to argue with him yet again, and so I said, "That's far too much to ask of you."

"I said I would drive you, and that's what I'm going to do," he insisted.

"God bless you," I said to him. And then to Dave I said, "Let's get back in his truck ... we're finally on our way."

"So what happened?" he inquired with a look of confusion.

"I'll fill you in along the way," I said.

I was happy. And I was more than willing to pay a bit more for the extra distance Muhamad would be taking us.

"So should I buckle my seatbelt?" Dave said jokingly as we once again got comfortable in Muhamad's truck. Sure, they had a word for it, but in reality there was no such thing as a seatbelt in most Yemeni vehicles.

6

The Police Chief

The first part of our trip to Sagayn with Muhamad was on relatively flat land. But it wasn't long before we reached the foot hills ... and soon after that, we were driving along through the mountains.

It ended up being a very comfortable, and thankfully uneventful, one and a half hour ride to Sagayn.

But since Sagayn was at the edge of Khawlaan territory, I decided it might be more profitable if we moved on a little deeper into the heart of the region. And so I asked our driver, "Muhamad, can you tell me what the next big town in Khawlaan territory is?"

"That would be Haydan," he replied.

"Can I bother you just one more time? Do you think you could drop us off somewhere here in Sagayn where we can find a ride to Haydan?"

"I'd be happy to. I wish I could take you there myself," Muhamad apologized, "but I need to return to Sa'da today."

I sure wished he could have taken us as far as we wanted to go ... and even better yet, after taking us to Haydan, stay with us, and then eventually drive us out all the way back to Sa'da again. "You've done so much for us already," I said.

Not only did Muhamad go out of his way to deliver us to the right spot, but then he also started asking around to arrange the next ride for us. And this time he was successful.

"Thank you very much for all your help and generosity," I said when it was finally time to go our separate ways. I was going to miss Muhamad.

"You're welcome, and may God be with you," he replied as he shook my hand and then Dave's in turn.

When I asked how much we owed him for the ride to Sagayn, he refused to take more than what two passengers would have paid. He certainly didn't end up making a profit on the trip, but he did make two new friends. What a generous man!

I should point out that Muhamad was driving a *Salown*, whereas the 4-wheeler he had arranged for us to ride in next just had the cab with an open truck bed.

I guess you'd like to know what a *Salown* is, right? Well first, I'll just mention that Toyota Landcruisers with an open truck bed were used for hauling around goods, and just as often people, or a mixture of the two (goods and people competing for space), like this one in the following photo that Dave (shown from the back ... sorry Dave!) and I ended up riding in.

As you will have gathered from the above photo, during the second leg of our trip, Dave and I ended up riding, not in the cab of the truck (since it was already full), but rather in the bed of the truck. In fact we stood up the whole way.

Okay, so standing up in the back of a truck may not sound all that comfortable to you, but it really worked out well for us. We had fresh air ... we didn't feel the bumps as much as someone who's sitting does ... we also had a much better view, a 360 degree view ... and that meant more freedom for taking photos too.

Now about Salowns ... that was how Yemenis referred to the totally enclosed Toyota Landcruisers (see following photo) in which more passengers could fit, with actual seats to sit on.

After another two hours on rather treacherous mountain dirt roads, as we were approaching a large town, the driver leaned out of his window and shouted back to us, "This is Haydan."

We drove into town, he pulled over the truck in front of a small store, and we all climbed out.

Now, why we did it, I can't recall, but I overheard that Haydan wasn't our driver's final destination. So we decided (actually I'm pretty sure I decided ... sorry Dave!) to ask our driver, "Excuse me. I'm wondering ... are you going to keep driving on to another location in Khawlaan?"

"Yes, I'll be driving all the way to Marran today," he replied.

"Well Dave, do feel up to going yet further?" I asked.

He replied, "It's up to you, but I'm willing to keep going."

So turning back to the driver I inquired, "Would you mind if we went all the way to Marran with you?"

"Not at all. We're just going to buy something in the store and then we'll be on our way again," he said as he and his two companions walked up to the store entrance.

Dave and I decided to buy some refreshment in the store, so we both jumped out of the back of the truck, and as we entered we received the reception, "who are they?" ... stated not to us, but rather to the driver who was at the time paying for a pack of cigarettes and a bottle of water.

"They're foreigners who are going to Marran with me," he informed the proprietor.

"Can we have a couple of Canadas?" I asked him, confusing him even more by speaking to him in Arabic.

"Are you Syrian?" he asked me.

"No, actually I'm Canadian," I replied.   He looked even more perplexed.

After placing the empty bottles on the counter and paying the man, we joined the others, taking our places in the back of the truck once more, and off we crawled continuing on our adventure yet deeper into the Khawlaan mountains.

We climbed higher and higher, and higher yet. Suddenly we were enveloped by a mist ... a mist that was at times so thick, we couldn't see much past the sides of the truck. Maybe the not being able to see was actually a good thing, since, as a result, the thousand meter or more drop to the right side of the truck was hidden from our sight as it wound its way around those mountain paths.

But when we were able to see, I was amazed at the beauty of the terrain we had covered, were covering, and were about to cover ... a very dangerous beauty, but beautiful nonetheless.

We finally arrived in Marran ... far far removed from Sa'da city and the comfort of Harry's mud house. I assured Dave that we would go no further.

I paid our driver the agreed on fare, we thanked him for the ride, and then started to walk, just enjoying the chance to finally stretch our legs and play the tourists, with no particular agenda in mind. And that's when the Police Chief's two men arrived on the scene to fetch us.

The Police Chief was sitting at his desk doing paperwork as we entered his office behind our escorts. I greeted him with, "Peace be with you."

He stopped what he was doing, looked up at us, and responded, "And with you be peace. Please, have a seat." He seemed a pleasant fellow.

After I translated for Dave, he was quick to respond with a "Shukran" (*thank you*) before sitting on the chair next to the one I had chosen.

The Police Chief got right to the point, "Can I please see your travel permission paper?"

I quickly produced a copy of my *to whom it may concern* government approved travel document, unfolded it and, making sure it was in my right hand (using the left hand would be inappropriate), I presented it to him as I said, "Please sir, this copy is for you."

It was clear that he was intrigued as he read it. Then he looked up at us and said with a broad smile, "Welcome to Marran. You are our guests."

"Shukran," I responded ... as did Dave, even though he had no idea why he was saying it.

I was thankful, but I was also still wondering if the Police Chief was going to ask to see Dave's permission paper ... which kept me feeling a little nervous. But it didn't happen. He must have just assumed if my paper was okay then Dave's should be fine too. I mean, obviously he wouldn't be there if he wasn't supposed to be, right?

So, rather than the interrogation I had expected, he merely started to engage us (well, actually *me*) in light conversation. That definitely put my mind at ease.

"Tell me about your research," he eventually said with sincere interest.

"Well sir ... blah, blah, blah ..." and I told him about the kind of research I was planning to do in North Yemen. And I won't bore you, my readers, by going into details here. Do I hear a sign of relief? But, if you do want to know more, then don't forget you can always read about it in Appendices 1 and 2.

The police chief seemed rather impressed by what I shared with him. Or maybe he was merely impressed because I was able to share the information with him all in Arabic. Many times throughout my Middle East travels, I found the more I interacted with someone in Arabic, the more honored the person would feel, and the more they relaxed.

The Police Chief finally turned to one of his men and said, "Show these men to the best hotel in town!"

That was a phrase Dave often reminded me of for years to come because of his shock when we walked up to the *best hotel*.

7

The Best Hotel in Town

The Police Chief had one of his men escort Dave and me to the best hotel in town.

To tell you the truth, I didn't think the hotel was all that bad ... but I had stayed in such dollar-per-night hotels before. Dave, on the other hand, wasn't used to such *humble* accommodations ... a rather run-down looking building both inside and out.

The owner of the establishment was friendly enough, although initially somewhat shocked at the sight of his guests to be.

The man who led us to the hotel introduced us rather formally, "These men are guests of Marran, treat them well," as if we were some sort of dignitaries.

The owner greeted us with, "Welcome to Marran."

"Thank you very much," I responded to both our guide and the landlord.

Having heard me produce another "Shukran," Dave did the same ... and that became a routine for him. I noticed Dave's eyes surveying the scene in front of us ... cot after cot, some with mattresses, some without, a TV on a table against one wall with a number of men sitting on cots watching the screen ... but also glancing our way from time to time as discreetly as possible.

I could hear Dave mumbling over and over again sarcastically, knowing that no one present would understand him except me, "the best hotel in town ... the best hotel in town ..."

"Would you like a private room?" asked the owner.

Surprised that there was even such an option, I replied, "Yes, please," without even consulting Dave, knowing he would most likely not be opposed to taking the 5-star option since it was available. "A private room would be very nice. Could we see it?"

"Of course," he replied with pride, "come this way."

I interrupted Dave's mumbling and told him to follow us, filling him in along the way on what was happening as the owner led us a little off to the left and then unlocked the padlock which secured the door of the private room.

The owner stood aside and announced, "here it is," with a manner of deep satisfaction that he had such a room to offer to special guests who show up in Marran.

Dave and I walked into a rather spacious room littered (I certainly don't want to give you the impression it was *orderly*) with numerous cots ... basically a smaller version of the large room. But it would indeed be private. Just what we needed.

"Thank you, this is very nice. It will do just fine," I said.

He looked pleased. He turned and walked off leaving us on our own to get settled ... while I'm sure he returned to the others in the main room and joined in on one of the many conversations going on about the two Westerners.

Dave and I were glad we finally had a few moments to ourselves. We closed the door, found two suitable cots situated not too far from the door, placed our belongings on them, and then sat down to catch our breath after the long tiring adventurous day.

Relaxation for Dave consisted of reading a few pages of a book he had brought along ... and for me, it was writing up some notes about our trip thus far.

"How about having another look around the town, Dave?" I finally suggested. "And maybe we should try and find a place to get a bite to eat."

"I won't argue with that," replied Dave. "You know me. I'm always ready to eat."

As we walked along Marran's main road, we suddenly heard a siren coming our way. It seemed strangely out of place in such a remote location, and yet my city instinct told me there must have been either a crime or an accident nearby.

Soon it was no longer just a noise, the 4-wheeler coming into plain view as it rounded a corner and sped towards us with its siren blasting and with a number of men precariously hanging off the back. I assumed they were part of the Marran police force. They were all talking and laughing, and a couple of them waved to us, which dispelled my theory of this being some emergency.

"It looks to me like they're just out for a joy ride," I said to Dave.

"Yeah, it's probably a show for us foreign dignitaries to demonstrate how advanced they are in Marran with the use of gadgets like sirens," he replied.

"I'm pretty sure you're right," I said as we instinctively shifted over to the side of the road to make sure we gave them plenty of room as they drew ever closer. I wondered if they were going to stop when they reached us, but they passed us by and headed in the direction of the Police Chief's office, and were soon out of sight.

The daylight was starting to fade. So instead of wandering around in the dark trying to find a restaurant, we decided to return to the hotel, knowing that we'd be able to get something simple to eat there. We topped off the meal with a cup of sweet milky tea and a little TV.

Of course, I always wanted to take advantage of every opportunity, and so I started interacting with a few of the men about my favorite topic ... Arabic dialects. Most anyone anywhere in the Arabic speaking world was more than willing to talk about their dialect because, as mother tongue speakers, they were the experts ... and I always treated them as such.

Dave couldn't exactly benefit from the TV or the interaction since it was all in Arabic. (Sorry Dave!)

Eventually we headed back to the privacy of our room where we could debrief about the day's events, and I could write down a few more observations before turning out the lights. For some time afterwards we continued to hear the sound of voices and the TV in the other room. But then suddenly it was silent ... most likely because the town generator was turned off.

The night passed slowly as I rolled from side to side, trying to get into a position where something wasn't poking me through the thin mattress and my sleeping bag.

As for Dave, he apparently had no problem sleeping, which was another reason I woke up from time to time. I would reach over and poke him so he'd roll onto his side and provide a little silence until the next time.

Morning finally arrived. Then over a delicious breakfast in the hotel consisting of fasoulia (finely mashed fava beans), some freshly baked flat bread and sweet milky tea, Dave and I discussed what our next plan of action should be. "So what do you think Dave, should we stay here or move on?"

"Hey, I'm just along for the ride. I'll follow your lead," Dave defaulted to me.

"We traveled quite a distance to get out here to Marran," I said. "So maybe we should start making at least some movement back in the direction of Sa'da."

I went to the hotel manager and paid him for the one night we had spent there in the *best hotel*, and then we went looking for a ride to Haydan, the smaller town we had passed through the day before.

8

My Mute Friend

"Yes, I can give you a ride to Haydan," the driver of the 4-wheeler informed us. "But you'll have to ride in the back."

"Praise be to God," I responded. "We'll be fine in the back."

This was only the second driver we had asked for a ride. I had anticipated a much longer search and wait. Dave and I quickly tossed our bags into the truck bed, climbed in ourselves, and the driver engaged the clutch jerking the truck forward before either of us had a chance to get a solid grip on the roll bar, nearly depositing us back on the road. But we both recovered, repositioned ourselves, and we were on our way. The trip to Haydan (pictured here) was pleasant and uneventful.

"Can you tell us if there's a hotel here in Haydan?" I inquired of the driver after our arrival as I handed him the fare.

"The hotel is just a short distance down this road," he responded, pointing with his hand before retracting it to help count the riyals I had deposited in his other hand.

As he drove off to his destination, we found our way to the hotel ... another top notch one based on our first impressions. The owner didn't seem too taken aback at the sight of us walking through the door. The hotel was a two story structure, and we ended up with another private room for ourselves ... a room with a view up on the second floor.

Upon entering our room, my ever observant travel companion turned to me and said, "There aren't any beds in this room!"

"What do you mean. The beds are right over there," I said with a big grin on my face, pointing at the thinnest mattresses I'd ever seen, placed right on the hard floor, lining the two-tone walls which probably hadn't seen a fresh coat of paint for a good 30 years or more.

"But there aren't any cots," Dave stated the obvious.

"Welcome to the second best hotel," I said.

Catching a quick ride in Marran, which resulted in an early afternoon arrival in Haydan, meant we still had plenty of daylight hours left, and so we started wandering around the town. And as usual, we ended up being the best entertainment they'd had there in a long time.

At one point a few brave young people (somewhere in their teens) came up to us and started talking with me (Dave was mute as usual). So I took advantage of the situation and started telling them about where and why I had studied Arabic, and explained that I was doing research about different Arabic dialects in the Middle East.

When I noticed how open and interested they were, I enquired, "Would it be okay if I ask you some questions about Yemeni dialects and write down a few notes?"

"No problem," answered the most verbal of them, who I found out was named Ahmad.

"I have some paper up in my room," I said with the intention of going up to get a notepad and pen and then return to the street.

But Ahmad took it as an invitation to accompany me, and said, "Okay, let's go." And before I knew what was happening, Dave and I and a crowd of kids (we had attracted quite a throng of younger children by then) paraded along the street, through the hotel's front door, past the owner, who just stared in disbelief, up the stairs and right into our room.

I pulled my notepad and pen out of my backpack and proceeded to interview Ahmad. "Have you ever been to Sana'a?" I asked him.

"Sure, I went to Sana'a just last year. It was my second time," he said, obviously quite proud of that fact.

Then looking at the rest of boys I inquired, "And what about the rest of you?"

The majority said, "No," but there were two more yeses.

"So how different is your dialect from the dialect spoken in Sana'a?" I asked.

"Oh, there's a big difference," was Ahmad's response. And a general chime of agreement came from all present. Even though the majority of them most likely would never have met someone from Sana'a, they'd probably heard it spoken on the radio or TV.

"Can you understand what they say?" I dug further.

"Of course we can understand their dialect," Ahmad claimed, "but they say things in a funny way and use words we don't use."

"Can you give me some examples?" I asked next.

"Oh sure, that's easy," Ahmad said, and proceeded to give me a few vocabulary items and phrases, while others present also added their input.

"And what about the south of the country. Have you ever met anyone from Ta'izz?" I asked.

"I've never been to Ta'izz," admitted Ahmad, "but I've met people from there. They speak a lot like Egyptians."

"Like Egyptians?" I said with surprise, even though I already knew that to be the case. I had some knowledge based on interaction with Ta'izzi speakers who worked in Sana'a.

"Oh yes, sometimes it's very hard to understand them," he said. And once again there was a general agreement.

No question about it, Dave and I were definitely a big hit! They hung around for well over an hour and never seemed to tire ... although I certainly did, and I was sure Dave did since he couldn't follow any of the interaction. And so I eventually decided to draw things to a close with, "Thank you all very much for your help. It was a pleasure to meet you all."

They got the hint, and Ahmad spoke for them all, "You're welcome. And if you need any more help, don't hesitate to ask." With that, they all stood up and trooped out of our room, leaving Dave and me on our own.

Later that same afternoon as we were on our way to the staircase, intending to head down to the main floor to inquire about an evening meal, we happened upon an open door. I noticed three men sitting in the room with a number of decorative janbiya belts and pouches piled in front of them. They looked up with curiosity written all over their faces as we walked past.

"Peace be with you," I said to them as I entered their room uninvited. Dave followed close behind.

"And with you be peace," the three of them said one after the other, not seeming bothered at all with my entrance.

"Nice work," I said pointing to the belts.

"Thank you," one of them replied. "We're getting ready for market day tomorrow."

"I didn't realize it was market day tomorrow," I said, and then asked, "Do you sell janbiyas too?" wondering if I'd be able to make a purchase right then and there.

"No just the belts and pouches," he said.

After a few more verbal exchanges I asked, "Do you mind if we take a couple of photos of your work?"

"Not at all," all three of them agreed ... and hence the following photo.

"Well, now I know what needs to make up part of our agenda for tomorrow," I said to Dave as we continued on our way.

The next morning, after a quick walk through the market, where neither of us bought a thing, we started the process of finding a ride back to Sa'da. Dave and I were sitting in front of a small store, both of us sipping away at bottles of *Canada*, while some of the younger children of Marran were watching us (as usual). Whether they had been part of the crowd present in our hotel room the day before, I couldn't say for sure. They noticed that Dave never said anything in Arabic ... never talked to any of the Yemenis directly. Of course, as I already pointed out, Dave didn't know any Arabic except for a few courtesy words.

Well, two of the boys eventually came up to me, and one of them asked, "Sir, does your friend know how to speak."

I said, "Sure, he knows how to speak. He just doesn't know how to speak in Arabic."

I could see their brains processing that bit of information. But it was obvious something still wasn't making sense to them. They whispered amongst themselves, and then the second boy asked, "What's wrong with him? Is he mute?"

I tried to explain that we both spoke another language. But with their limited experience (they might have been 9 or 10 years old), they couldn't comprehend that anyone existed who couldn't speak Arabic. If someone didn't speak Arabic, then they were obviously mute.

Much to Dave's discomfort, they just kept staring at him in amazement.

9

Left Lying
on the Side of the Road

I don't recall how long we had to wait for a ride in Haydan, but Dave and I were glad when a Salown Toyota Landcruiser came along from Marran with room for two more passengers. I negotiated the fare and we were good to go.

The very rear of this model of Salown had enough room for four passengers who had to sit facing each other. They were not the kind of seats anyone really ever desired to occupy, and that was why, on this particular occasion, with only room for two more passengers, they were the only seats still available. I didn't think anything of it, and was just glad to have found a ride.

So Dave and I crawled in, took our seats, placed our meager belongings on our laps, and off we went.

It only took us three and a half hours to get from Sa'da city to Haydan ... that's not counting the waiting time between rides. But this time it was a straight drive all the way to Sa'da city, our driver's stated destination. And so within three and a half hours, give or take a bit of time depending on how this guy drove, we would be back in the comforts of Harry's mud house once again.

Do you happen to recall what I wrote earlier, that by Yemeni standards I was rather tall? Well, Dave was taller yet. Have you ever sat in the back of a station wagon ... I mean in the very back where the extra seats fold out ... you know, where only little kids fit because the seat is so low down to the floor? Well, that about describes the type of seats we were sitting on. So poor Dave was sitting right across from me with his knees right up near his chin ... with no room to stretch out in any direction whatsoever.

And as you know, the very rear of *any* kind of vehicle is pretty awful when the driver hits a bump in the road. Well let me tell you, we were sure bumping around in the back of that 4-wheeler.

I learned something new about Dave that day. He had a weakness. Okay, so maybe he had more than one weakness ... but the weakness I learned about was that he doesn't do well in small, enclosed, cramped, hot, stuffy, bumpy places ... and that's a good description of the situation we were facing in the back of the Salown.

And so, after being under way for just a very short distance, I noticed that Dave was looking very uncomfortable ... and he was very pale. "Are you okay?" I asked him.

He responded in a rather raspy voice, "I think I'm going to lose it."

"Dave, do you want me to ask the driver to pull over?"

He merely nodded, unable to utter another word. It looked to me like he was about to pass out.

I immediately shouted up to the driver, "Excuse me! Excuse me! Please stop the truck!"

The man sitting next to me, and also facing Dave, couldn't help but notice what was happening, and so he also started to shout, and much louder than I did, "Stop the truck!"

Those who were sitting on the middle bench seat all immediately turned around, and then one of them leaned forward and quickly explained to the driver, "one of the foreigners is sick."

This was nothing unusual for Yemenis. In the future I would end up seeing the same thing happening to some of them on trips. And I already told you what happens on those big fancy intercity buses ... you know, about the driver handing out plastic bags because of you-know-what. Well, enough about that topic.

The driver stopped the truck.

I quickly opened the back door, scrambled out of my seat onto the road, grabbed Dave's bag from off his lap, and then helped Dave get out ... all in a matter of seconds.

All eyes were turned on us.

The driver didn't even bother getting out from behind the steering wheel. So leaving Dave for a moment (somehow he managed to stay standing after getting some air), I went over to the driver and said, "Please wait for a minute until I see how my friend is doing."

"Okay," was his brief response.

The driver and the passengers were, of course, all anxious to get under way again. A number of them had probably already been waiting quite some time to find a ride in Marran and didn't want any more delays.

Dave didn't look at all well. There was no way he'd be able to continue the trip sitting in the back of the truck ... and no one offered to trade seats with him. Well, even if someone had offered Dave their seat, it most likely wouldn't have done any good at that point. Dave was in no shape to travel any further, no matter what part of the truck he sat in. So there was no use in asking the driver to wait for us any longer.

I finally returned to the driver and said, "We can't continue on the trip with you."

"Okay," he said again. I couldn't tell if he felt any sympathy for Dave or not ... but he could see very well for himself that Dave was in no condition to go on.

"Wait a second. I'll pay you for the trip," I said, feeling obligated to pay the driver the whole fare all the way to Sa'da, even though he'd probably end up picking up other passengers along the way to replace us. I thanked him for his patience and handed him the money. He didn't hesitate accepting the payment, and off he drove without us. I didn't have time to worry about his attitude. I quickly headed back over to Dave.

Many heads were still turned, watching us until the truck rounded another corner and we were finally out of their sight. I'm sure that incident gave everyone in the Salown something to talk about for the rest of the trip. (Sorry Dave!)

Dave slowly (very slowly) made his way to the side of the road and sat down. He looked awful. And it wasn't long before he stretched himself out right in the dirt. I had quickly made a pillow out of his jacket so at least his head could find a little comfort.

I just stood there looking down at him, and was at a loss about what to do next. I hadn't even taken the time to look at our surroundings ... I was just trying to figure out what to do with Dave. Were we going to have to find our way to the nearest village ... maybe back to Haydan, and spend the night there? Would he be able to travel if another truck came by with an open bed and allowed us to sit in the back? I rather doubted it.

I certainly couldn't carry him anywhere, and I didn't think he'd appreciate me dragging him through the dust. So I finally sat down right beside him as he calmly lay on the side of that lonely road.

Then suddenly some movement off to the right, in the direction we had been traveling, caught my attention. I looked up the road and spotted a house. I was amazed I hadn't even noticed it before. What had actually caught my attention was a man who must have just gone up onto the roof of his house. He stood there looking down at us. And then, much to my surprise, I noticed that he was signaling to me.

Have you ever been in a situation where you think someone is waving at you but it actually turns out he's waving at someone behind you? That can prove embarrassing. So just to be sure, I turned my head to have a 360 degree look around me and, not seeing anybody else, I decided the man indeed had us in mind ... he wanted us to come to his house.

I was overcome with joy! What a welcome sight!

I waved back at him to let him know I had seen him, and then leaned over and asked Dave, "Do you think you can manage a short walk?"

With his eyes still closed, he asked feebly, "Where to?"

I replied, "There's a house just a short distance up ahead, and a man on the roof indicated he wants us to come there."

With that bit of welcome news, he opened his eyes and said with a groan, "okay."

Sure enough, Dave managed to find enough energy to sit up, get up to his feet, and then start walking, slowly but with determination, the short distance to the house, while I carried the bags and walked beside him ready to steady or catch him if he suddenly felt dizzy or took a turn for the worse.

I looked up at the house again as we walked along, and noticed that the man had disappeared from the roof. But then as we drew closer, he suddenly reappeared, this time at ground level. He just stood there waiting for us.

As he watched us approaching him, I wondered if he had any second thoughts about offering to help these two very strange strangers. He most likely would have been concerned about how he'd communicate with us.

I thought I better speak first to help put his mind at ease. "Peace be with you," I greeted the kind man in Arabic.

"And with you be peace," he replied. And then he asked, "Does your friend need a place to lie down?"

What a welcome statement to both of us. Dave, of course, only understood because I had translated for him. "Yes please ... Thank you very much for your hospitality ... That's very kind of you ... God bless you ..." etc, etc, rolled off my tongue, to make clear how very grateful we were.

Dave didn't say a thing ... at the time probably not even being able to recall the few Arabic words he had learned. He just kept unhurriedly putting one foot in front of the other, plodding along behind the good Samaritan who was now leading the way.

When we arrived at the front door, I made sure to help Dave do the culturally appropriate thing and took his shoes off for him. Then I took off my own shoes, before following our host inside.

He led us straight into the very nicely furnished sitting room where guests are normally entertained and said, "Your friend can lie down here."

The sitting room had the usual Yemeni style plush mattresses (much more practical than our western style couches) lining the walls. I led Dave to one of them in a corner of the room.

Without any hesitation, he got back down on his knees, and with a sigh of relief, lay down and closed his eyes. I was glad I had brushed some of the dirt off of him on the way to the house.

I sat down on the mattress next to him.

Before I was able to engage our host in conversation, he left the room, only to return before long carrying a tray with some steaming hot tea. Dave was sound asleep by then.

As for me, I enjoyed the opportunity to sit and relax ... so very thankful to have found such a kind, caring man in that time of need. What a great unplanned opportunity it was to sit and visit with a local man. I joined him in a cup of tea while I told him where I was from and talked about the reason I was in Yemen. He listened very attentively, and also shared his insights about the language situation in the Khawlaan region, in Yemen, and in the Arab world in general. It was clear he was a very well-informed person.

I had to think through what Dave and I would do next. How long would it take him to improve? I mean, I had no doubt he would recover. Should I assume that this kind man would allow us to spend the night if Dave wasn't able to travel any further that day?

It was about an hour or so later when Dave finally started to stir. He opened his eyes, sat up, looked over at me, and merely said, "Hi."

"How are you feeling Dave?" I asked.

He replied, "I'm feeling much better. I sure needed the rest."

"That's great," I tried to encourage him, but still had my doubts about his recovery considering the way he looked only an hour earlier. I still suspected we'd be spending the night ... but maybe, just maybe ... was there possibly some hope we could be moving on that same day?

The tea had been kept hot in a thermos, and so when our host saw that Dave was awake and doing better, he poured some in a cup and offered it to him. Dave, with a "shukran," accepted it and drank it down.

"So what do you think Dave. Do you feel up to looking for another ride to Sa'da?" I inquired, still harboring some doubt.

Without any hesitation he said, "No problem. I'm ready." And then with a smile he added, "As long as we don't get shoved into the back of another one of those Salowns."

We thanked our host over and over again for his hospitality, and then made our way to the side of the road where we sat and waited for a vehicle to pass by that way. Our host stayed right beside us.

We could hear a truck coming before we actually caught sight of it. And as it came around the bend, where Dave had not long before been lying in the dirt, our host signaled for the driver to pull over, which he did. He was driving a truck with an open bed ... exactly what we were hoping for. We could see that the cab was full of passengers. No problem. We'd stick with the fresh air any day.

I was happy to let our host do the speaking on our behalf, and whether it was the way he presented it, or whether the driver would have taken us anyway, I was relieved when our host informed us, "The driver will be going all the way to Sa'da, and he's willing to give you a ride."

"Praise be to God," naturally rolled off my tongue first, followed by another "thank you" to our host. Then Dave and I climbed into the back of the truck, and we were once again under way.

As we drove along, I looked over at Dave standing beside me feeling as good as ever, with a smile on his face, taking in the fresh air and the spectacular scenery. You would never have known that he had been looking so pitiful just a couple of hours earlier.

I was glad the adventure would soon be over, and then we'd be getting a good night's sleep in Harry's mud house.

That very same evening I was quite sure Yemenis in Marran, in Haydan, in the kind man's house, and in Sa'da (namely, those who had been in the Salown when Dave got sick), were all talking with relatives and or friends about their memorable encounter with the two Westerners.

10

Entertainment

Only a few days after my good friend Dave flew out of Sana'a, taking with him many memories (hopefully more good than bad), I was back up in Sa'da staying in Harry's mud house while preparing for my next trip. I would be heading to Raazih, one of the four chosen regions to be included in my research. For some reason I decided not to include Khawlaan. I'm sure the rationale for the decision was a brilliant one at the time, but somehow it escapes recollection.

This time I would be traveling all on my own. No one to share the experience with ... except for the Yemenis I would be encountering, of course. No one to talk to in English, of that I was sure. Immersed in the language and culture ... the ideal way (although sure to be exhausting) to really experience and observe things ... totally dependent on the local population. I was looking forward to the trip, but at the same time dreading it.

The morning of my departure I ate a hearty breakfast (not knowing when or where I would get my next meal), and then I headed to *Baab Al-Yemen, (the gate of Yemen)*, the main entrance to the old city.

The first time I heard someone referring to *Baab Al-Yemen* in Sa'da city, I was confused, and sure I had heard wrong, because I knew for a fact that the main gate leading into the old city of Sana'a was called *Baab Al-Yemen*.[12] Well, it just so happened that the exact same name was being used up in Sa'da. Why not.

Anyway, I had inquired the day before, and was told 4-wheelers departed from *Baab Al-Yemen* for Raazih. I didn't mention earlier that Harry lived inside the old city, and so it was only a short stroll from his house to the gate of Yemen.

I walked through the gate, looked across the street, and spotted the row of narrow buildings, just as it was described to me. Only one of those buildings appeared to be ready to do business at that hour ... it was the only one with its doors open ... large metal double doors

---

[12] See chapter 2, *City of Wonders.*

providing a wide inviting opening. That's where I would start my inquiries about a ride.

I marched over, glanced in, and spotted three men inside. Two of them were sitting on well-worn mattresses on the floor, one leaning against the wall to my right, and the other against the opposite wall. The third man sat behind a desk straight in front of me, with a cup of tea in one hand and a cigarette in the other. I assumed the man behind the desk was in charge, so I walked up to him and, after the usual exchange of greetings, I inquired, "Can you tell me if there's a place around here where I can catch a ride to Raazih?"

"Yes, you're in luck," came the words from the man to my right, diverting my attention to him. "My truck is right over there," he continued, pointing to a Salown parked to the right of the building. "I'll be leaving soon."

"That's great. How much per passenger?" I asked.

He told me the price. I don't remember exactly how much it was, but I do remember agreeing and then sitting down next to him, at his invitation, to wait for the imminent departure. I was rather proud of myself for securing a ride so quickly and without any assistance. Hey, it was only 10AM, and I would soon be on my way.

An hour later we were still sitting there with no sign of *leaving soon.* So I asked, "How much longer before we leave?"

"We'll be leaving soon," he assured me. "I'm just waiting for a few more passengers."

"Yeah, right. We'll be leaving soon," I said to myself mockingly after another hour had passed.

Now it's not like I was merely sitting there twiddling my thumbs. I spent a fair amount of time interacting with the men, and especially the driver who was a real talker.

"I'm going to get something to eat," I informed the driver after a gentle breeze carried the smell of cooking my way from a small hole-in-the-wall restaurant across the street, reminding me that I should take care of my physical needs while I had the chance to do so.

"Okay, take your time and enjoy your meal," he replied.

"I should take my time, he says. I guess that's an indication that it'll still be a while before departure," I thought to myself.

I ate at a leisurely pace, returned to my *guaranteed* ride and continued the wait. It was 2:30 when we finally started on our way!

Four and a half hours after I had *found my ride*! I had hoped to be at my destination by then, and I was just getting started!

We hadn't driven more than ten minutes before we stopped and the driver jumped back out of the truck. "Where are we?" I asked one of the other passengers. "And why did we stop here?"

"We're in Taalih," he informed me. "The driver wants to find a few more passengers."

Taalih was a large market town just to the west of Sa'da. I found out that the best plan of action was to take a local taxi straight to Taalih, and then look for a ride out to the remote areas. Live and learn. That was definitely what I planned to do the next time.

Once our driver was satisfied with the number passengers, we were ready for the real take-off. I'm not sure when that was ... I finally stopped keeping track of time, since all it did was frustrate me and definitely wouldn't make things happen any faster anyway.

So here is the passenger list ... on the front bench seat sat one woman (next to the window) and two men ... plus the driver. They were really crammed in. On the middle bench seat sat one woman and three men ... also a tight fit. Then a young boy, a man and I sat in the back amongst the baggage.

Hey, wait a minute. How did I end up sitting way in the back again?! ... especially since I was probably his first passenger to sign on! "Well, at least I had breathing room," I consoled myself.

Heading out of Taalih, we traveled west on a stretch of paved smooth road ... with the emphasis on *smooth*. But the most comfortable part of the drive ended all too soon as we turned off onto a dirt road. The dirt road actually turned out to be relatively flat (albeit bumpy) for quite some time, but that changed as soon as we started the slow climb up into the mountains.

Along the way, as we were passing through a tiny village, we came across a man who was looking for a ride. He had the misfortune of having a tire go flat a little ways back on the road, and not having a spare, caught a ride to the village we were now passing through to have it repaired. He asked our driver if he could take him to his truck ... along with the tire, of course.

I didn't really catch much of what transpired during their conversation, but in the end the driver decided to give the guy a ride ... most likely because the price was right.

The driver tossed the tire up on the roof rack, and then opened the rear door so the new passenger could climb into the back, which was, of course, where I was sitting. I loved the expression on his face when he caught sight of me. He had to sit right across from me, and as he took his seat, he turned to the other man in the back and asked, "Who's the foreigner?" not suspecting that I could understand what he was saying.

And just to add a little more to the surprise, I said to him in Arabic, "I'm German and I'm here in Yemen doing research."

Why did I say I was German? I often (but not always) resorted to my roots because that's what's important to Arabs. My parents were German immigrants to Canada, and so I could claim German descent. Then if it required further clarification, I would add that I had Canadian citizenship. And as I already pointed out, most people just thought *Canada* was a drink.

This new development would involve some backtracking for us to get the man to his truck. I didn't think that was such a good idea. I really didn't want to end up winding along those narrow treacherous mountain roads in the dark. Besides, it had already been a long day just to get this far. Yes, I was feeling rather selfish at the time.

But, of course, the driver didn't ask for my opinion. I was a mere passenger, like any other passenger ... all of us at his mercy. And so back we went, dropped off the grateful man with his tire, and then started moving, it seemed ever so slowly, towards our goal once again.

Progress was made, and not much further up the road we dropped off one of the other passengers. But soon afterwards our driver was *kind enough* to pick up yet three more passengers, which made for an even tighter squeeze for the rest of us. This particular driver was definitely bent on making as much profit on this trip as possible.

Okay, okay, not many trucks were on the road at that hour of the day, and so giving people rides really was a service.

The trip went on ... and on ... and on. Then what I had dreaded the most came to pass ... the sun was starting to set. And my understanding was we still had some distance to cover before reaching our destination.

Next, to make things a little more eventful, the on-coming darkness combined with the rough roads finally got to the woman sitting in the front seat ... who was thankfully sitting beside the window. She leaned out of the window (after pulling up the veil from her face) and ... need I say more? I guess I really didn't have as much to complain about as she did.

It bothered me that the driver didn't pull over right away. Instead, he casually looked over at the woman's husband and (not sure if it was even said sincerely) he asked, "Do you want me to stop the truck?"

But the woman managed to speak up for herself and said to the driver, "No, don't stop, go on." She obviously wanted to get the never-ending trip over with as quickly as possible (as did the rest of us!). That proved to be the better choice, since it wasn't much longer before the couple climbed out of the truck.

I couldn't see the relief on the woman's face ... of course, I couldn't see her face at all because of the veil. But I'm sure the relief was there nevertheless.

By then darkness had set upon us in earnest, and it was only then that the driver finally turned on the headlights ... I had been wondering if he would ever do so. He carried on as if driving in the dark didn't bother him in the least.

Soon we dropped off a few more passengers, and I was invited to move up to business class seating on the middle bench seat ... definitely a welcome change. From my new vantage point I managed to keep myself entertained by watching our truck's lights illuminate the shrubs and rocks, and even the odd creature, along the way, never knowing what was going to pop up ahead of us next, whether on or beside the road.

Once, as we came around a curve in the road, I noticed another vehicle's headlights appear off in the distance. It was eerily rocking back and forth as it approached us. It really was an amusing sight to behold. And yet those kinds of encounters were no laughing matter, since the two trucks would soon have to pass each other ... the catch being, there wasn't enough room for two trucks to pass each other on those narrow mountain roads. Although a solution existed ...

As they drew ever closer, the driver of each vehicle started watching for a wider spot in the road where he could pull over and hug the side of the mountain, so the other vehicle would be able to pass safely. Such *passing lanes* were purposefully made for just such occasions when the roads were originally cut out of the sides of the mountains. That very day we had already passed a number of other vehicles along the way ... but that took place in the daylight! The darkness definitely added to the unwanted suspense.

Personally, I always hated being on the outside of the road if it was our driver who had to go around another vehicle on those mountain goat trails, knowing that if the ground gave way even just a little, we were all doomed. So on this occasion, when we came upon a hug spot first, I gave a sigh of relief. We waited. The other vehicle soon reached us, and then very slowly drove past, the two drivers exchanging smiles and greetings during the short-lived moment that their windows were side by side.

Other lights we passed along the way were stable ones, produced by kerosene lamps, shining out at us from inside lonely houses we rather infrequently passed along the way. Off in the distance I could see yet more lights spread out over the mountains as generators fed at least some segments of this remote electricity hungry population with power.

Eventually we dropped off the last of the original passengers, leaving us with only two of the additional ones we had picked up along the way. As we drew ever nearer to our final destination, and the end to the trip was becoming a reality, the three Yemenis started joking and laughing.

I didn't participate in the frivolity. That was partly due to exhaustion, but mostly because I couldn't always follow what they were talking about. In fact, I didn't understand much of what the Yemenis had been saying throughout the entire trip ... sometimes including phrases directed right at me. Their dialect almost always threw me when it came at me full speed. At least the driver was one of those who was willing to slow down his speech and adjust his vocabulary to accommodate me. But when interacting with other Yemenis, as he was doing at that moment, he would usually lose me too.

It was after 9 PM when I finally arrived in Nadhiir ... almost twelve hours from the time I first started looking for a ride. Nadhiir was the largest and most central town within the district of Raazih. I was physically, mentally, and emotionally exhausted! But the trip wasn't quite over yet ... I still needed to find a place to bed down for the night.

As I paid the driver the fare (fares are agreed on before the drive starts, but typically paid after arrival), I asked him, "Can you tell me if there's a hotel here in Nadhiir?"

"This is the hotel right here," he said pointing to the building right beside us. "I'm planning to spend the night here myself."

In fact the other two passengers ended up staying there too, which was a clear indication that none of them were from Nadhiir.

With my backpack in hand (rather than over my shoulder), I followed the driver up a few wooden stairs. I could hear the din of many voices coming through the closed door, and then once the door was opened, it hit me like a tidal wave. But suddenly it subsided, and the contrast was stunning. The clamor was suddenly reduced to a whisper. The change in the atmosphere was, of course, due to my appearance in the doorway. Thankfully the cranked up volume of the TV helped reduce the uncomfortable contrast somewhat.

I walked into a large room which had cots lining all the walls, with a few scattered rather randomly in the middle. Small groups distributed here and there were the source of the talking, laughter and general buzz of the original relaxed ambience. There would be no privacy, of that I was sure.

The smell of many bodies, mixed with cigarette smoke and old mattresses all blended together to form a now somewhat familiar aroma for such surroundings.

Since the driver and I entered together, he introduced the idea of my staying in the hotel to the owner before I even had a chance to open my mouth. "I brought a foreigner with me and he needs a bed."

That didn't bother me since it got things rolling without my having to introduce myself. I tried hard to ignore everyone else and just focused my attention on the owner. But I could feel the eyes of every guest there gazing at me. "Is there even a bed available for me?" I wondered.

"He can have the bed right over there," the owner said pointing out a cot against one of the walls.

"Thank you, that will do fine," I said, letting the owner know I understood him and could manage to communicate in Arabic ... albeit in my strange dialect.

Realizing that he could interact with me directly, he asked, "Where are you from?"

"I'm German, and I'm doing research in Yemen," I responded.

"Welcome to Nadhiir," he said, and then returned to what he was doing prior to my arrival, asking no further questions.

With the initial curiosity having worn off, everyone was more or less back to their pre-interruption activities and volume. I walked through the midst of them and, arriving at the cot assigned to me, I placed my backpack on it to claim it as my own. 20 riyals ($2 US) per night provided a guest with a metal frame cot, some rope woven around the frame to form a base, a well-worn lumpy mattress, and a multi-colored wool blanket. A pillow was not included.

It wasn't what I would call a sanitary environment. And that was one of the reasons I always carried a sleeping bag with me. Although, whatever little creatures happened to be crawling around on those mattresses and blankets would probably eventually end up in my sleeping bag with me anyway. A reassuring thought, right?

So there I was. You know how some hotels provide piano players, some have singers ... well this hotel could boast a Westerner as part of their entertainment package. Yup, I'm sure I was most likely the focus of many conversations that evening. It was something I just had to get used to, being in the line of work I was in. I had to keep reminding myself that the immersion experience was good for me.

I also found the Yemenis very entertaining. A number of guests started playing a game. The game consisted of one man standing with his back to a number of others. The one with his back turned placed one of his hands, palm up, over his shoulder (if it was the right hand it went over the right shoulder). Between one and three men stood behind him, and one of those slapped his hand. The one who got his hand slapped had to guess who slapped him, and in addition guessed which hand (right or left) the man had used. The game went on for hours while others laughed along with the participants or joined in themselves. I wasn't asked to join in the fun, and I didn't ask to be a part of it either. I just observed and enjoyed watching how much fun the others were having together.

As I pointed out, the TV was already going when I first walked into the hotel. I found out it was tuned to a channel coming in from Saudi Arabia, and I was surprised at how clear the picture was. Since I was far too exhausted to hold an intelligible conversation with anyone, and since there was no way I was going to get any sleep before everyone else turned in, I decided to join the *cot potatoes* with eyes glued to the TV.

I can't recall what the first program was, but I certainly couldn't forget what program came on next. It was All-star Wrestling! Yes, the American WWF (World Wrestling Federation) style of wrestling with Hulk Hogan and his buddies.

"Do you enjoy this program?" I asked one of the men. I already knew the answer based on the expression on his face as he watched, but thought it would be a good way to create some interaction.

"Yes," he said. "They are very big and strong."

Ha, for Yemenis with their slight builds, those wrestlers must have looked like giants.

"How often does this show come on?" I inquired.

"Twice a week," he answered. "Once in English and once translated into Arabic."

As I watched their reactions to the program, I had the feeling the Yemenis believed they were watching real wrestling rather than mere entertainment. So I decided to find out if that was true, and asked the same man, "You do know that those wrestlers are acting, don't you?"

He looked at me in disbelief, and said, "You're kidding."

"No," I said, "it's not real. They're actors."

"Of course it's real," he argued. "Look at them!"

I decided it wouldn't be worth my while to argue the point, and so I just sat there observing and enjoying the Yemenis' reactions to the wrestling and didn't really pay much attention to the program itself ... a form of entertainment I didn't particularly care for. I found the Yemenis' reactions much more entertaining.

After the wrestling, a circus program came on, although not too many people seemed interested.

Things finally wound down at about 11:30. By then I was beyond exhausted.

I headed over to my cot and started to unroll my compact sleeping bag, which I'm sure was another strange sight for the other guests ... and I imagine they were just waiting to see what I would be pulling out of my backpack next.

As everyone was getting ready to lie down, a little squabble arose over who should have which mattress. I was just hoping the owner hadn't inadvertently assigned me someone else's mattress to sleep on. But since no one said anything to me, I assumed all was well. The whole place was full up for the night.

I just tried to ignore the aroma coming from my well-used, never cleaned mattress and crawled into my sleeping bag, making sure that the few valuables I had along were safely tucked away beside me right in the bag. I lay there, totally worn out but with too much adrenaline still flowing to allow me to get to sleep quickly. I eventually slept, although it was a rather restless sleep.

11

The Shack

I woke often throughout the night hours ... and eventually my eyes sensed that the dispelling of the darkness had begun. Then I started the wait for others to stir before I made any move to get up myself.

The stirring eventually came, and I joined in ... rolling out of bed and organizing my few belongings. I heard a few of the hotel guests order some breakfast ... one of the services I wasn't aware the hotel offered. The smell of food cooking reminded me that it had been a long time since I last had a decent meal.

I walked over to the manager, bid him a "good morning," and then ordered what everyone else was eating, something I always thoroughly enjoyed, good ol' mashed fava beans, freshly baked flat bread, and sweet milky tea.

Feeling somewhat revived after a few hours of sleep (very few indeed!) and a scrumptious meal, I felt ready to attempt some interaction with a few of the other hotel guests who were still mingling around the premises.

I was quite sure that all of them were curious to know more about the Westerner who had suddenly shown up yesterday evening, most likely the first one they'd ever had the opportunity to observe up close. They probably only ever heard rumors about Westerners, or had ideas based on TV shows ... a scary thought considering the kind of garbage so much of western TV offers to the world. So it was up to me to give them some new ideas based on what at least this one representative Westerner was like ... a rather daunting responsibility.

So I started up a conversation with one of the men standing closest to me, and was soon surrounded by a few others. Besides telling them something about myself and why I had come to Nadhiir, I found out something about them too. All of the men staying in the hotel were from other parts of North Yemen. Not one of them was from any of the villages of Raazih. They were only there for the work ... employed as laborers in the fields ... fields I had yet to see with my own eyes, the darkness having prevented me from doing so upon my arrival. Those men had no other place to stay except the hotel.

Hmmm, so I fit right in. All of us were outsiders. Of course, I was much more of an outsider than the others were.

Now even though they all turned out to be extremely friendly, I decided not to spend my time getting to know any of them better. That's because my goal was to meet people from Raazih. And so it was time to venture out and have a look around the town, and hopefully bump into a few friendly locals who would be willing to interact with me.

I paid my bill, grabbed my backpack, and headed out the hotel's door, ready for further adventure, wondering who or what I would encounter. And my first encounter was the town itself.

As you can see, it was quite a spectacular town, built right on and part way down the side of a mountain. I could see why they needed laborers to work the vast terraced fields which started just underneath the town and then crept layer by layer far down the sides of the mountain.

I gazed in the direction from which we had come in the dark the day before, and marveled at it all ... something I assumed (maybe wrongly) the locals took for granted.

Off in the distance, on the next mountain, and the mountain after that, the villages were scattered, just like the villages I had seen from the window of the Boeing 727 the first time I flew into Yemen.[13] And now I was right in the midst of them.

I hadn't walked far from the hotel before I happened to look back and noticed a man opening up a small door located right underneath the hotel itself. It was a store, and I decided to pop in and buy something.

The storekeeper proved to be exceptionally friendly. In fact, at his invitation, I sat down on a stool and spent the next one and a half hours visiting with him. We didn't actually talk the whole time ... part of the time I just sat slowly sipping away at a *Canada*, watching and listening as customers came in to buy various products from him.

Every customer who came through his door was clearly startled when they noticed me sitting there. They'd enter, catch sight of me, start interacting with the storekeeper, but kept glancing my way every few seconds. Overcome by curiosity, each one eventually asked the storekeeper, "who's the foreigner?" I actually had the feeling that some of them were rather suspicious of me, and it made me a bit nervous not knowing what was going through their minds.

Right near the beginning of our encounter I had explained to the storekeeper about the research I was doing. He thought it intriguing, and actually related that information to his curious customers, to which most reacted positively, as if it was something acceptable and *normal* ... and here's the reason why ...

---

[13] See chapter 4.

"Do you know Shaala?" the store owner asked me soon after he found out I was a researcher.

"No, I don't," I responded to him ... while to myself I thought, "How should I know anybody out here? I've never been to Nadhiir before in my life."

"Shaala was a very nice girl," he said.

This was getting more and more confusing. Why would I know a Yemeni girl from Nadhiir? I needed more input, and so asked, "Who is Shaala?"

"Shaala is from Britain. She lived with Sheikh Ahmad while she did research here," he informed me.

"Ah, so that's it ... he's been saying the name *Sheilah*. Okay, so another foreigner has been doing research here," I processed in my mind before asking the man, "What kind of research did she do?"

"She was doing research about the use of qat," he said with obvious pride.

"What is *qat*?" you, my readers, are probably asking.

Very briefly now, but dealt with in more detail in chapter 13 (entitled *The Chew*), qat is a type of plant, and Yemenis chew the leaves to extract a stimulating drug.

Okay, so Nadhiir was not as remote and untouched by foreigners as I had at first thought it was. A town leader named Ahmad Muhamed Jebran had hosted a British researcher named Shelagh Weir a couple of years before my arrival (I found out her full name and actual spelling later at AIYS). Shelagh had spent two 7-month periods in Nadhiir researching qat consumption, and then wrote a book[14] about it. Many Nadhiir residents (including the store keeper) were very proud of the book. I found out later that her book was banned in North Yemen (by the government) because of its support of qat.

Everyone in Nadhiir would have known about Shelagh ... and so I was merely another researcher. It sounded normal to anyone inquiring. As for me, I decided what the store owner told his customers was good advertising that may pay off in the end.

The storekeeper eventually suggested, "You should meet Ahmad. He might be able to help you."

He probably assumed that Ahmad, based on his vast experience, would know how to handle foreigners wanting to do research. Or maybe it was a way to inform someone significant of my presence in

---

[14] *Qat in Yemen: Consumption and Social Change* (published in 1985).

town. Or maybe it was a way to get me out of his store? No, I'm sure the latter wasn't the case.

I concluded that Ahmad may turn out to be a good contact, and so responded, "I would enjoy meeting him. Does he live close by?"

"Just a second," he said, and went off, leaving me all on my own in the store.

"Oh great, what do I do if another customer comes in," I asked myself, not having any idea where he went or for how long.

But less than a minute later he returned with a boy following close behind. I didn't know what relation the boy was to the storekeeper, but he told the boy, "Please take this man to Ahmad's house right away."

So off we went, winding in and out between houses, not too far, but far enough so that, as someone unfamiliar with the town, I ended up quite disoriented. When we reached Ahmad's house, he wasn't home. That was disappointing.

"Thanks for your help," I said to the boy.

"You're welcome," he replied. "Can I help you in any other way?"

"No, I'll be fine," I responded.

I imagined he was glad to be freed from his obligation, and he quickly ran off leaving me stranded. Well, not really stranded ... the town wasn't all that big, and I was sure I'd be able to find my way back to the store, if not on my own, then by asking. And so I started to head in what I considered the right direction.

Okay, so my sense of direction failed me. But that wasn't necessarily a bad thing, since as a result, I happened upon the local school. I consciously slowed my pace as I drew nearer to the facility. From the number of students playing outside, it appeared they were out for recess.

I could tell that a few of the students spotted me, and word was getting around. Soon many pairs of young eyes were looking my way.

I was scanning the scene hoping to catch sight of a teacher, when I noticed one of the braver students heading my way. He must have been about 14 or 15 years old. He came right up to me and said, "Hello, how are you?" in English, with a very heavy but understandable Yemeni accent.

"Fine, thank you," I answered him, also using English. But I quickly made the switch to Arabic, knowing that his English would most likely be very limited. During our brief interaction I was able to explain to him why I had come to Nadhiir, hoping this encounter would lead to some help with my research.

But much to my disappointment, the boy suddenly said "goodbye" in English, and turned and walked off.

Strange. I couldn't tell if I had said something to offend him. But while I was still thinking it through, he suddenly reappeared and asked (in Arabic), "Would you like to drink some tea?" So it seemed his earlier English "goodbye" was to be understood as "excuse me for a minute." He just didn't know how to phrase it properly in English yet. I still recall how poorly I stated things when I was first learning and using Arabic in Jordan.

"Yes please," I said, expecting to go to a coffee shop with him, or maybe to his home where he lived with his parents. "That's it. He must have gone home to get permission to invite me for tea," I said to myself.

Then directing my speech at him, once again speaking in slow clear English for his benefit, I asked, "What is your name?"

He answered, continuing to use the school English he'd memorized and practiced many times over, but probably never had a chance to use on a mother tongue speaker of English before, "My name is Mansoor. What is your name?"

"My name is Butros," I answered.

Butros is the equivalent of *Peter* in Arabic. In Jordan I would often use the name Butros, mostly because it was easier to pronounce than *Peter* since Arabic doesn't have the English 'p' sound. And so when Arabs tried to say *Peter*, it always came out sounding more like *Beater* (with a flap 'r' at the end). Butros just sounded better when coming from Arabic speakers.

As for my family name *Twele*, if I changed the first letter to a heavy Arabic 't' (technically referred to as a pharyngeal sound), it could be pronounced *Taweel*, which means *tall* in Arabic and was a well known family name in Jordan.

In fact (bear with me as I continue down this rabbit trail), I found out later that the name Taweel was also a common name in the south of Yemen. I learned that bit of information during my departure after another visit to Yemen some years later. I was sitting next to a Yemeni man on the plane and we naturally started to exchange a few words. Somehow, while talking about where he came from, I found out his family name was *Taweel*. So I piped up, "Hey, my name is Taweel too," pronouncing it the same as his name.

He smiled, thinking I was obviously jesting.

So I pulled out my passport and showed him my name, *Peter Twele*. He looked at it in disbelief.

Then I said jokingly, "So we must be from the same tribe."

We both had a good laugh.

Mansoor and I strolled along together, chatting as we walked, when he abruptly stopped in front of a small shack ... an old wooden structure that, from the outside, didn't look very safe to me. He reached up, turned the door handle and walked in.

When he noticed I wasn't following him, he returned to the open door and motioned for to me enter.

I still hesitated. I assumed was he was living with family, and so that meant a female could very well be inside ... maybe a sister, or his mother. If that was indeed the case, then it definitely wouldn't be appropriate for me to enter without his father being the one to invite me in.

He continued to look back at me from inside the shack, wondering why I was still hesitating, and finally said in Arabic, "Come on in Butros and I'll make some tea for us."

I concluded that his family wasn't home, and so it must be okay. So I climbed the few wooden stairs and went inside.

The shack was a one-room structure packed full of furniture ... three beds, a table, and some sort of cupboard with a TV on top. On the table sat a few pots, pans and glasses along with a single kerosene burner.

As you can see in the photo, the walls were covered in graffiti, and clothes hung here and there on nails. It was simple, but very well organized.

While I was scanning my surroundings, Mansoor lit the kerosene burner and put some water on to boil. Then we sat and sipped our strong tea (just what I needed to keep me going) and exchanged information. I found out Mansoor wasn't even from Nadhiir, but rather came to Nadhiir from another Raazih village to study. His own village didn't provide any higher education past grade six. So as it turned out, he wasn't living with his parents after all, but was rather living with two other students.

After some time, the door opened and in walked three boys, who all appeared to be in their teens as well. One of them was Saari, one of Mansoor's roommates, and the other two were friends. They didn't seem at all surprised to see me in the shack, and so I assumed Mansoor must have filled them in about me during his earlier absence. I was formally introduced and then the five of us started to interact.

At some point an exchange took place between Mansoor and one of the two visiting friends. "I want to invite him to be a guest in my home," said his friend.

"No, he's my guest and he's going to stay here," insisted Mansoor.

My opinion obviously didn't seem to matter, since they didn't ask for it. They were discussing my fate, assuming I would be staying with one of them. I just listened, and wasn't sure if I should interject any thoughts or not. In the end Mansoor won out. Even though he wasn't from Nadhiir, he seemed to be rather influential among his peers.

"Thank you very much," I finally spoke up, "but I don't want to be a bother to anyone. I'll stay in the hotel again tonight."

"That's not possible," Mansoor replied. "You're going to stay here as our guest," first looking over at Saari, who nodded his head in agreement, and then back at me again.

"Thank you very much. You're very generous," I finally conceded, although I still had my doubts. How would it look ... me staying there with two teenagers. I just had to trust they knew what they were doing, and I didn't want to insult anyone. I concluded that it would be an opportunity to spend more time with some Raazih Arabic speakers rather than in the hotel with a bunch of Yemenis who weren't even from the region.

I mentioned that there were three beds. Well, one of his roommates was off in his home village visiting his family, and so that left a free bed in the shack for me to sleep on ... a solid wooden frame bed with wooden slats on which lay a mattress. The bed was somewhat wider than the cot I had slept on in the hotel, but it seemed rather short, causing more lumping of the mattress than I thought necessary, as well as forcing the head to be raised. But I wasn't going to be picky ... as far as I was concerned it was going to work out just fine.

The hours flew by, and eventually we agreed it was time to get some sleep. I once again pulled my compact sleeping bag out of my backpack, unrolled it, crawled into it, zipped it up, put down my head, and hoped for a restful sleep. And sleep I did, until ...

"What was that noise?" I said groggily to myself.

Then I heard it again. Footsteps. Not big footsteps, like from a human, but rather little footsteps running across the raised wooden floor of the shack.

When the footsteps stopped, the sound of nibbling started. Some sort of animal was inside the shack with us. A little animal had obviously squeezed in through some breach in the shack's defenses.

I moved, and whatever it was scuttled off. Complete silence. Had I scared it off for good? I lay there on my side with my eyes wide open staring at the floor. But there was no chance of seeing anything in the pitch black that ruled the shack.

I closed my eyes wishing for sleep to overtake me quickly, but the tapping feet returned first. And this time I was sure I heard two of them. "I bet they're rats!" went through my mind. "Oh great. What should I do?"

I listened attentively. They would scramble around, nibble, then scramble some more ... most likely eating the feast of crumbs spread out on the floor ... leftovers from our supper.

I made some noise, and off they scampered again. Silence. But sure enough, they were soon back at it.

I always carried a flashlight with me, and I slowly and silently pulled it out of my backpack which I had conveniently placed beside me on the bed. I hesitated to use it since I didn't want to wake up Mansoor and Saari, and yet I wanted to get a look at those little creatures that were tormenting me.

I turned on the flashlight, and then heard the little feet scamper off, but saw nothing. I turned it off and waited until they returned. Then I pointed it in the direction of the noise and turned the flashlight on again. Nothing ... they reacted too fast.

I finally gave up with the flashlight and covered my head. I managed to doze from time to time, but never got a solid sleep that entire night. Eventually I just lay there waiting for the sun to rise.

12

The Endless Story

The darkness slowly abated, and with it the noise of the tiny invisible monsters. I waited for Mansoor and Saari to get up before attempting to show any signs of life myself.

Finally I heard some welcome human movement (as opposed to the unwelcome rodent movement I had put up with all night). "Good morning," I said as I crawled out of my sleeping bag and stretched, trying to fake looking refreshed.

"Good morning mister Butros," Mansoor greeted me. "How did you sleep?"

"I slept very well, thank you," I said, but was sure my bloodshot eyes would betray me. Boy did I ever want to get my hands, actually my shoes, on those dirty little rodents!

"Praise be to God," both of them said almost in unison.

"Praise be to God," I said after them.

"Are you hungry?" Mansoor asked.

"Yes," I said honestly ... then quickly adding an appropriate, "but I don't want to be any bother."

"No, no, it's no bother at all," he quickly said, although I saw no sign of food or any sign of either of them trying to procure food. The three of us just sat talking.

Soon there was a knock on the door. It startled me.

Mansoor went to the door, opened it and exchanged a few words with someone. I couldn't see who it was from the angle where I was sitting, but it sounded to me like it was an older woman's voice. I never got a glimpse of her. Mansoor's hands went out, and then came back in with a tray containing food and drink. Hmmm, so it seemed that Mansoor and his two roommates were at least partly taken care of by someone in the town. Mansoor didn't say who the woman was, and I didn't think it was appropriate for me to ask.

We sat down and Mansoor handed me some bread which I willingly accepted. Then he poured some coffee into a glass for me. It was white coffee. Not white because it contained milk, but rather white because it was made from coffee bean pods rather than from actual coffee beans.

I had gained some experience drinking the white pod coffee while in Sana'a. The first time I tried some was at a special function held at the American Institute for Yemeni Studies. It was an evening event and I gladly accepted a cup of the white brew when it was offered to me ... I was always open to trying new things. Well let me tell you, it was bitter (very bitter), and it really took some getting used to. Then later, after the occasion, when I was trying to get to sleep, I found out it was quite a potent brew. It pretty well kept me awake for the entire night.

Well this time it was morning, and I was certain it could only do me some good ... namely, it would help keep me awake after the last two sleep-deprived nights. So I gladly accepted a glass of it.

I'll never forget that first sip. I had never in my life tasted anything so bitter ... probably ten times more bitter than what I had experienced in Sana'a. It was pure torture! I'm quite sure my face must have gone through all sorts of contortions which Mansoor and Saari obviously didn't notice, otherwise they would have immediately asked me about it. They were contentedly drinking their own coffee and eating.

I quickly stuffed a piece of bread into my mouth to try and get rid of the horrible taste the coffee had left. I continued eating, but couldn't bring myself to take another sip of the coffee. It was pretty much the first time in all my travels that I couldn't get down something I was offered ... and I had eaten and drunk some very *interesting* things, believe you me.

I surveyed my surroundings to try and spot a place where I could pour out my coffee without being noticed. Not a chance. Maybe I could walk to the door with it, pretend to get a breath of fresh air, and then *accidently* drop my glass on the ground. But then Mansoor would merely pour me another cup.

I was their guest, and their full attention was on me almost all of the time, and so Mansoor did eventually notice that I wasn't drinking. But first he merely asked, "How is the food, Mr. Butros?"

I answered truthfully, "The food is delicious, praise be to God."

"Praise be to God," he said, and then noted, "But you're not drinking your coffee."

Okay, what should I say? I definitely couldn't force it down. But I didn't want to insult my host. In the end, I decided to be truthful, and said, "I'm sorry Mansoor, but I'm not used to this kind of coffee. It's a little too strong for me." What an understatement!

Without any hesitation, and not seeming to be offended whatsoever, Mansoor quickly boiled some water and made me a cup of tea instead. The tea was strong, but familiar and swallowable. I was very thankful. What a gracious host, having his guest's comfort first and foremost in his mind.

Now I had explained to Mansoor what my research was all about the day before. I informed him that I needed to find people to help me with a couple of things. First, I needed someone to tell me a natural story in the Raazih dialect. Second, I needed someone to translate some specific material into the Raazih dialect for me. If you want to know some more details about my research, then please read appendix 2.

Mansoor was more than willing to help me. Actually, he was quite enthusiastic about it. So right after breakfast, he decided it was time to get to work. "Wait here Mr. Butros," he told me. "I know someone who should be able to tell you a good story in our dialect."

To which I responded, "That's great. Thank you for your help Mansoor. I'm sorry to be such a bother."

"No bother at all," he said as he disappeared through the shack's door, leaving me and Saari on our own.

"This is working out great," I said to myself.

He soon returned, and then he, Saari and I walked a short distance to another house in the village. When I entered, I saw a couple of men around my age sitting next to a very old man. The two younger men stood up.

"This is Mr. Butros, the researcher I told you about," Mansoor introduced me.

"Peace be with you," I greeted them.

"And with you be peace," they responded.

The two younger guys didn't seem very relaxed as they shook my hand, but I didn't think much of it because a lot of people tend to get nervous if their voice is going to be recorded.

As for me, I was totally focused ... ready and anxious for one of the young men to start telling me a story. This was exactly what I was hoping for.

Mansoor could tell I was pleased, and he was beaming with pride that he'd been able to set up this appointment for me.

"Are you ready to tell us a story sir?" Mansoor said to the older gentleman.

"Why's he talking to the old man?" I wondered.

"Grandfather, the professor is here to record a story," one of the men said rather loudly to the old man.

"Oh great, Mansoor arranged to have the old man tell me a story," I thought, rather dismayed at this unexpected and unfortunate turn of events.

Both of the younger men were now interacting with their grandfather with raised voices, which indicated to me that the old man was hard of hearing. And from the way he moved his head and eyes, it was obvious he also couldn't see very well. And when he opened his mouth, there weren't many teeth to speak of. This would be the last person I'd pick to tell me a story. But Mansoor had carefully thought it through, and as far as he was concerned, the best person to help me was obviously the oldest man in the village.

I hope I didn't show how very disappointed I was. I should have seen this coming. I've seen it happen before. It's such a typical way of thinking ... namely, believing that the oldest person in the village is the one who speaks the *purest form* of the language, closest to the way everyone *used to speak*.

It's a fact that with the passing of time, languages change. And what I was looking for was natural material with *current* language usage. In addition, since I would be getting others to listen to it, I wanted a story that would be easy to listen to, and an older man with a wavery creaky voice and missing teeth wouldn't provide me with the kind of material I could use.

But I couldn't insult Mansoor, and I certainly didn't want to offend anyone else, and so I tried to act as pleased as possible about this *invaluable* opportunity ... and believe me, it would take some impressive acting on my part. I had already hesitated a little too much, and everyone was starting to sense my dilly-dallying. So to break the tension, I quickly placed my backpack on the floor, pulled out and set up my tape recorder, plugged in the microphone, and said, "Sir, I'm ready to record your story."

"What?" said the old man.

"He's ready to record a story!" one of the two men said with his volume turned up high.

And so, with obvious pride at being selected to provide information for the foreign *professor*, the old man started speaking while I held the microphone close to his mouth.

The elderly gentleman waxed eloquent. He went on and on and on, as the other two men prompted him and encouraged him to go on and on and on. It turned out to be a very long recording. I wouldn't exactly call it a story, since at times he would talk, and then he would sing or chant something, and then he'd start talking again, with constant interruptions coming from the other two men.

Usually I would take the time to go through any recorded material with the person who told it, so I could do a quick translation to get meanings for any vocabulary I wouldn't have understood ... and believe me, I hadn't understood much of what the old man had said. But it would have taken me hours to go through such a long recording, and it was material I knew I wouldn't be using anyway. Since I hadn't warned them about needing to go over the story with them, they didn't expect it, and so I could get away with not doing it.

When he was finally done, I said, "Thank you very much for the wonderful story, sir." And I added many other praises and thank yous to him and all the others involved. Then I turned to address just the two younger men and asked, "Would one of you be willing to tell me a story as well?"

"Oh no, we're not good at telling stories," they protested.

"Well it was worth a try," I said to myself as I started packing up my equipment. Then I thanked them all again and left with Mansoor and Saari.

As we walked along, Mansoor suddenly informed me, "I arranged to have the elderly man come over to my place later today so you can record some more material."

I couldn't believe my ears. "Oh, that would be great," I said quickly, hoping he'd think I really meant it. I had obviously fooled them by showing a little too much enthusiasm over what I had recorded.

Saari disappeared, and Mansoor started giving me a tour of the town. On my mind the whole time was, "How can I get someone else to tell me a story that I can actually use?"

We eventually headed back to Mansoor's shack. As I sat talking with Mansoor, my mind wasn't totally on our conversation ... my mind was trying to come up with a new plan for finding someone to get a recording from.

Suddenly a few of Mansoor's friends showed up. "Work with what you've got, Peter," I decided. And so I went ahead and asked, "Can any of you tell me a story so I can record it?"

"Sure, I can tell you a story," piped up one of them.

Ah, cooperation at last! Out came the tape recorder, and with the mic in his face, the boy proceeded to tell me about how a friend of his lost his watch while they were on a trip together. It was something, although it didn't quite flow naturally (a little too choppy), and the length and detail also wasn't quite what I was looking for. "But it might have to do," I said to myself, "if I can't come up with anything else."

I felt rather discouraged, and decided I needed to get out on my own for a while. So I excused myself and went for a walk. Along the way I spotted a store and decided to pop in and buy something to drink. The fellow running the store introduced himself as Faisel. He was probably in his mid 20's and was very friendly. I, of course, talked with him about my research, and deciding I had nothing to lose, asked if he'd be open to telling me a story.

He rather surprised me with his answer, "I'd be happy to."

Then he proceeded to tell me a story about a medical need he had and how at one point he traveled to Saudi Arabia for treatment, and then another time went to Sana'a. Great story. In addition, he helped me with the translation of the other research material. Success!

Having finally gotten what I needed, I felt relaxed later when the old man showed up at Mansoor's shack. I was okay with recording some more of what he had to say, and planned to file it away with the other material I had recorded from him earlier in the day.

In the end everyone was happy.

At Mansoor's invitation, I decided to go ahead and spend one more night in the shack with Mansoor, Saari and my rodent friends, who I was sure would show up again sniffing out and devouring whatever tidbits we had inadvertently left for them during the daylight hours. I was determined to ignore them, and get some well deserved and badly needed sleep that night.

I made it through the night, woke up ready to travel, said my goodbyes, caught a ride, and was on my way back to Sa'da.

13

The Chew

Soon after my arrival in North Yemen, as I was walking along the streets of Sana'a early one morning, I happened to notice, mixed in among some of the other rubbish, a green glob lying in the middle of the street. And just a few meters away, in a gutter, I saw another one. It was quite obvious to me that they were some kind of animal droppings. But what kind of animal had they come from? I wasn't an expert on animal scat, but it sure didn't look like those droppings came from any animal I'd ever seen before. I looked around to see if I could spot the depositor, but no animal life was to be seen. I examined the samples no further, lest anyone passing by think I was a little on the strange side.

Later that same day, in the early afternoon, while out for another stroll in an effort to get to know the city yet a little better, I came across a group of men, two of them haggling over the cost of something that at first I couldn't make out. As I stood at a distance and covertly observed the goings on, I noticed the seller eventually wrapping a bundle of thin leafy branches in a plastic bag, and the buyer contentedly handing him the agreed on price. It was quite clear (to me) that the leaves were some sort of greens the man was bringing home for his wife to cook as part of the family's supper.

The next day, sometime in the afternoon, when I entered a small store to buy a few canned goods, I couldn't help but observe a pile of branches with leaves protruding from a ripped open plastic bag lying on the counter in front of the seller. They looked exactly like the ones I had seen being purchased the day before. The man was sitting behind the counter watching TV. He had a glazed look in his eyes as he slowly and selectively picked leaves off the branches and popped them into his mouth. He hardly even acknowledged my presence.

As I searched through the store for certain goods, with no help even offered by the worker, I would glance his way from time to time, wondering about some disfigurement I had noticed on his face. I thought he must have been suffering from some sort of ailment ... and admittedly I wondered if it was something that could be contagious.

I found what I wanted to buy, walked over to the counter, all the while discretely watching his leaf picking activity, asked him how much I owed him for the goods, paid him, and went out, still not knowing the truth about the leaf chewing and the *disease*.

Leaving the store, I walked along and suddenly noticed a couple of men sitting on some concrete stairs in front of a building. A pile of branches was lying between them, and they were busy with the same activity as the man in the store ... slowly and deliberately picking off some of the leaves and stuffing them into their mouths. Both of them had the same kind of lump on the sides of their faces, something I would come across time and time again throughout my travels.

It was definitely time to ask someone about this peculiar phenomenon. That's when I was first introduced to the word *qat*. And that's when I found out about the daily event most Yemenis participated in, known as *the chew*.

Qat[15] is a type of plant that was (and still is) widely grown in North Yemen ... and actually in a number of other countries as well (for instance, Somalia, Eritrea and Ethiopia). It's a slow-growing plant that can apparently grow quite tall ... although the plants I saw were usually no more than a few meters in height.

"So why do Yemenis chew qat leaves?" is the question I assume you must be asking yourselves ... the same question I had asked myself that day so long ago. And what's with the lump in the cheek?[16]

---

[15] Scientifically referred to as *Catha edulis*.
[16] Photo taken by Bert.

"You need to chew some qat," Ahmad told me. "How do you expect to understand Yemenis if you don't chew qat?"

This was part of Ahmad's regular scolding every time I saw him. It was said jokingly, and yet he would have been thrilled had I given in and actually participated in a qat chewing party, something which was part of his regular (although for him not daily) routine.

"Okay, I'll come and join you and your friends when you have your next qat chew ... but it's only so I can visit with you. I'm not going to chew qat," I insisted.

"We'll see," he said with a laugh. And I returned his laugh as we parted.

In fact, the day of the chew, I actually accompanied Ahmed when he visited his qat supplier so I could watch him in action. He had a careful look at the seller's wares, picking up bundle after bundle of qat, looking each one over very carefully, looking for the best leaves for his money. Other customers were doing the same. That particular seller had his qat bunches all wrapped up in banana leaves rather than plastic bags, giving the same desired effect ... moisture retention. The qat leaves are always wrapped because it's important to keep the leaves moist. Qat leaves contain a drug that acts as a mild stimulant, and the leaves are chewed to release the drug to obtain the desired effect. As soon as qat leaves dry out, they're not as potent.

When he was satisfied, Ahmad pulled out the agreed upon price and the exchange was made. Ahmad left a happy man, ready for the chew party.

With his qat in hand, Ahmed and I walked back to his apartment where he washed his precious leaves in the shower, cleaning them and keeping them moist. Soon we were joined by some of his friends, each carrying their own bundle of qat and a bottle of water or pop.

Chewing qat is something of an art. Ahmad picked the fresh leaves from the tops of the branches, carefully selecting the small, soft fresh leaves, and even some of the slender soft branches. He explains, "Only the small fresh leaves are good. The larger leaves get thrown out along with the branches." That definitely matched what I had observed.

The small tender leaves are placed in the mouth where the molars grind away at them, chewing them into a mush. The mushed leaves then get stored in a ball in the cheek. The ball of leaves slowly grows until it forms a bulge. The larger the ball of leaves, the larger the buldge ... and a large bulge is something to be proud of. Men and boys walking down the street in the afternoon with bulging cheeks was a sight I soon got used to.

"Butros, do you want to try it?" Ahmad asks. I hadn't bought my own bundle at the qat market, but he waved a branch close to my face, taunting me.

"Okay, I should at least see what a leaf tastes like," I say to give Ahmad some satisfaction.

He picks some nice tender leaves and holds them out to me. So I choose one and pop it in my mouth. "Yup, it tastes like a leaf," I said to myself.

"So, what do you think?" he inquires.

"It's not bad, but that's as much as I'm going to chew, thank you very much," I tell him.

They all have a good laugh, and the party goes on ... it goes on for hours. And we talk.

The remnants, the hard branches and the undesirable leaves, pile up in front of the party of chewers.

During this whole process, the chewers don't actually swallow the juices which the leaves produce. They spit out the juices into small spittoons which are stationed around the room. Each person has his own drink which they sip on throughout the party.

As I understand it, the chewer essentially experiences three stages ... and no, I have never gone beyond the tasting of one leaf to experience it for myself!

Stage one ... about 15 minutes after the wad of chewed leaves is formed in the cheek, the drug will have started its effect on the chewer's mind and they become very talkative. Stage one lasts for a couple of hours or so.

Entering stage two, the chewers are calmer and contemplative. They'll just sit silently or take part in quieter conversations with each other.

Stage three consists of irritable and depressed partiers.

Apparently a considerable amount of business and local political decisions are made during qat-chewing sessions ... hopefully before stage three!

There's definitely some controversy about this widespread habit. "Exactly how widespread is the habit," you ask? I'm not positive, but I've heard that as many as 80% of men and 45% of women chew qat on a daily basis for long periods of their lives. So Ahmad was in the minority, only partying on a weekly basis.

Anyway, the controversy is about whether or not this qat-chewing habit is harmful. Some say that chewing qat is nothing more than a socializing habit, and it hasn't been proven to be addictive or to have any serious medical side effects ... it's just a part of being a Yemeni.

Others, including the World Health Organization (WHO), argue that it's definitely a bad habit. These opponents say qat produces a mild to moderate psychological dependence. It also kills the user's appetite ... which explains why I rarely saw any overweight Yemenis.

Insomnia is another side effect. In fact many students chew qat for the very reason that it keeps them awake through the evenings as they study.

Apparently long-term qat usage can also lead to problems with the liver, and may result in ulcers.

Then there's qat's effect on the economy to consider. Some claim that chewing qat is reserved for leisure time, after the main work of the day has been completed. Well, that wasn't my observation. I saw the qat markets full of buyers by late morning. And even when people were working, it seemed their minds were on the purchase of and the chewing of qat. So, as far as working hours was concerned, qat made for very short work days. In addition, researchers estimated that families spent about 17% of their income on qat.

As for qat's effect on the environment, it's cultivation consumes far too much of the country's agricultural resources. About 40% of the country's water supply goes toward irrigating qat plants ... and it's a water supply that is quickly running dry.

When I traveled in the Khawlaan region I could see for myself the qat fields covering much of the landscape. I was told by locals that they used to grow more coffee beans, corn and wheat, but because qat brought them more profit, many stopped growing the other crops and planted qat instead. Qat is about five times more profitable than coffee.

I guess I've given more space to the negative side than I have to the positive ... so my bias is showing.

When the qat chewing party is all over and the chewers disperse, on their walk home they dislodge the ball of chewed qat from their cheeks and spit it out on the road or the sidewalk. Hence the green globs all over the city streets the next morning.

14

Who's Manipulating Who?

"You want to go where?" the man asked me.

"I'm trying to find a ride to Munabbih," I repeated.

"Stay in Sa'da," he said in a commanding voice before shaking his head and walking away.

He knew as well as anyone that foreigners couldn't just go wandering off into the unknown, especially not into the region known as Munabbih ... a very remote part of the country, high up in the mountains (over 2000 meters in elevation) in a region to the northwest of Sa'da city ... about as northwest as you could possibly go before crossing into Saudi Arabia. Munabbih was a region that Yemenis from around the country considered a wild and uncontrolled area. Most Yemenis would never even consider going there themselves ... and yet Munabbih was my destination.

I was determined to get there ... and so the search for a ride continued unabated. Munabbih had a significant population, and I knew that people came from that region to visit the big city, namely Sa'da, to purchase goods. I was determined to find a ride with someone who would be heading back out that way. And so I approached yet another person and asked him if he knew of anyone who would be driving out to Munabbih.

It was March 3rd, 1987. I had woken up early and left the safety of Harry's mud house by 7:30 AM. My previous trips to other regions had taught me that finding a ride could take quite some time. I walked through the streets of Sa'da to get to the appropriate intersection so I could catch a ride to Taalih (the market town to the west of Sa'da ... the place where I should have started my trip when I headed to Nadhiir in Raazih). It was always easy to get to Taalih, but then the real challenge of finding the ride to the outlying area started. And so there I was, in Taalih, asking about rides to Munabbih.

So far no luck. But then suddenly, "What was that?" I was sure I had heard someone mentioning the word *Munabbih*. "It came from that truck," I said as I quickly headed in the direction of a Salown which was almost full of passengers, and where three men were standing beside the vehicle talking.

As I drew closer, two of the men were getting into the vehicle leaving the third man on his own. "Excuse me, are you going to Munabbih?" I asked the man who I now assumed to be the driver.

He replied, "Yes I am. How can I help you?"

"Do you have room for me?" I inquired.

After a slight hesitation, obviously due to my foreignness, he said, "Sure. It'll cost you 100 riyals. You can sit in the middle."

He opened the door and asked the other three passengers already sitting on the middle bench seat to make room for me. So the man sitting beside the door hopped out and indicated I should get in first. I guess he wanted to keep his window seat. I was fine with that. Hey, I was just glad to find a ride.

Soon two more passengers showed up and joined the lone passenger sitting in the back, and we were on our way. Wow, I didn't even get stuck in the back this time! Progress! And it was only 9:15, not even two hours from when I started the search.

It was going to be a long ride through the mountains to get to Munabbih ... so I was told anyway. It would be like all the other rides into the mountains ... no pavement, only one lane dirt roads carved out of the sides of the mountains. By now I should have been used to such things, right? Well, I'm not sure I could ever really *get used* to it ... but I did learn to *endure* it. To tell you the truth, every trip through the mountains of North Yemen had me scared, believe you me. And now I was heading into one of the most isolated parts of the country.

As it turned out, that particular driver really didn't have the best interests of his passengers foremost on his mind. After he had his guaranteed paying passengers, he just took his time. He stopped once to buy gas, and then again shortly after that to buy some personal things. And then he even had the gall to stop yet again to buy himself some breakfast, while the rest of us were left sitting in the truck waiting for him!

Well, actually a couple of the male passengers also jumped out, including the guy to my right. I had been interacting with him some ... a very friendly fellow. As he was making his exit, he turned to me and said, "Would you mind watching this for me?" and much to my surprise he handed me his rifle. Well, he didn't exactly hand it to me, he just leaned it over into my hand.

"Okay, so if someone tries to take this from me, what am I supposed to do then?" I asked myself, feeling a little awkward about such an unexpected honor.

Everyone in the truck carried a rifle (and enough ammunition to last them under most circumstances) except for the driver, a woman passenger and myself. The rifle's owner smiled and thanked me as he got back in and took charge of his rifle once again.

When the driver reappeared, two more men were with him, and he announced matter of factly, "You need to make room for two more passengers."

Okay, he already had nine passengers crammed into his vehicle ... two in the front with him, four of us in the middle, and three in the back. Where was he going to stick these two additional ones? Presumably in the very back. They obviously weren't going to fit in the front or the middle ... at least I hoped he wasn't planning for one of us to have someone on his lap.

This driver was determined to make as much money as possible on this trip at the expense of the comfort of the passengers he already had.

Well things suddenly started to get a little lively. You should have heard the protest coming from behind me, "There's no room back here," said one of the men.

Another one said, "If they're supposed to get in here then we're getting out, and then you'll be worse off."

I should point out that typically no one ever puts down a deposit, so the passengers do have some control and can abandon the vehicle if the driver oversteps his bounds. Anyway, the rather heated discussion ended with us getting under way again without having taken on the extra passengers ... much to my relief. It was all very entertaining though.

Well, it wasn't only the driver who was trying to take advantage of the passengers. When we arrived at a fork in the road, the two male passengers sitting to my left had an argument with the driver. Although it was hard to catch all the details of their fast flowing speech, the gist of it was, they insisted the driver take them all the way to their village, which meant driving along the right fork, whereas our destination was along the left fork. It would result in a lot of back tracking for us to get to our final destination. As I understood it, it would have added an extra one and a half to two hours of driving time. I certainly didn't want that to happen.

One of them said, "We're only going to pay half of the fare unless you take us right to our village." The agreed-on price was 100 riyals ($10 US).

"No, I won't do it!" the driver said, refusing to give in to their demands.

"Okay, have it your way," said one of them as they made their exit, slung their rifles over their shoulders, handed the driver some money, and walked off along the right fork.

So the driver lost 100 riyals. Actually he lost a potential profit of 300 riyals considering that the passengers in the back had refused to let him cram in those two extra passengers near the beginning of the trip.

Since the driver acted like a real jerk a lot of the time during the trip, I had a hard time feeling sorry for him. And actually, on my return trip, I found out that the going price for a one-way trip to Munabbih was usually between 50 and 75 riyals, and so this driver was actually overcharging us. Thankfully most of my encounters with drivers were not like this one.

One of the guys from the back moved up to the middle seat so there were now three of us. Everyone had much more breathing room.

A flat tire along the way, at a place called Wadi al-Jabir, allowed us a short break while the driver changed the tire.

Soon after we got back under way again, the man sitting on my right started snoozing. The reason I even mention it is because his relaxed hold on his rifle resulted in it either pointing at my head or into my side. It made me a little nervous, and I wished he would position his rifle a little differently. More importantly, I hoped he had his safety catch on. Thankfully the person sitting on my left was a little more careful with his rifle, so I only had to keep my eye on the guy on my right.

The mountain road to Munabbih wound through a beautiful green area. And as a pleasant surprise, the trip didn't last half as long as I had prepared myself for. We arrived in a small village called *Suq al-Munabbih*[17] (translated, *the market of Munabbih*) before 2 PM.

---

[17] You've already seen a photo of this village in chapter 1.

15

Chains

I was led through the main entrance into the lower level of the stone defensible castle-like structure, and ended up in a small narrow damp courtyard.

As my eyes adjusted to the change from the bright direct sunlight to the somewhat less well lit interior, I was suddenly aware of a number of faces nearby, slowly turning to gaze up at me. Men were sitting here and there on various shaped concrete blocks which I assumed were part of the building's foundation.

"Why are those men all just sitting there?" I wondered.

But I didn't have to wonder long, because one of them suddenly moved his legs aside to allow the passing of another man who was coming our way. I assumed the man approaching us worked for the Police Chief. When the lethargic man was forced to exert himself, I was somewhat startled by the rattling of chains.

The guard (for that's what he was) came up to us and, after taking a good long look at me, asked one of my two Egyptian escorts, "What do you all want?"

"Could you please inform the Police Chief that there's a foreigner here who would like to see him?" he replied.

I had turned my head at the sound of the chains, and my eyes remained focused in that direction during the brief interchange taking place between the Egyptian and the Yemeni. I noticed that those chains were fastened to metal bands, and those bands were wrapped around the man's ankles. My eyes then did a quick scan of the other men, and every one of them (about half a dozen) was also outfitted with the same hardware.

Based on the evidence before me, I made the quick brilliant Sherlock Holmes style deduction, "This is a prison! Where have the Egyptians taken me?"

I assumed, and hoped, that somewhere in this building was an actual office where the Police Chief was sitting. I also hoped he would be a kind person. At the same time, I imagined myself spending more time in Munabbih than I had counted on ... in chains!

Then I started to speculate about what these prisoners had done to deserve this kind of treatment. Were they murderers ... were they thieves ... what?

The guard said, "Just wait a minute." Then he forced (with a command rather than a shove) the same man who had to move aside earlier to stand and hobble away from the bottom step of the set of stairs where he had been loitering, proving to me that it was indeed not an easy matter to walk with chains clamped around the ankles. The guard then ascended the stairs.

It only took a few minutes for the Police Chief to appear, slowly descending the stone steps. His eyes were glued on me, and in those eyes was a look of astonishment. He was probably in his mid-forties, and slightly more heavy set than the average Yemeni. He emanated an aura of being in charge ... giving a clear signal that his authority was not to be challenged. He did not necessarily look unkind ... and yet he had not even the slightest hint of a smile as he examined me with his gaze.

My mouth suddenly felt dry, and I found it hard to swallow.

When he finally reached the second to bottom step, he stopped his descent and just continued looking down at me. He was in no hurry to speak, but when he finally did, the Police Chief said nothing at all to the Egyptians, and said nothing that would make me feel like he was happy to see me there within his jurisdiction. His first words were merely, "Where are you from?"

The first thing I did upon my arrival in Suq al-Munabbih was inquire about the location of a restaurant so I could buy some lunch. As I approached the eatery, I was fascinated by the sight of a woman sitting on the ground not far from the restaurant's entrance. A round metal tray, containing a pile of uncooked flat bread, sat within arm's reach to her left. Then to her right she had a flat woven basket with a stack of cooked flat bread. Right in front of her was a gaping hole in the ground.[18]

I watched closely as she quickly stuck her hand down into the hole, and then just as quickly pulled it out again holding a round of cooked bread which she accurately tossed onto the growing mound on the basket. In and out, in and out went her hand, removing the fresh cooked bread. And then suddenly it went in and out, in and out again, once more in rapid succession, this time depositing some of the uncooked bread. As I drew ever closer I could see what I already deduced to be the case, that I wasn't looking at a mere hole in the ground, but rather at a pit oven, and I could clearly make out the individual bread rounds plastered to the side of the oven as it cooked. Amazing.

Suddenly a waiter dashed out of the restaurant holding an empty shallow bread basket in one hand. He slowed down his pace when he spotted me standing there, but continued on his way until he reached the baker lady. He swiftly scooped up a number of pieces of cooked bread, placed them on his basket, and then commenced with his return trip. As he passed by me again, with the smell of the freshly baked bread, now within arm's reach, filling my nostrils, he turned to me and

---

[18] The photo was taken by Bert in a different district. The photo is used here to illustrate the same technique which was used in Munabbih.

said, "Come on in," before quickly disappearing back inside the building.

I didn't have to be asked twice. With stomach growling, I continued towards my goal, right behind the waiter, desiring to get my teeth into some of that fresh pit-baked bread. Add to that some chicken with vegetables, and I felt revived.

I was pleased when a few of the men sitting in the restaurant showed an interest in getting to know me. Of course, I was always thrilled to make as many contacts as possible ... and it was easier when the feeling was mutual.

I learned from my new acquaintances that two Egyptian teachers worked at the local school. When I mentioned that I'd like to meet them, one of the men summoned a boy who was standing nearby and told him to take me to the school. I said my nice-to-meet-yous, paid my bill, and then followed the boy who seemed more than willing to serve.

But just as we were leaving the restaurant, I happened to cross paths with a few more local residents who took a double take when they spotted me. A couple of them greeted me and then proceeded to engage me in conversation. They were curious about my presence in Munabbih and found me intriguing ... and I found them just as fascinating. They had a wild look about them. It must have been the headdresses they were wearing ... very different from what I was used to seeing Yemeni men wear in other parts of the country. One of them was wearing a very colorful thin beaded band, and his friend was wearing two bands. In all the other parts of Yemen I'd been to, men usually wore some sort of cloth head covering.

I noticed that some of the Munabbih men also wore different knives from the more typical Yemeni janbiya with its curved blade (see photos in chapter 2). The Munabbih knives had a straighter blade and were worn at a slant rather than straight up and down. One of the younger men also wore a sword in addition to his knife. Otherwise their loose robes or wrap-arounds with suit jackets looked pretty much like the clothes worn by men in other parts of North Yemen.

My young guide had waited patiently for me during the encounter, and then we continued on our short trek to the school.

Needless to say, the two Egyptians were stunned to see me, a Westerner, heading their way. I could see it in their motionless stances and on their focused gaze. The only movement was a very slight turning of the heads and a movement of the lips as they talked amongst themselves while I drew ever nearer. I wondered what was going through their minds.

"How did he get out here?" one would likely be saying to the other.

"This is unusual," the second would say. "I wonder what he's doing here."

"How's your English?" the first inquires.

"You go ahead and speak first," the second says.

"Peace be with you," I said once I was within audible range.

"And with you be peace," they both responded.

"My name is Butros, and I'm from Canada. I came to Yemen to do language research."

I could see the relief on their faces to hear me speaking Arabic, albeit not the dialect from their homeland where many foreigners are known to study Arabic, but understandable nonetheless.

"Welcome! Welcome!" came from the lips of both of them.

"My name is Ibrahim," said one of them as he shook my hand.

"And I'm Hassan," said the other, also reaching out his hand in turn to take hold of mine.

I could sense they were feeling very honored that I would seek them out. In return, they treated me as their honored guest, which thankfully started with a cup of strong tea as we sat and became acquainted.

It was quite evident that Ibrahim and Hassan felt just as foreign in Munabbih as I did. In fact, I think in some ways I was able to fit in better than they did with the Yemenis because I always did my best to take a learner's approach to things. They, on the other hand, saw themselves as *the highly educated experts* and far superior to Yemenis in every way. From the way they spoke (speaking freely, obviously assuming I would feel the same way), it was clear that they really didn't have much (if any) respect for Yemenis, especially not for country bumpkins like the Munabbih folk.

The teachers lived simply. One of the school rooms functioned as their home away from home. They just had a couple of mattresses on the floor, some clothes hanging on nails on the walls, a kerosene burner, and a few pots, pans and dishes.

When the Egyptians found out I hadn't reported to the Police Chief upon my arrival, they suggested I do so right away. I think the advice they gave me may have been just as much for their own benefit as for mine ... namely, so they wouldn't be accused of helping some foreigner who didn't belong in the area.

The school was situated a very short distance from the main section of the village. Then just a little further up the mountain was the Police Chief's office, located within the small castle-like building.

"Sir, I'm from Canada," I said rather nervously to the Police Chief, answering his inquiry. "And I'm here in Yemen to do language research through the Yemen Centre for Research and Studies."

I thought mentioning the Yemeni institute was better than bringing up the *American* institute (AIYS). Throughout my time in the Middle East I usually tried to distance myself from American connections as much as possible.

"Where is your permission paper which allows you to travel out here to Munabbih?" he asked next.

I was prepared. I quickly and confidently produced a copy of my *to whom it may concern* document, and as I handed it to him I said, "here it is sir. You can keep this copy I made for you."

He looked it over, but gave no facial expression to indicate whether he was satisfied or not. But his next request broke the suspense. "Where is your permission paper from Sa'da security allowing you to come out here to Munabbih?" he enquired.

"Sorry, but I don't understand what you mean, sir," I replied with honest confusion.

"You can't come out to Munabbih unless Sa'da security gives you permission to do so," he explained.

"I didn't realize that," I said respectfully. "But this paper gives me permission to go anywhere in the country, and so I thought it would be enough."

"That's okay, I give you permission to stay this time. But if you decide to come out to Munabbih again, you'll need to bring along written permission from security in Sa'da," he said firmly.

"Thank you very much for your kindness, sir," I said, showing him the honor and respect due him.

He hadn't even bothered to take me up to his office. As we stood interacting in the midst of the chained prisoners, more of them had appeared from hidden corners and rooms ... all of them curious and most likely enjoying the unexpected and unusual excitement. I wished I would have been brave enough to ask for permission to take photos of the prisoners in their chains, but decided such a request would be deemed very inappropriate.

As I turned to make my exit, the Police Chief suddenly blurted out, "Please feel free to come to my office later. Then you can have the chance to listen in on some discussions I'll be having with people in our local dialect."

That was an invitation I never would have expected to hear from him, but I definitely planned to take advantage of it. "Thank you very much sir. Peace be with you," I said.

"And with you be peace," he replied as he turned and made his way back up the uneven stone stairs.

16

The Meeting

Ibrahim and Hassan had been standing there the whole time listening in, with great interest I might add, on the interaction I had with the Police Chief. When it was all over, the three of us left together and walked at a rather leisurely pace back down toward the school. The Egyptians stayed at the school while I continued on into the village itself, determined to start making some more contact with the locals that very afternoon.

My first stop was the auto mechanic's shop. He had the front wheel off a Landcruiser and was examining the brake pads. He looked up as I approached, and our eyes met. He nodded his head as a greeting, which I took as an invitation to stop and talk, "Peace be with you," I said.

"And with you be peace," he replied, but without offering to shake my hand because of the grease on his.

"Nice village you have here," I continued, merely for the sake of engaging him in conversation.

"Yes it is, but it's not my village. I'm from Ta'izz," he said.

I was disappointed to hear that, although I tried not to show it. "From Ta'izz?" I said. "You're a long way from home."

"Have you been to Ta'izz?" he inquired.

"Yes, it's a beautiful city," I replied, at which his eyes lit up with pride. I had stayed in Ta'izz during part of my two-week long exploratory trip six months earlier. It was located way down in the south of the country. That mechanic was indeed a long way from home.

There appeared to be quite a mixture of people from all over Yemen working in Suq al-Munabbih ... most likely because it was a market village. For example, the cooks, whom I had met earlier on in the restaurant, came from the south of the country too.

The mechanic and I chatted a bit more, and he would have kept right on talking, but I finally excused myself, "It was nice meeting you. I think I'll look around the village some more. I'll see you again later." In such a small village I definitely would see him again.

"Nice meeting you too," he said, and I was sure he meant it.

What I really wanted was some interaction with Munabbihites. I had met a few of them earlier, on my way to the school, but they had since disappeared. I would obviously have to use a different strategy to get to meet some of the Munabbih residents.

Well, at least I had the Police Chief's invitation to sit in on some discussions in his office that evening, and maybe it would result in some good contacts.

At about 7:30 I made my way up to the castle once again, where I was met by a few guards stationed outside the main entrance. "Can we help you?" one of them asked very politely.

I was quite sure that by then all of them would have heard about the presence of the foreigner in town. "Yes, please. The Police Chief told me I could come and sit in on some meetings he'd be having in his office this evening," I informed them.

By the looks on their faces, they obviously weren't aware that such an invitation had been extended to me.

"Wait here a minute," one of them said before disappearing inside the building.

In the meantime I engaged the other two guards in some light conversation.

A couple of minutes later the man returned and said, "follow me."

And so I did ... walking past the gawking prisoners, and then up the uneven stone stairs the Police Chief had descended to meet me earlier in the day.

At the very top of the stairs was a large landing ... and on that landing was a mound of flip flops ... and down the middle of the mound was a thin path leading to a door at the opposite end of the landing. Obviously the door would lead into the Police Chief's office.

I stood on the top step in front of the landing and stared at the sea of blue flip flops scattered there while the guard made his way along the path to the door. He slipped off his own flip flops, placed his hand on the door handle, and then turned to look at me. He signaled for me to follow him.

It was too late to turn back now. The Police Chief had been informed I was coming to the meeting, and so to the meeting I now must go.

I walked along the path to where the guard was still standing, waiting for me to catch up. I took off my shoes (I was not wearing flip flops at the time), and dropped (not literally) my backpack beside them.

The guard turned the handle and the door creaked open. He went in first and I followed. Actually, truth be known, I only just *started* to enter the room ... but then suddenly hesitated. As I had already deduced, but what was only then confirmed, it was not a small office. It was a large room ... a very large rectangular room ... and there was a person in that room to go with each and every pair of flip flops out on the landing. At least 50 men were present, all sitting against the room's walls, and every one of their heads turned as I entered.

My mind suddenly went fuzzy. I wasn't sure where to go. And the cloud of cigarette smoke added to my discomfort, for as I took in a deep breath to calm myself, I almost choked. All I wanted to do was back out on to the landing again, pick up my backpack and shoes and retrace my steps down to the safety of the school with my Egyptian friends. But I refrained from doing so. And believe you me, it took all the courage I could muster not to make an exit.

The Police Chief was sitting at one end of the room. I distinctly remember noticing that he was seated to my left as I entered, because I was looking for him. And what made it particularly easy to spot him was the fact that he (along with another man who I will introduce later) was sitting on a large raised platform which was about the height of one stair, and took up one whole wall. Everyone else sat at a lower level, down on the floor, all around the remaining three walls.

When I caught sight of him, with my head turned in his direction and my eyes seeking out his, wanting some sort of reassurance, I was rather disappointed when the Police Chief never even looked up to acknowledge me. He paid no attention whatsoever to my presence. It was as if this was a normal everyday occurrence to have a Westerner popping in like that at such a meeting. A thousand thoughts raced through my mind in those few seconds of shock ... as if my whole life were flashing before my eyes. I thought that only happened when you're drowning!

"What on earth am I doing in this situation?!" I shouted inside my own head.

I quickly recovered from the shock and caught sight of the guard who had led me up the stairs. He was walking right across to the opposite side of the room. Once again he turned to look back at me. I hadn't even budged an inch. Again he had to signal for me to follow him. I had no choice ... I followed the guard while fifty pairs of eyes watched my every move. My heart was pounding as I thought, "Why couldn't he seat me right beside the door so I could sneak out after a few minutes!"

About two thirds of the way along the wall from where the Police Chief was positioned, the guard stopped in front of a couple of Yemenis and asked them to make room for me.

They were already packed in like sardines, and yet they did their best to obey, one moving to the left and the other to the right, forcing the next five men in both directions to move over a couple of inches each as well. By then I had caught up to the guard and I squeezed in between the two men as best I could, trying to get as physically comfortable as possible ... *comfortable* being a relative term considering it was virtually impossible to get really *comfortable* in the few square inches of space I was allotted to occupy. My knees were pulled up towards my chest. I was unable to stretch out my legs lest the souls of my feet point at the men sitting on the opposite wall and I thereby offend them.

I just sat there ... trying not to look nervous ... not looking anybody in the eye ... my gaze focused on the Police Chief ... trying to look genuinely interested in what was going on, as if it was very important for me to be present in that room for those meetings.

I could distinctly make out some whispering from one person to another sitting close by asking, "Who is the foreigner?" ... probably representative of many whisperings taking place.

The Police Chief was being very official. He was totally in charge. Did I understand anything he was saying? Well, not much, to be very honest. "Blah, blah, blah, blah, blah ..." he went on and on. The purpose of the meeting and the topics covered were not very clear to me, especially since the business was all being conducted in the local dialect. Of course, considering the setting, and from what I could catch, it was plain he was dealing with legal matters.

One of the topics of discussion, which I could follow at least a little, was about the use (actually the *misuse*) of weapons. As you already found out in chapter 1, weapons were always at hand and ready to be used ... a little too ready! And from what I gathered, inter-village conflicts occurred and were on-going. I assumed at least some of the men chained up in the prison below us had been arrested for participating in such conflicts.

Most of the time the Police Chief was the one who brought up specific topics. But from what I could gather, this was a public meeting (hence the large gathering) during which men from the various sectors of Munabbih were allowed to voice matters of concern. Words were exchanged, notes were taken, and decisions were made.

I didn't ask any questions ... I didn't take any notes ... I didn't take any photos ... and I didn't turn on my tape recorder ... which was in my backpack on the landing outside the door anyway. But oh how I wish I could have recorded what was going on and taken some photos! I merely sat there and observed.

In typical Yemeni style, and very fitting for the business-like atmosphere, many, if not most, of the men sitting in the room were chewing qat leaves[19] ... plastic bags laid out before them, hands automatically and skillfully selecting the most tender of leaves, popping them into their mouths, bottles of water or pop at the ready, spittoons spread around the room, cigarette ends glowing ... constant activity throughout the never ending discussions.

In addition to chewing qat, the Police Chief, and a few of the other men sitting closest to him, were doing their part to add to the cloud of smoke by handing around the long hose attached to an unpolished brass argileh (translated, *water pipe* or *hookah*) which was located at the end of the room where they were sitting. I wasn't sure who was allowed to participate, but it was definitely limited to a select group of those present ... most likely those of highest social standing. I was relieved that I hadn't been seated in a place where it might have been offered to me. I wouldn't have known what to do with it, having lived such a sheltered life.

I mentioned earlier that another man at the meeting was also sitting cross-legged on the platform a short distance to the right of the Police Chief. Beside him was a low table, and he appeared to be functioning as the Police Chief's personal secretary. In his hands he was holding an object which, from where I was sitting, looked like a short thick white stick. I strained my eyes to try and make out what its function was. I was quite sure it wasn't a bludgeon. Suddenly, after some remark made by the Police Chief, the secretary started to unroll the *stick*.

"It's a scroll," I mumbled under my breath. I was quite familiar with such things from reading about them and seeing them in museums, but I never thought scrolls would still be in use in the year 1987. It wasn't parchment, but rather paper ... I assumed it was composed of numerous papers which had most likely been taped together.

---

[19] See chapter 13, *The Chew.*

Anyway, the secretary unrolled the scroll just enough to jot down a few notes ... presumably written after previous notes which had been made the last time it was unrolled for the same purpose. With that accomplished, he rolled it up again. Then a few minutes later he went through the same procedure again. Fascinating!

"Now what's he doing?" I wondered as I unconsciously leaned forward blocking the view of the man sitting beside me, and then corrected myself so as to fit back into my allotted slot along the wall. The secretary, wearing a very stern face, started unrolling a much larger segment of the scroll, obviously to refer to something that must have been written at some previous meeting ... unrolling it as only someone experienced in the art could do ... finding *the something* he was looking for, reading *the something* out loud, and then slowly rolling the scroll back up as he talked. It was quite a long scroll, And the movements of the secretary's hands manipulating that scroll almost had a hypnotic effect.

The Police Chief gave another short spiel, and someone else responded. The secretary then had to refer to *something* again, and so he went through the whole unrolling and rolling procedure again ... and then another time ... sometimes writing something down, sometimes reading something.

I couldn't help but wonder if anyone ever challenged the Police Chief's authority. I wondered whether he even came from that particular part of North Yemen, or whether he was just stationed there. I very much doubted he would have been appointed by the federal Yemeni government, since as I pointed out in chapter 4, the federal government was not appreciated in the north. More likely he would have been appointed by the local Sa'da provincial government.

I must have been sitting in the meeting for about an hour and a half before I finally got up enough courage to shift any part of my body more than an inch (besides the inadvertent leaning forward I had done to observe the scroll ceremony). I half expected some part of my anatomy to go permanently numb if I didn't get out of that cramped position soon ... and so I decided it was definitely time to make my exit.

I didn't know if I needed to follow a specific procedure to leave the meeting. I had observed a few others leave over the past half hour, and so I decided to try and imitate what I saw them do. I stood up slowly but decisively, and then looking straight ahead at the door the entire time, never looking at a single face in that room (not even the Police Chief's), I started to walk.

When I arrived at the door, I turned the handle, opened it, went out, and closed it again. I'm quite sure I didn't take a single breath during the whole departure process. I then quickly slipped on my shoes, picked up my backpack, and made my way down the stone stairs.

"I made it!" I said to myself with both pride and relief.

I remembered the prisoners downstairs, and so descended at a slow pace until I spotted a guard standing at the bottom of the stairs having a smoke. I casually stopped right beside him and proceeded to chat with him about who knows what while continuing the evening's inhalation of second hand smoke. I just felt like I had to talk to someone, and he seemed willing enough to do so.

A few minutes later a servant came up to me and asked, "Would you like to drink some tea?"

"Yes please. Thank you," I replied. Boy did I ever need a cup of something!

Rather than bring the tea to me, he escorted me into a side room. That gave me the opportunity to sit and enjoy a relaxing cup of tea while having the benefit of the servant's company. It was so nice to be out of the spotlight.

I don't recall how much time passed before a guard showed up and informed me, "The Police Chief would like you to return to his office."

I thanked the servant for the tea and then followed the guard back up the stairs to who knows what next.

When I arrived at the landing, the sea of blue flip-flops was gone ... all but a few of them. That was a relief. I once again removed my shoes before re-entering the meeting room. Only seven men remained. Whether they were some of the same men or new ones, I had no idea. Sherlock Holmes would have been appalled at my lack of observation. All I knew was I felt so much more at ease with the smaller numbers. I reclaimed my spot at the side wall, a short distance from where the interaction was happening, and observed.

The same man who had served me tea earlier showed up and offered me another dose, which I gladly accepted. And a little later he came in yet again, this time placing in front of me a dish of mushy beans with bread for supper.

While I sat there observing the proceedings, a guard led one of the shackled and chained prisoners trudging into the room. On his way in he gave a glance in my direction, most likely wondering what I was doing there. He sat down against the wall opposite me and the Police Chief proceeded to interrogate him, one question after another.

When the grilling ended, the secretary, who was still present, produced an ink pad. The prisoner first pressed his right thumb on the ink pad, and then on a number of papers before he was led out of the room.

While that was going on, a second prisoner entered the room. And so the evening went on.

When the last person had finally made his exit, the Police Chief came over to me and asked, "Did you enjoy listening in on the discussions we had?"

"Yes sir, I did," I responded ... a half truth at best. "Thank you very much for giving me that opportunity!"

"You're welcome," he replied. "Good night."

"Good night to you, sir," I said.

And with that he walked out the door, just as the servant re-entered. By then it was 11 PM. "Do you want to go down to the store with me and watch some TV?" he asked.

"Yes, thank you," I lied. What I really wanted to do was find a bed somewhere so I could lie down and get some sleep. In fact I was ready to collapse right then and there on the floor. But I thought going with him would be the appropriate thing to do. And so off we went.

I was surprised to find a number of young boys in the store along with a couple of adults. They were all sitting around the TV waiting for All-star wrestling to start.

It was midnight before we left the store. I was exhausted, but still had no idea where I'd be sleeping that night. It was only then that the servant informed me I'd be spending the night in the Police Chief's office.

We arrived at the prison, or castle, or whatever you want to call it, the servant dropped me off at the meeting room while he went to find me a foam mattress. He placed it on the Police Chief's sacred raised platform, and then disappeared to who knows where. I promptly collapsed on the mattress.

So there I was, a guest right above who knows how many chained prisoners just one floor down. I didn't hear any rattling of chains. I was quite comfortable, and glad to have some quiet time with no one else around for a few hours.

17

The Argument

I had been lying wide awake for quite some time even before the darkness started to subside ... my mind processing yesterday's many events ... the aroma of cigarette butts and ashes, and rejected qat leaves and branches still hanging thick in the air ... most likely not to be cleaned up until later this morning, sometime before the Police Chief's administrative duties recommenced.

When it was finally light enough, I pulled out my notebook and started jotting down some of those thoughts I definitely didn't want to forget ... prior to embarking on the new day's activities. I would type up and expand those precious notes at a later date, once I was reunited with my computer.

The minutes ticked by ever so slowly. I just assumed that a prison guard or a servant would eventually show up to let me out of the oversized *guestroom*. "Should I wander down the staircase all on my own?" I wondered.

Of course, downstairs was full of prisoners, so I wasn't sure it was such a good idea to descend unaccompanied. But if nobody showed up soon, I was determined to at least walk over to the door and look out to see if any non-prisoners were just outside ... that is, unless the door happened to be locked.

The same servant from yesterday evening eventually showed up with a friendly, "Good morning mister Butros! How did you sleep?"

And I responded with, "Good morning. I slept very well thank you. Praise be to God!"

"Praise be to God!" he said. "Are you hungry? Would you like to have some breakfast?" Breakfast had already entered with him on the tray he was carrying.

"Thank you very much! Sorry I'm being such a bother," I said.

"No bother at all, mister Butros," he said as he put down the tray on which was a bowl of mashed beans, some freshly baked bread, and two glasses of sweet milky tea. I was living the good life!

The meal was obviously meant for both of us, and I was glad to have his company once again. We got along well.

When we had finished eating, I decided it was time to find someone who could provide me with a story in the Munabbih dialect. The evening before gave me a lot of exposure to legal proceedings, as well as to a bit of the local culture, but I couldn't use that for my research. I needed to record a story.

Then the obvious suddenly hit me, "There's a local person sitting right across from me. Why not ask him for help." The two of us had talked about my research at length. And so I got up the courage and said, "As you know, my reason for coming to Munabbih is to try and learn as much about your dialect as possible. One of the things I need to do is record a story spoken in the Munabbih dialect. Would you be willing to tell me a story?"

My question clearly caught him by surprise. "Mister Butros, I'm not good at such things," was his humble reply.

"I just want you to tell me about something you've experienced ... like a trip you had, or something that happened to you or to someone else you know," I persisted.

"No, I can't," he said with finality in his voice.

"Okay, no problem," I replied, deciding not to push any further, not wanting to strain our relationship. It was time to implement plan B ... head down to the school and talk to the Egyptian teachers. Perhaps they could get one or two of their older students to help me out.

Ibrahim and Hassan taught grades one to five, and those five grades were divided into two classes. If any of the students wanted a higher education, then they'd have to go somewhere else to get it. I ran into the same situation in Raazih where I met and stayed with Mansoor[20] who, along with his roommates, had to live in Nadhiir to get their higher education.

Only boys attended the school in Suq Al-Munabbih ... which was quite typical throughout most of North Yemen at the time. School was not mandatory (also typical), and from what I heard (and also observed), not all boys in Munabbih region were attending school.

I also observed that school was often a frustrating experience for many Yemenis. Learning was hindered because students were expected to deal with the foreign teachers' dialects as well as Modern Standard Arabic, both of which were very different from what the local population spoke. Part of the reason for my research was to show that such linguistic barriers to learning were built into the education system.

---

[20] See chapter 11.

If those barriers were removed, or at least lessened, then the quality of the Yemeni students' education would improve.

Now since school was a relatively new phenomenon in most Yemeni villages, it wasn't uncommon to find a number of older boys mixed in with the younger ones ... having started their education somewhat later in life. I had already detected students in their teens studying at the school. It was one or more of these older boys I hoped to get help from ... via the teachers.

After arriving at the school, I presented my need to the teachers ... of course, leaving out the part that I was doing my research to put them out of their jobs. I merely stated, "I need someone to tell me a local story and translate some material for me. Would you be willing to ask one of the older boys to help me?"

"Of course we'll help you find someone," Ibrahim said without any hesitation. "But you'll have to wait until school is over for the day."

I was happy (actually, I had no choice but to be happy) with that.

After a short jaunt through the village, taking time to exchange greetings with the southern friends I had made the day before, I returned to the school, and sat down right outside the classrooms, where I waited and listened. One of the subjects focused on the Quran. Another dealt with reading fluency.

When classes finally ended, I watched anxiously as the teachers and students all exited from the two rooms. Much to my relief, Ibrahim headed in my direction, and with him was a student who was definitely in his teens.

"Mister Butros, this is one of our best students and he would like to help you," is how Ibrahim introduced him. The Egyptians hadn't forgotten me!

"Thank you very much," I said, holding out my hand to shake the story teller's.

"I'm glad to be of service," he said politely.

We entered one of the classrooms, and about a dozen other students of various ages filed in after us. They were all curious to see what I was going to do, and most likely also wanted to hear the story. That was great, since having the young man tell the story to a Yemeni audience would make him less nervous, thereby providing me with a much more natural text ... definitely better than having him speak into a microphone with only a foreigner with a blank expression (due to a lack of comprehension) looking on.

I explained to him what kind of a story I was looking for while I pulled out my tape recorder and set it up on a desk. He appeared totally relaxed. When everything was ready, I asked for silence, pushed the record button, and told him to go ahead.

He began, "One day we were walking in a wadi ..."

"Boys, shut up," Ibrahim yelled at a couple of stragglers who entered the room.

"Not helpful," I kept my thought to myself. "Could you please start over again?" I instructed the story teller, due to Ibrahim's outburst rather than the late comers' conversation.

"Okay," the story teller agreed, not as bothered as I was by the interruption. "One day we were walking in a wadi. We arrived at a place far from here, inside Saudi Arabia, where we happened upon some soldiers ..."

Right from the outset I could tell that this boy was a natural at telling stories. He told us a great story about the time he and some of his friends snuck across the border from North Yemen into Saudi Arabia and then back again, and how they managed to avoid being caught by the Saudi military patrolling the area. His account, along with his observable maturity, caused me to conclude he was most likely somewhat older than I had initially thought.

Now, to be very honest, during the original telling of the story I didn't understand much of it. But a clear indication that it was first-rate was from the reaction of the other students who all seemed thoroughly enthralled by it. I watched their wide eyes, and heard their laughter, and observed the tension as they lived the story with the story teller. As for me, I was able to appreciate the story much more after I played it back to the story teller, section by section, and had him explain the difficult to understand parts to me while I made notes. Success!

"Thank you very much. That is a great story!" I complimented the story teller.

"You're welcome sir," he said as he rose to his feet and shook my outstretched hand, clearly pleased by my flattering remark. Then he headed to the door and made his exit, followed by the few students who had stayed behind for the explanation component.

"Butros," I heard one of the teachers say. I turned around to see it was Hassan speaking, "we want you to stay here at the school with us tonight as our guest."

I rather doubted that I was expected to return to the *guestroom* up at the prison. No one had informed me that I should plan to head up that way to spend another night, or attend more meetings. So I assumed I was free to accept the kind invitation of the Egyptian teachers. "Are you sure I won't be a bother?" I said appropriately, knowing very well the answer would be, "Not at all!" ... which it was. Then after a few more verbal exchanges, I finally ended with, "That would be very nice, thank you."

After spending a nice relaxing evening with the Egyptians, they graciously provided me with a foam mattress allowing me to share their school room with them so I could rest my weary bones.

The next day I managed to get other material translated and recorded. And so, having accomplished what I intended for that first trip, I was looking forward to returning to Sa'da the following day.

For the rest of the day I hung out with my new found friends, the day came to an end, and my third night was spent once again sharing the Egyptians' quarters.

My last morning in Suq al-Munabbih was when I happened to stumble upon the blanket of weapons being sold in the market,[21] and eventually found myself standing next to a metal water tank anxiously awaiting the outcome of a rather intense argument.

Dozens of armed men, spread throughout the village with fingers on their rifle triggers, waited as well. And I assume you've also been waiting.

The argument raged on, words passing from one antagonist to the other, flowing past the heads of those who formed a human barrier between them. The peacekeepers were very aware of the many rifles standing at the ready.

A number of other voices on each side were contributing to the racket ... smaller arguments attempting to help settle the main squabble. Thankfully they were having success, being able to distract the chief contenders so that each of them eventually turned their attention to the gathering on their side. And finally, after what seemed like an eternity, but was in reality only minutes (although my eyes were not on my watch), the argument grew less intense and eventually evolved into a mere loud, but no longer threatening, *conversation*.

Others throughout the village also sensed the change in the level of tension, and started to relax. Rifles were lowered and repositioned to

---

[21] See chapter 1, *The Wild Wild North*.

their preferred location (at least where I preferred to see them), dangling by their straps over the shoulders of their owners. Not a single shot had been fired. I hope you are as relieved to read that as I was to experience it at the time of the incident.

People started moving again ... going about their business ... talking ... in all probability much, if not all, of the discussion revolving around the topic of *the argument*.

As for me, I was still just standing there. I felt like I was waking up from a dream ... actually from a nightmare, where you feel like you need to be running but your feet have turned into lumps of lead, and some sort of danger is charging at you, and you can't move fast enough, and then suddenly ... you wake up in a sweat.

It wasn't much longer before I found myself sitting comfortably in a 4-wheeler on my way back to Sa'da ... to Harry's mud house where a shower, privacy and sleep (but no rifles!) awaited me.

18

Soup Bowls

The weariness from my trip to Munabbih only two days earlier had not yet subsided, and yet I had to keep moving. I wanted to make sure I'd be able to gather all the data I needed for my research within the limited amount of time I had available to do so.

"You're off to a late start," Harry observed as we leisurely sat at his dining room table on chairs, something I never get to experience during meals with my hosts in the villages.

"I told Mahmoud and Abdu that I'd meet them in front of the mosque at 9:30," I explained. "They said they'd help me find a ride to Hishwa."

This time I would travel in the opposite direction, away from the mountainous regions, heading eastward on somewhat flatter ground. My destination was Barat, a district located within the Jawf[22] province.

I had become acquainted with Mahmoud and Abdu in Sa'da city. They filled me in on the route I should take. To get to Barat, I first needed to head to the town of Hishwa which was located right under the Barat plateau. Then from Hishwa I should easily (yeah sure!) be able catch a ride up to Barat itself. As I pointed out to Harry, they offered to help me find a ride that morning.

"You still look tired," Harry observed. "You've only had one day off after your last trip."

"I'm fine," I insisted.

Harry went off to work at the hospital, and then at 9:25 I walked over to the mosque located not far down the road. Not much activity was going on around the mosque at that hour, the last prayer time having finished some time ago.

"Good morning Butros," Mahmoud greeted me.

After the three of us had exchanged appropriate greetings, Abdu said, "Let's go."

"Where are we going?" I inquired as we started on our way. I was glad to be receiving help from a couple of locals.

---

[22] See the map and some information about Jawf in chapter 4.

"Trucks leave for Hishwa just outside *Baab al-Yemen*," Mahmoud explained.

"Oh no," I thought. But sure enough, they took me to the same stretch of buildings where I had to wait for such a long time after finding a ride to Nadhiir in Raazih.

"Our friend wants to go to Hishwa," Mahmoud said to a man reclining just inside one of the buildings. This was bringing back some not-so-pleasant memories.

"Suleiman will be leaving for Buga'a soon," the man said pointing to a second man sitting across from him, who was obviously the driver of my soon-to-leave ride.

"Where's Buga'a?" I asked.

"Buga'a is much further than Hishwa, but I can drop you off in Hishwa," explained Suleiman.

Now since Mahmoud and Abdu helped me find transportation, I felt obligated to take whatever ride they arranged for me. "Hey," I thought, "maybe it wouldn't end up being such a long wait this time."

Then to Suleiman I said, "Okay, I'd like to reserve a seat."

"That will be 100 riyals as a down payment," Suleiman informed me.

My experience thus far had been that payment was only ever made at the end of a trip, and so I hesitated. But Abdu explained it's not unusual to pay part of the fare prior to departure. I went ahead and handed Suleiman ten ten-riyal bills prior to thanking my friends for their help. Then they left, and I started the wait. That was at 10 AM.

By 4:30 PM, when Suleiman was satisfied with the number of committed passengers, we got under way. So once again, most of my day was spent hanging around waiting.

Well, in reality, a fair amount of interaction was going on during the waiting period. In fact, Suleiman was a very talkative fellow. He was an older gentleman who, once we did get under way, ended up talking non-stop the whole trip. And to tell you the truth, sometimes I preferred that to dead silence.

I followed him to his vehicle and was surprised to find that Suleiman drove an old Mercedes car. I had just assumed we'd be traveling in a 4-wheel drive because that's what I was used to from my previous trips. It just confirmed for me that on this trip the terrain shouldn't be too rough.

Something else that amazed me was that after six and a half hours of waiting, he only had two other passengers in addition to me ... although he did end up picking up two more along the way.

During the first few kilometers we passed one mud house after another ... hundreds of them. Most of the houses were fairly large, with a good sized yard enclosed by a high mud wall.

Initially, the unpaved road didn't seem all that bad ... bumpy, yes, but okay. But my opinion soon changed after we hit the first real pothole. I was lifted right off my seat, and wacked my head on the ceiling of the car.

The problem was that I happened to be sitting in the rear of the car (yes, again!), and so I couldn't see the potholes coming, and therefore didn't know when I needed to brace myself. Then it happened again.

After the third time, I decided the only solution to avoiding a serious concussion was to sit in a slouched position so I wouldn't bounce up quite so high when hitting the now seemingly endless potholes. I slouched uncomfortably the rest of the way to Hishwa. And because of the potholes, it was slow going most of the time.

When we came across the first military checkpoint, a guard asked Suleiman, "Who's the foreigner and where's he going?"

"He's Canadian. I'm going to drop him off in Hishwa," he replied.

"Let's see his permission paper," the guard asked.

I had a copy of my *to whom it may concern* paper all ready in my hand, gave it to Suleiman, who in turn handed it to the guard.

I must admit I was a bit nervous after my experience with the Police Chief in Munabbih who had demanded I produce a second document from Sa'da security. What if this guard asked for a similar document and I couldn't produce it. Would he send me back?

The guard only took a moment to look at the paper and seemed satisfied. Before he said anything more, I piped up, "That's a copy of the original, so you can keep it."

"Go ahead," he said to Suleiman as he walked away with the paper.

"Okay, so it looks like all should go well on this trip," I mumbled to myself. And indeed it did go well as we passed through a second checkpoint without a hitch.

Soon the sun set, and we drove along in the darkness. But this definitely wasn't as bad as maneuvering in the dark with the vehicle hugging the sides of the mountains out to the west. And to make things even better yet, a quarter moon shone its light so I could actually see something.

Suleiman chatted away about this and that as we traveled ... "This is Wadi Aslah," he said at one point as we shifted onto the packed sand of a dry river bed. We continued winding through that same wadi the rest of the way to Hishwa, much of the time with high ground and greenery to both the right and the left of us.

It was already past the actual evening prayer time, but everyone had agreed they should wait and pray as a group once they spotted a good place to do so. My opinion didn't matter since I wasn't a Muslim, and so they wouldn't expect me to join them. Moments like that at times proved a little awkward ... but then again, I was used to being in much more awkward situations!

When they finally stopped to pray, I went off on my own and prayed too, in my own way. I enjoyed those few moments of solitude, while the moon and the stars vied for my attention. Suddenly, off in the direction we were heading, I saw a flash of lightning.

We had only traveled a little further before we came upon a village where Suleiman stopped yet again.

"Now what?" I said to myself in some frustration.

Suleiman turned to me and said, "There's a restaurant here and we're going to get something to eat. Do you want join us Butros?"

That was a welcome question. I hadn't even thought about food, but his mention of a meal set my stomach to growling. I responded, "Yes, that sounds like a good idea."

The six of us headed toward the three-sided crude structure. It was totally open at the front ... no door, and no wall. As we made our entrance, I followed the others who started to form a lopsided circle on a large woven rectangular reed mat. The heavily soiled mat covered enough of the dirt to just barely accommodate all of us. The waiter approached us and proceeded to take our order, which resulted in some discussion about what was on the menu. My only contribution to the conversation was, "I'll eat whatever everyone else is going to eat."

A decision was made, and I heard what was ordered, but I still had no idea what it was. "This should be interesting," I thought ... and it certainly was.

First we were served what I assumed was a loaf of bread, although it didn't look like any bread I had ever seen before. The loaf (I didn't know what else to call it) was kind of the consistency of play dough ... a large half-round lump sitting on a metal plate. I had no idea what we were supposed to do with it. Then beside the loaf, the waiter set down a large bowl of rather oily looking broth. But we weren't given any spoons, and so I couldn't deduce how we were supposed to consume any of the soup. I obviously couldn't use the *bread* to sop up the soup since it had none of the liquid soaking attributes that regular baked bread did. Rather awkward!

I decided it was time to apply some *participant observation* ... namely, let the others start eating (the observation part) and then I'd just do whatever they did (the participant part).

I watched carefully as one of the men ripped off a piece of the loaf and then molded it into a small round bowl ... and I mean small, something that can wrap around the end of the thumb ... and that's precisely how he had formed the miniature bowl, on the end of his thumb. This tiny bowl then served as an eating utensil, used to scoop up some of the broth from the *real* bowl. The bread bowl was then consumed along with the soup which it held. Fascinating ... and how convenient.

I did well with the observation part, and then it was time to apply the participation part. I assumed the men I was sharing the meal with all detected my hesitation, and also noticed that I was watching them closely ... but they never seemed to let on ... although Suleiman did say, "Eat Butros, eat."

"Thank you," I replied, as I ripped off a piece of the play dough just like they were doing.

I'm sure they were all rather amused as I stuck my thumb into the dough and formed my first little bread bowl so I could partake of some of the soup.

Okay, I could tell that my bowl was going to leak ... and I mean really leak. My bread bowl had a hole in the bottom that needed to be patched. The only solution I could think of was to re-roll my failed bowl back into a ball and start all over again. I knew I should have paid closer attention during the play dough course I took in kindergarten!

"This is hard work," I said out loud with a laugh, reminding myself that it's better to laugh and not take things too seriously.

They laughed right along with me, rather than at me.

I formed a new bowl over my thumb, this time making sure I didn't poke a hole through the bottom. It looked good.

Next, I dipped my bowl into the soup, and then actually made it safely with some broth all the way into my mouth ... probably still dripping a little more liquid than the rest of the participants, but I had every right to be proud.

Just to give you a little hint ... if you ever have the opportunity to eat a meal like that, don't take too much dough to make your bowl or you won't be able to fit it into your mouth very easily. I should also point out that the broth was very tasty. But at the pace I was going, I don't think I ever ended up getting my fair share.

That was the challenging part of the meal. Fortunately, I knew exactly how to partake of the next course which consisted of a platter of bite-size pieces of tasty tender goat meat, a basket of freshly baked flat bread and a bowl of salad. Once again pieces of bread were ripped off the loaves and were used to pick up the meat and/or salad. The bread was then consumed along with its contents. Usually only a small portion of meat is ordered, because it's always the most expensive part of any meal. Then we topped it all off with some tea and a sweet desert. The whole meal lasted well over an hour.

Once we were done, we all crowded back into the car and moved on. It was 11 PM when we finally arrived in Hishwa.

Hishwa was my destination, whereas Suleiman's destination was Buga'a ... but he wouldn't be continuing that day. "A few us are going to sleep in the local mosque," he informed me.

That was new information to me. I had no idea people could go and sleep at a mosque when they're traveling. That sounded like something I'd like to try, so I asked, "Can I join you?"

Suleiman responded, "That's not possible because you're a Christian."

"Oh, I see. No problem," I said ... although in fact I was rather disappointed.

So as I pulled money out of my pocket to pay him the rest of the agreed on fare for the ride, I asked him, "Can you tell me if there's somewhere here in Hishwa where I can spend the night?"

He pointed to a small shack with a well-lit outdoor area and said, "That's a hotel over there. It costs 20 riyals to rent a mat and blanket for the night."

A few of the other passengers were already walking in that direction. I didn't understand why any of them bothered heading to the hotel-shack when they could have gone to the mosque.

"Thank you for the ride Suleiman. God be with you," I said.

"And God bless you," he said as he walked off.

I sauntered in the direction of the shack, but instead of paying the 20 riyals, I pulled out my sleeping bag, laid it out on the sand, and crawled inside.

We never did hit any rain. I couldn't even spot any clouds, so the stars filled my view as I lay on my back reflecting on the day's events and drifted off.

19

The Exchange

"Where are you headed?" Ahmad asked me.

I met Ahmad while eating breakfast at a little hole-in-the-wall restaurant in Hishwa after a not-so-comfortable sleep on my bed of sand. You can probably guess what I was eating ... beans and all that typically accompanies them.

"I'm planning to travel up to Barat," I replied.

"I'm driving to a town in Barat ... Suq al-Inaan. I can give you a ride in my truck," he offered.

Ahmad was a really friendly guy, very easy to talk to, and I wasn't going to pass up an opportunity like this, so I responded, "That would be great. Thank you."

That was the quickest ride I ever found! But little did I know at the time that the ride with Ahmad would involve a bit of a detour, resulting in another adventure, before I arrived at my planned destination.

After we finished breakfast, Ahmad shouldered his rifle, and the two of us walked toward his Landcruiser. It looked brand new, which made me think he must be quite well off. I couldn't help but wonder what kind of business he was involved in. We hadn't discussed that topic yet.

A man was standing next to Ahmad's truck, and it appeared he was waiting for him. He was watching intently as we approached... his eyes clearly focused more on me than on Ahmad.

"This is my new friend Butros," Ahmad introduced me to him.

"Nice to meet you Butros," he said, holding out his hand. "My name is Ali."

My first impression was that Ali was a much more serious fellow than Ahmad ... but very friendly nevertheless. My hand went out to meet his as I replied, "It's nice to meet you too Ali."

I had the feeling he was wondering where I had come from and why I was hanging out with Ahmad.

"Excuse us for a moment," said Ahmad as he grabbed hold of Ali's arm and led him a short distance from where they left me standing so they could have a private discussion. I assumed it was about the presence of the foreigner. I hoped I hadn't misread them, and that they were indeed as kind as I had first judged Ahmad to be. I guess I would find out soon enough.

It seemed to me that the two of them were traveling together ... something Ahmad hadn't bothered mentioning when he offered me the ride. I started to get a little concerned, while they were off talking on their own, that maybe Ali would disapprove of my being there. But apparently it wasn't an issue, since when they returned to where I was patiently (and a little anxiously) waiting for them, Ahmad invited me to get into the passenger seat of his truck. Ali hopped into his much older looking red truck (and surprisingly not a Landcruiser) parked next to Ahmad's, and off we went, Ali in the lead and Ahmad following close behind.

From Hishwa, we traveled a short distance through Wadi Aslah (back in the direction of Sa'da), then veered off to the left, passed through one village, and soon arrived at another village where we pulled up in front of a house which I found out belonged to Ali. I would never have been able to retrace our route, and I had no idea what we were doing there.

As I climbed out of Ahmad's truck, I was suddenly face-to-face with a few more men, who were also (of course) rather surprised to see the Westerner. All eyes turned to Ahmad for an explanation ... and explain he did.

I was introduced all around, "This is Butros from Canada ..." He also told me all of their names, "This is so-and-so, etc, blah, blah, blah ..." (names which I forgot soon after I heard them).

I still had no idea what we were doing at Ali's house or who all those men were. I finally concluded it was nothing more than a stop along the way so Ahmad could visit some of his friends. They obviously weren't relatives, otherwise they would have been introduced as such.

Then three more men came out of the house. They were quite elderly, and as I was introduced to the first one, Ali said, "This is my father."

"It's a pleasure to meet you father of Ali," I said respectfully as I took hold of his extended callused hand.

"Have a seat Butros," Ali invited me to join them as the crowd all started positioning themselves on the ground in a circle.

I sat down ... what else could I do? But somehow I had an uneasy feeling that I didn't belong there. "This is definitely some sort of meeting," I said to myself. I was getting more and more curious, wanting to know what this *meeting* was all about.

Everyone was chatting away, and it all seemed rather laid-back, as a thermos of tea was brought out with some cups and everyone was served something to drink ... including me. Then the casual chatting changed to a more formal discussion, mostly between Ahmad and Ali, but with others feeling free to give input. And that's when I finally found out what kind of *business* they were all involved in. They all worked together in a smuggling racket!

Ah yes ... now let the real adventure begin!

I immediately had a scene go through my mind ... Ahmad racing along a dirt road, with me sitting beside him, and Yemeni soldiers in a couple of vehicles behind us in hot pursuit with a loud speaker roaring out the words, "Stop or we'll shoot!" And then I hear the sound of bullets hitting the metal of Ahmad's truck.

"Are these the kind of guys I want to be hanging out with?" I asked myself. But it was obviously a little too late to be asking that question. It was the ride I ended up with, for better or for worse. Maybe the next time (if there was going to be a next time) I'd ask a few more questions before hopping into someone's truck with him.

To tell you the truth, those smugglers turned out to be some of the friendliest people I'd met thus far. They were merely earning a living like anyone else. I just kept hoping that they wouldn't get caught during the next few hours I'd be hanging out with them.

What really surprised me was how open they were about what they were doing. No one seemed to think it was important to hide anything from me. It was as if it were a common occurrence to have a Canadian show up and be an observer.

I took another sip of my tea and then decided to ask, "Where do you get the goods you sell?"

Ali informed me, "I sneak across the border into Saudi Arabia, buy the goods from a supplier, and then smuggle those items into North Yemen."

Ahmad added, "Then I buy the goods from Ali and take them to Sana'a where I sell them to our contacts there."

"And then those goods get into the stores and are sold to people like me, right?" I added.

They laughed, and Ali said, "That's right."

Wow, a very well-organized smuggling network with all the links in place. "I just hope a weak link doesn't get them all thrown in jail," I thought ... the scene of the chained prisoners in Munabbih coming back to mind.

I should also point out that nearly everyone carried rifles, just like in Sa'da. I just hoped they wouldn't have to use their rifles as long as I was with them!

The bargaining over the quality and price of the goods continued. These kinds of transactions take time. After they had settled on a price, another thermos of tea was brought out and everyone's cup was filled again.

Then Ahmad walked over to the cab of his truck and brought out something wrapped in a bundle. He set it down on the ground in the middle of the circle and unwrapped it, revealing large packets of money, each packet with a rubber band around it.

Ahmad knew exactly how much money was lying there. He grabbed the exact number of packets needed and handed them to Ali. Then he wrapped the remaining money into a now somewhat smaller bundle and carried it back to his truck, while Ali and his men proceeded to count the money.

I haven't really talked about North Yemen currency yet, except to inform you that in 1987 one American dollar was worth 10 Yemeni Riyals. Well, when I first arrived at the Sana'a airport, and before I was given my entry stamp in my passport, I was required to exchange $150 US. I did so, and was handed my Yemeni riyals all in 50's (that's like receiving $150 all in fives at a bank). I didn't think anything of it at the time.

But within the first few days I found out that 50 riyal bills were almost unheard of, and that 20 riyal bills were almost just as rare ... even if you happened to get money from a bank. One day I went into the American Express office to change some money, and I must have looked rather shocked when I was handed a stack of bills with the comment, "Sorry we only have 10's and 5's today."

When I related my experience to the director of AIYS he laughed and told me, "That's nothing. When I bought my truck I literally had to go to the car dealer with a suitcase full of money to pay cash for it."

Ahmad had handed Ali the money all in 10's, so there were literally stacks of bills to count in the courtyard that day. The men talked and sipped tea as they counted. By the time they were done, we were working on our third thermos of tea.

Then it was time for the next stage ... namely, it was time to load Ahmad's truck with the goods he had just purchased ... which I assumed was going to turn into another long process.

So, finding a *quick* ride didn't result in a quick trip after all! But it was definitely turning out to be another one of those unforgettable experiences.

They drove off somewhere (without me) in Ahmad's truck to get the *stuff*, which I was told consisted of telephones, TVs, radios, and other electronic items, all of which are usually highly taxed by the government. There was definitely a demand for those commodities through the black market.

I had the feeling that, if I had wanted to, I could have gone along to observe the loading. They probably just wanted me to relax during the boring labor intensive part of the process. I was quite sure I'd get to see the goods once they returned with the loaded truck.

When the laborers returned, I couldn't believe how high they had the merchandise piled in the bed of the truck ... stacked much higher than I would have thought safe. A tarp covered and secured it all, unfortunately hiding all the products from view, which I assume was not so much to keep it hidden from me as from straying eyes along the way to Sana'a.

After *the exchange* was over, everyone was all smiles, and "congratulations" flew back and forth along with "good byes" and all sorts of God-focused Muslim phrases. I took part too as I prepared for my departure with Ahmad.

"We're going to return to Hishwa first," Ahmad informed me. "You ride with Ali and I'll meet you there."

"Okay," I said, not quite understanding why I had to ride with Ali ... another mystery. I obediently clambered into the cab of Ali's truck.

I watched as Ahmad took off in his loaded truck. "One bad bump and the whole thing is sure to tip over," I thought to myself.

Ali followed behind Ahmad for a mere 10 seconds before he passed him, leaving him in the dust ... literally. Ali was driving like a maniac ... most likely trying to impress his foreign passenger ... who in reality was *not* impressed.

I assumed we were on our way to Hishwa, and had no reason to believe otherwise. But when Ali suddenly stopped beside what appeared to be army tents, I asked him. "Are there soldiers stationed here?" I hadn't actually seen anyone yet.

He chuckled as he remarked, "No, these are Bedouin tents."

That surprised me. I had spent a significant amount of time with the Bedu (short for Bedouin) in Jordan (something you'll have to read about in my next book), and their tents were the traditional Bedu tents made of hand spun and woven goat hair.

Ali jumped out of the truck and called out to let someone know he was there. I remained seated in the truck and watched.

Suddenly a man appeared from behind one of the tents and approached Ali, his eyes straying enough to catch sight of me.

The two of them went through the expected greetings, then talked some (I couldn't hear the topic), and finally Ali and the Bedu man disappeared, leaving me all on my own ... but not for long. They soon returned with a small bleating goat in tow. "It must be time to celebrate the big transaction that just took place with Ahmad," I concluded.

Ali handed the Bedu man some of the profits he had made from the day's sale, and then took hold of the rope tied around the goat's neck. He lifted the goat into the truck bed, and then climbed in himself, so he could secure the other end of the rope to the frame of the truck just behind the cab window. And so the goat finally gave up its useless struggle, but not its bellyaching, most likely sensing the impending doom.

We made one more stop along the way, but I'll wait until the next chapter to fill you in.

As we started on the final stretch to Hishwa, Ali turned to me and said, "Butros, I'd like you be my guest. Why don't you stay here with me and my family."

What an honor! I really hadn't expected such an invitation from him. I didn't know what to say. I had already promised Ahmad that I would ride with him. Should I flex on my plans? I hated having to make such quick decisions. I mean, sure I had my plans, but this would be a great opportunity to get to spend some quality time with the locals. And as I think back, I wish I would have taken the opportunity to do so, but ...

"Thank you very much," I said to Ali. "I really appreciate the offer, but I need to get to Barat today."

"Okay, but promise me you'll return for another visit," he insisted.

"I'll try my best," I responded, knowing it was highly unlikely.

As we approached Ahmad's truck I wondered, "Who are those three men interacting with Ahmad?"

"This is Butros from Canada," Ahmad started the introductions as Ali and I walked up. He told me their names, etc, and then informed me, "These men will accompany me to Sana'a."

"So these guys are also involved," I thought. "This racket sure employs numerous people." Or maybe they were just going along for the ride ... I didn't ask.

"God be with you," Ali said.

"Peace be with you," I responded as we shook hands and went our separate ways.

I wondered how the five of us were all going to squish into the cab of Ahmad's truck. But as it turned out, only four of us (and thankfully I was one of the four) had to squeeze into the cab. Ahmad informed me that the fifth fellow would be riding on the front bumper.

"You must be joking. He can't do that," I protested. "I'm sure I can find another ride."

"Don't worry about it. He'll be okay," he assured me.

Sure enough, the man climbed onto the front bumper, crouched down, held onto an ornament on the hood, and we started on our way. The guy on the bumper didn't seem to resent the fact that I had taken his place in the cab of the truck. He actually had a big smile on his face as we got under way. But I'm not so sure he was smiling the whole way.

The drive to Hishwa had been on relatively flat ground (except for the potholes!), but it was a long climb up to the Barat plateau, and it was much rougher.

There had been some greenery in and around Hishwa, but as we drove along, the land around us grew barren. I was told it seldom rained in Barat ... and that was rather easy to believe. Neither shrub nor tree was to be seen ... just dry dirt and rocks.

We were under way for a couple of hours before we arrived in Suq al-Inaan. And if you're wondering about the poor guy on the front bumper, well he traded off with a couple of others guys along the way.

As we all got out of the truck to stretch, Ahmad asked me, "Would you like to join me for lunch?"

"That would be nice," I replied.

As for the other three men, they disappeared I'm not sure where.

Ahmad ordered a delicious meal consisting of goat meat, bread and vegetables ... a real feast. And even better than the meal was the high quality interaction with Ahmad.

When it was all over, Ahmad pulled out a wad of bills, peeled off a few, handed them to the waiter, and pushed away my hand when I tried to pay for my part, telling me, "It's already taken care of."

To the waiter he said, "keep the change." And from the look on the waiter's face I could tell it was a generous tip.

"No, I want to pay," I protested, pulling out my *tiny* wad of bills I had along with me (I'm not sure it even qualified to be called a *wad*) which made me look like a pauper in comparison. And to tell you the truth, if I would have paid for the meal, I would have been in real financial difficulty, since I was actually running low on funds at that point in time and still had a couple of traveling days left before getting back to Sana'a.

"You're my guest," Ahmad insisted. And I knew it would be an insult to argue with him anymore.

"Thank you very much," I said ... and then added, "But I do want to pay you for the ride."

He just gave me a look that made it clear and final he wouldn't accept any recompense from me whatsoever.

So I decided all I could do was say another sincere "thank you very much!" as we shook hands, said our good-byes and nice-to-meet-yous and God-be-with-yous.

So the trip from Hishwa to Suq al-Inaan ended up costing me absolutely nothing.

Ahmad hopped back into his truck with his three companions, who had suddenly reappeared, and he drove off to sell his load to the next link in the smuggling network. What a life!

20

Yet Another Race

After *the exchange* took place, and while I was Ali's passenger, in addition to his stopping to purchase the goat from the Bedouin man, we made one more stop prior to our meeting up with Ahmad in Hishwa.

Ali pulled up in close proximity to a house, stopped his truck, and then called out to a man who was bent over working on something (I couldn't quite make out what) near the house.

The man looked up. From his rather neutral reaction, I couldn't tell whether he recognized Ali or not. If he was a friend, then I assumed he would have shown some pleasure at the sight of Ali. If he was a foe, then I thought some reaction would have made that clear as well. Maybe this was to be another business transaction ... I had no idea.

Ali didn't bother getting out of his truck, but merely called out to inform the man, "There's someone here I want you to meet."

His statement caught me by surprise. "Why does he want him to meet *me*?" I wondered.

The man started walking in our direction ... and it seemed that he was approaching rather slowly ... and I might even say cautiously.

As he drew nearer, Ali pointed out to me in a subdued voice, "He's a Jew."

But even before Ali informed me of that fact, the man's racial background became apparent to me, since as he drew ever closer, I could make out the long flowing curls reaching down the sides of his face just in front of his ears, swaying back and forth ... the telltale hairstyle which distinguished the male members of his religious group from their Muslim neighbors. That unique feature was based on the teaching of the Old Testament which states, "Do not cut the hair at the sides of your head ..." (Leviticus 19:27).

"Yes, can I help you?" the man asked Ali as he stopped near, but not too close to, the truck.

"Go ahead, talk to him," Ali entreated me.

"Okay ... well that's a rather awkward introduction," went through my mind ... and still keeping my thoughts to myself, but clearly stated by my facial expression as I looked at Ali, "So what am I supposed to say to him?"

The Jewish man just stood there. Having now turned his attention to me, he waited for me to say something profound. But it was Ali, never at a loss for words, who actually started the verbal interaction by informing the man, "This is a German professor doing language research here in Yemen."

I then took over, very briefly explaining a little about my research and exchanging a few (very few) words with him, although the whole time he seemed rather aloof.

The whole experience was to a certain extent rather embarrassing, since it was quite obvious Ali's real goal in summoning the man was merely to show off the fact that Jews lived in the region. I was quite sure the Jewish man himself realized it.

Rather abruptly, Ali blurted out a goodbye to the man and drove off, just leaving him standing there on his own. If I were in that man's shoes I would have felt insulted and humiliated. From what I observed, I had the impression that not much comradeship was shared between the Jews and the Arabs of Yemen.

"We have a lot of Jews living in this area," Ali informed me rather matter-of-factly, while my mind was still attempting to process what had just transpired.

One day, during my very first trip to Sa'da city, I explored the market located within the mud walls of the old city. As I meandered from one merchant to another, my eyes happened to rest upon one particular man who didn't boast a stall like the majority of other sellers did. Instead, he was squatting beside a colorful blanket upon which jewelry and other handiwork was spread out for the viewing ... and from his perspective, for the selling. Something made him stand out from the rest of the men in the market place ... it was the long curls. So Ali wasn't telling me anything new about the presence of Jews in Yemen. I had already learned of their presence in that region early on. But I hadn't been aware of how far in an easterly direction from Sa'da city communities of Jews were living.

When Dave and I were heading back out of the Khawlaan district located to the *west* of Sa'da city,[23] as we were passing near a village in the vicinity of Haydan, suddenly one of the passengers in the truck cab

---

[23] See chapter 9, *Left lying on the side of the Road.*

leaned out of the window to get my attention. Then he pointed towards the village and shouted, "A lot of Jews live there."

Interesting statement. I assumed he was just stating a fact for my benefit. Or was he looking for a reaction?

On another occasion, I was sitting in a store, and I can't recall which village I was in any more, but the fellow I was interacting with unexpectedly looked me right in the eye and remarked, "I heard about another person once who was traveling around from village to village asking questions, and as it turned out, he was an Israeli spy trying to find out more about our Jewish communities."

Now *that* man was without a doubt looking for a reaction from me. I kept calm (on the outside that is ... while on the inside I was admittedly rather uneasy), and I merely replied truthfully, "That's interesting. As for *me*, my only purpose for coming to Yemen is to learn more about Arabic dialects."

Apparently satisfied, he said nothing more about the Jews, and was more than willing to return to the topic of dialects.

What I heard from expatriates was that the government apparently didn't want foreigners mingling with the Yemeni Jews. They always tried to keep the Jews rather isolated.

Back to Ali the smuggler ... he informed me, "The Jews have their own education system, and they speak only Hebrew at home, and speak Arabic with us Arabs." Those were claims I couldn't confirm one way or another.

So when was it that Jews originally settled in Yemen? Historians argue about it. Was it at the time when King Solomon ruled, in the 900's BC? Was it before the destruction of the First Temple, in the sixth century BC? Some suggest it was after Titus destroyed Jerusalem, in 70 AD. Those dates are all based on diverse traditions. What we do know, is that by the early 500's AD a thriving Jewish population was living in Yemen. In fact, a couple of successive Yemenite kings at the time converted to Judaism.

Then when Islam gained control over the region, the Jewish population's status changed quite drastically, moving far down the social ladder. Later in the 10th century, when the Shi'a-Zaydi branch (discussed in chapter 4, *Base Two*) started to rule, things deteriorated even further. Jews were suddenly treated as if they were impure, and rules were implemented about how they needed to behave whenever they were in the presence of a Muslim. They weren't allowed to build their houses taller than a Muslim's house. They couldn't ride a camel or a horse, only mules or donkeys. And if a Muslim decided to beat on one of them, a Jew wasn't allowed to defend himself. His only defense was to run, or hope that some kind Muslim would intervene.

As for their contribution to Yemeni society, the Jews of Yemen were the expert silversmiths, blacksmiths and masons. They repaired weapons and tools, did weaving, made pottery, etc.

Jumping forward on the time line, eventually the Ottoman Empire took over and started to rule the region. Then at some point in the late 1800's, the Turks decided to allow its citizens to travel about more freely, which resulted in waves of Yemeni Jews emigrating to Palestine.

Next came the establishment of the state of Israel in 1948. Soon after that historic event, in the summer of 1949, a huge operation referred to as *On Wings of Eagles* (also known as *Operation Magic Carpet*) was implemented. British and American transport planes made approximately 380 under cover flights from Aden, in a secret operation which carried 49,000 Yemenite Jews to the new state of Israel. The operation lasted over a year.[24]

Well, obviously in 1986 when I was traveling around North Yemen, a sizable Jewish population was still present ... I would guess somewhere in the 1000's.

---

[24] Some of the dates and figures given in the last few paragraphs of this chapter were taken from Wikipedia articles "Operation Magic Carpet (Yemen)" and "Yemenite Jews" (2012) (http://en.wikipedia.org).

21

Everything Foreign

Ahmad and company, my new smuggler friends, headed west to find their fortune, leaving me all on my own in Suq al-Inaan.

So the few men I had just become acquainted with throughout the first half of that rather adventurous day were now nothing more than a memory. I was sure I would never see them again. But I was just as certain I'd never forget them, and that they would most likely never forget the experience they had interacting with me ... a strange foreigner wandering around where foreigners were never meant to be ... someone who took the time to participate in their lives, who listened to what they had to say, who could even communicate with them, albeit using a rather foreign but understandable (for the most part) Arabic dialect.

I can just picture Ali or Ahmad now, 25 years later, sitting around a fire, drinking tea and telling their grandchildren about this friendly stranger who they had found wandering through the hinterlands of North Yemen, and who they had the chance to rub shoulders with for a brief time. And here I am doing the same for my family and others who are now reading about it.

For me the adventure would continue. I had to move on. Deep down I regretted not having stayed with Ali after he had invited me to do so. I longed for some stability and familiarity.

As was the case in Sa'da city, and in all the other localities I had passed through on my eastbound excursion, the dwellings of Suq al-Inaan were all constructed of mud. Many of them were tall buildings, sometimes four, five or even six stories high.

Suq al-Inaan was a large town, and so I was certain they'd have a school somewhere within the city limits. Schools had so far turned out to be productive places to commence the contact-making process.

The school was easy enough to locate. The building was large and was made entirely of brick. It was quite a contrast to all the mud structures surrounding it. Its foreign appearance made me think it was most likely funded, designed and built by outsiders to that region. I made a beeline for it.

Much to my delight, an Egyptian teacher and I spotted each other, making eye contact from a distance. As a result, I made a slight adjustment to my bearing, and headed straight for him. He just stopped in his tracks and stood there watching me approach.

"Peace be with you," I started the conversation, holding out my hand to shake his which came up automatically to meet mine.

"And with you be peace," he said with his distinct Cairene Egyptian accent.

"Are you a teacher here?" I queried, knowing the obvious response.

"Yes I am," he replied, and then asked, "How can I help you?"

"My name is Butros, and I'm doing research in North Yemen ..." etc, etc, etc, as I gave him a brief introduction to what I was doing, hoping it would spark enough of an interest so he would agree to recruit some of the older Yemeni students to help me.

During my initial interaction with him, I discovered that hundreds of students were attending the institution, from elementary right through high school. Most importantly, quite a few of the high school students were in their 20's, and one or two in their 30's ... the very age bracket I was hoping to get help from.

I was also informed that Suq al-Inaan had a separate school for girls with women Egyptian teachers. Not many girls were getting an education in North Yemen in 1987, so I was impressed.

My new Egyptian acquaintance, Mahmoud by name, took it upon himself to give me a tour of the school. I thought that was a great idea, since it would result in exposure, and hopefully introductions to some Yemenis.

As we walked through the school, I received lots of stares from the students, and I'm sure some of them would have been very open right then and there to meet and interact with me. But unfortunately Mahmoud had latched on to me, and wasn't giving me any opportunity whatsoever to connect with Yemeni students. I was a highly educated

Westerner (hey, I'm not boasting ... I'm just telling you how I was usually perceived), and this was a prestige moment for Mahmoud, having me hang around with him, as if I had come all that way just to visit with him.

"Okay, so how do I get myself out of this situation without appearing rude and ungrateful?" I asked myself.

But the tour continued ... now beyond the borders of the school. My guide decided the next most relevant sight for me to see was the town hospital, where I assumed he was going to introduce me to people he knew ... most likely Egyptians who worked there. And sure enough, as we walked along, Mahmoud informed me, "An Egyptian doctor works at the hospital."

The same architect must have designed both the school and the hospital. It looked just as much out of place for that setting as the school did.

A man exited what I assumed to be the main door of the hospital as we approached. He wasn't Yemeni, and he certainly wasn't Egyptian.

"Hello Dawood," Mahmoud greeted him.

"Welcome Mahmoud," he replied. "Who's your friend?"

"This is Butros. He's from Canada," Mahmoud introduced me.

"Welcome Butros. I'm Dawood, from Somalia," he introduced himself.

"Wow, he speaks Arabic quite fluently," I thought. Then to Dawood I verbalized, "Nice to meet you."

"Is Abdallah here?" inquired Mahmoud.

"No, he needed to go to Sana'a for a few days," Dawood replied.

Dawood worked as the doctor's assistant. He invited us inside so we could visit in a more comfortable setting. We entered and sauntered down a long hallway. About a third of the way down, we entered an open door on our right, and found ourselves standing in a large sparsely furnished room. The room boasted a few cots, a couple of cupboards, a table, and another Somali man.

"Mohamed, this is Butros from Canada," Dawood informed his startled friend.

"It's very nice to meet you," Mohamed said using English. The more I interacted with him, the more impressed I was. He spoke English at a very high level. I was glad to hear he was teaching English at the boys' school. I had met other instructors of English who couldn't even hold a simple conversation in the language, so it was a real treat to speak

English with Mohamed ... and the feeling was mutual. He wouldn't often get the opportunity to talk with a mother tongue English speaker ... albeit a Canadian brand of the English language ... which my kind friend Chris from Oxford, England so often pointed out to me was an acceptable albeit inferior variety.

"We'd like you to be our guest," Dawood eventually said. "We have a room here in the hospital where you can stay as long as you want."

"Should I stay here?" I asked myself, as I quickly assessed my situation. Since the time Ahmad the smuggler left me, so far I had spent all my time with Egyptians and Somalis ... very nice helpful people, but they weren't part of the local population. And yet most of the day was already gone.

"I can try and get to know some Yemenis tomorrow," I concluded. "In the meantime why not have a nice relaxing evening with the Somalis, one of whom speaks English."

"Thank you Dawood. That's very kind of you to offer, and I accept. I would enjoy staying here with you," was my answer.

"Praise be to God," both Dawood and Mohamed said. They seemed sincerely glad.

They actually had a lot of spare room, since, from what I understood, it didn't sound like any patients ever stayed at the hospital, but rather only came during clinic hours in the mornings.

I could tell this turn of events didn't go over well with Mahmoud, even though he tried not to show it. His high-status guest was just snatched out from right under his nose. I hadn't even thought of him when I accepted the Somalis' invitation, but I should have. Now it was too late. The four of us continued to visit, and by the time Mahmoud left, I don't think there were any hard feelings.

A very relaxing evening it was. And when it was time to turn in, I ended up with a room all to myself on a not entirely uncomfortable bed.

22

The Dark Stairwell

With no surprises throughout the night hours, including no strange nocturnal creatures (at least none that I was aware of) or bizarre dreams, I woke in the morning feeling rather refreshed and ready for action. And so, after breakfast, I started on my way back to the school with the intention of encountering and acquiring help from some of the Yemeni students.

I was making good progress towards my intended target, when I suddenly caught sight of a group of curious children heading in my direction. They were giggling and talking and acting silly ... just being boys. Then the bravest of them stepped forward with a big smile and verbalized a thunderous "Helloo meester," demonstrating his communication skills in English.

"Hello. How are you?" I replied in very slow clear English.

"Helloo, helloo," the rest of them chanted, thrilled that I was taking the time to befriend them.

"Suura! Suura!" (translated, *Photo! Photo!*) a few of them entreated, having caught me with my camera in hand.

That was enough of an invitation for me. I gladly obliged them.

Feeling somewhat encouraged by that friendly encounter, I felt even more optimistic once I arrived at the school and a couple of young Yemeni men, Abdallah and Ahmad, came up and introduced themselves. Knowing that opportunities can vanish as quickly as they materialize, I promptly tried to bait them into discussing Arabic dialects. They not only took the bait, but were easily reeled in, showing a sincere interest in my research.

I really felt on a roll when I asked them, "Do either of you know of anyone who could tell me a story in your dialect?" and Abdallah responded, "I'd be happy to tell you a story."

"He's gifted when it comes to telling stories," Ahmad added.

"That's great," I responded, but then suddenly heard the school bell ring indicating classes were starting. "Don't you have to go to class?" I asked.

"No problem," replied Abdallah. "Let's go over there," he said, and then led me to a the end of the school building where we made ourselves comfortable on a covered concrete landing.

I quickly produced my tape recorder to capture his story, and Abdallah started, "About three years ago I traveled to Saudi Arabia with my uncle and two other relatives because we were led to believe there was an opportunity to work awaiting us. But when we arrived, we found nothing but disappointment ..."

The story turned out to be a perfect length, lasting about two and a half minutes. They didn't have time to go over the story with me to explain things I hadn't understood very well, but Abdallah suggested, "Why don't we review the story later at my house while we drink some tea."

That was exactly the kind of opportunity I was hoping for. "Thank you very much," I replied. "I would enjoy that."

"Okay, I'll come later to pick you up at the hospital," he offered. And with that, they left.

I was sitting outside of the hospital with the Somalis when our conversation was suddenly interrupted by the sound of a motorcycle approaching. Dusk was upon us, and so at first I didn't realize it was Abdallah until he stopped and dismounted and commenced walking in our direction. By then I had actually given up hope that he would even show up.

"Good evening," he greeted the three of us, and then turning his attention to me, "Are you ready to come to my house, Butros?"

"On a motorcycle?" I wondered. Honestly, I would have much rather walked, having observed how motorcycles are often driven in this country. But I was Abdallah's guest, and he was going out of his way to treat me special. And so, I decided not to focus on the potential danger, but rather just be grateful for his kindness. "Hey," I encouraged myself, "I'm sure he rides this thing all the time ... and he's still around."

I shouldered my backpack, hopped on the back of the motorcycle, and we were on our way ... and I never even fell off once!

When we arrived at Abdallah's house, Ahmad was at the front door waiting for us. The two of them entered the doorway and I followed. I suddenly found myself ascending some stairs behind them. The stairs wound around, and I quickly lost sight of them ... and of everything else for that matter. With the failing light outside, and no windows, the stairwell was dark ... I couldn't see a thing. Abdallah and Ahmad, being very familiar with the stairwell, moved at a rapid pace, not thinking it possible that anyone could ever go astray. Well, the Canadian proved them wrong ... I felt very lost!

Now if the stairs had been laid out like stairs in Canada are, with consistent heights and lengths, then my dilemma would not have been as immense. But by then, after having ascended and descended Yemeni stairwells on numerous occasions, my experience told me the height and length of steps could vary by a great deal ... and that was definitely the case at Abdallah's house. I had no idea how high to lift my foot, or how far to step forward.

After the first few stumbles, I stopped, remembering the flashlight in my backpack. So I reached in, pulled it out, and the ensuing light was an immediate comfort. It dispelled enough of the darkness to allow me to resume my ascent, and with confidence restored, I quickened my pace. In fact, I almost ran right into my hosts as I rounded one corner. They must have realized their mistake in leaving me behind and had stopped to wait for me. We proceeded together, with the two of them setting a much slower pace for the bumbling foreigner.

We must have climbed at least four flights of stairs ... it seemed endless. Finally, we halted on a landing, although the stairs continued upwards, I assume leading up to yet another floor, or to the roof. We entered a door where a pleasant sitting room awaited our arrival, a kerosene lamp already lit to provide a dull light.

"Have a seat," Abdallah said, and the three of us sat down on soft mats and reclined on pillows ... a dangerous position for someone as tired as I was. But the interaction was sure to keep me awake.

We had only been lounging for a few minutes, before a voice called out for Abdallah from outside. He went to the window and shouted down, "Come on up Ali! The door is open!"

Ali must also have been accustomed to that stairwell since it didn't take long at all before he entered the room and we were introduced to each other. The more the merrier! And the three of them would soon be even merrier once they started chewing on the supply of qat Ali had purchased in the market and carried into the room with him.

"Butros, would you like to chew with us?" asked Abdallah, putting me into an awkward position ... although not intentionally on his part.

Hmmm, to chew or not to chew. "Thank you very much, but I don't chew," I said sticking to my convictions. We only interacted a little more on that topic before they ceased the pressure upon me to conform.

As they entered stage one of the chew session (the stage where they become very talkative), it was the perfect time to get down to the business of going over Abdallah's story and translating other material into the Barat dialect.

Once the work was done, we continued socializing until I eventually indicated it was time for me to return to the hospital.

Abdallah was quick to offer, "I'll take you back."

I didn't even attempt to refuse his offer.

After the appropriate number of thank yous and blessings were exchanged with Ahmad and Ali, Abdallah and I entered the stairwell once again, where the darkness was still lurking, hoping to cause confusion so as to provide its partner in crime, the uneven stairs, another chance to try and victimize me. But I disappointed my foes yet once again by putting the darkness to flight with my flashlight.

And thus having survived the descent, Abdallah and I rode off into the dark night on his motorcycle.

23

The Resort

After another comfortable night in my private room at the hospital, and having visited with the Police Chief (at his request, with nothing unusual happening during the encounter with him), and having accomplished all that I had hoped to achieve in Suq al-Inaan, it was time to move on.

Travel was tiring, and so was the constant interaction in a second language ... a language which consisted of various dialects constantly forcing me to deal with differences in vocabulary and pronunciation from one district to the next. The overall experience was always quite taxing. And so my preference would have been not to visit more than one region per trip. It would have been nice to return to Home Base #2 in Sa'da city so I could recuperate a bit ... especially since I didn't really get much of a break after my previous intense trip to Munabbih.

On the other hand, it really didn't make any sense to head west all the way back to Sa'da when I was already so far out east, and especially since my next destination was actually located even further to the east within Jawf province. To be more precise, my next target was situated more in a south-easterly direction, which, if I followed that path, would be taking me closer to Home Base #1 in Sana'a. So it would definitely be a better use of my time if I kept right on going in the south-easterly direction to my next destination, and then head to Sana'a from there.

The only potential problem was a financial one. I didn't have many riyals left when I arrived in Suq al-Inaan, so how could I manage to add on some extra days with the need to pay for travel, food and lodging? I couldn't borrow any money from anyone, and I had to at least offer to pay for any services rendered. Who would believe that the *rich foreigner* didn't have any money? Poor planning on my part (pun intended).

Then I started to recall the many incidences of hospitality that had been extended to me thus far, both on this current trip and on previous trips. Even the poorest Yemeni, Egyptian and Somali had proven themselves generous. They've all been willing to share their food and lodging with me, and I was quite sure I would be experiencing more of the same. Therefore my main concern was paying for rides, and I calculated I just might be able to manage. So I decided to take a chance and see if I could make what little money I had left stretch.

My Somali hosts were disappointed to see me go, and I would miss the quality times we shared. We said a face-to-face goodbye, and then I gave one more wave from a distance, as I headed to the market place of Suq al-Inaan to start the search for a ride to Al Hazm.

"I'm not going to Al Hazm," the driver of a Salown told me. "But I'm going as far as Kharab, and that's right on the way to Al Hazm. It will be easy to find another ride in Kharab to take you the rest of the way."

I sure disliked hearing the statement *"it'll be easy to find another ride"* so effortlessly rolling off the tongues of Yemenis, as if they really expected me to believe it.

Noticing my hesitation, one of the other passengers leaned out of the truck window and informed me, "When we get to Kharab I'll be looking for a ride to Al Hazm too," substantiating what the driver had just told me.

"Well whatever happens, I guess some movement in the right direction is better than no progress at all," I reasoned ... and then said out loud to the driver, "Okay, I'll ride with you."

With that settled, I suddenly started thinking about the name of the town, *Kharab*. "Okay, I've learned the word kharab, and its meaning has to do with *destruction* ... or it could be a reference to *wasteland*. Is that really where I want to be heading?"

As we started along the road leading out of Suq al-Inaan, we first climbed a little higher in elevation, and then started the descent, coming off the Barat plateau on the opposite side from which I had gone up two days earlier.

The driver informed me, "We have a choice of two roads off of this side of the plateau, an old one and a new one. The newer road is used more often now, but we're traveling on the old road."

"Why are we on the old road?" I inquired.

He answered, "Because the old road leads us in a more direct route towards Kharab."

We headed down into a valley where we sadly left the paved road and started driving alongside a waterless river bed in the midst of parched surroundings, with the odd forlorn shrub sticking up here and there. It was a welcome sight when we eventually started to encounter some greenery.

We had to slow down to a crawl when we came across a large herd of goats indulging in lunch. They were occupying both sides of the narrow road, and were wandering back and forth across the road itself, with a total disregard for the periodic traffic. Their presence was a sign that Bedouin must be living close by. And sure enough, it wasn't long before we passed a number of Bedouin tents. The only visible residents were a few barefoot children who interrupted their play long enough to give us a wave, and then a more intent stare once they spotted me gazing back at them.

In addition to our vehicle, some of the intermittent traffic consisted of trucks laden with various items. One was carrying goats, probably with the intent of selling them in the city. Another truck carried firewood. I was told firewood brought a good price in the city. In Sana'a I often saw trucks parked on the side of the road, full of firewood, just waiting for some buyer to come along. I heard that women preferred to cook their bread over a wood fire rather than use gas. I'm not sure I was enough of a connoisseur of bread to taste the difference.

The driver directed the vehicle right into the dry river bed itself ... it's width indicating that an abundance of water must have been flowing through the region at one time, whereas now the bed merely consisted of a mixture of sand and gravel.

We had been moving along at a good pace and soon arrived at the village of Kharab. Much to my delight, I discovered that Kharab wasn't a wasteland after all. A large quantity of greenery met my eyes. Maybe the town took on the name *wasteland* (if that's indeed what Kharab meant to the locals) based on some past natural disaster ... or perhaps it was built next to some ancient historical site ... or perchance it was named that way to deceive any potential distant enemies into thinking it was a horrible place, and so not worth attacking. I can't tell you the real reason.

I only had to spend about an hour in Kharab between rides. That was admittedly not due to my amazing ability at finding my next ride. Rather, all the credit goes to Hussein, a Yemeni man who had traveled from Suq al-Inaan in the same vehicle with me. In fact, it was Hussein I had interacted with prior to joining the passenger list to Kharab. Knowing that I planned to travel on to Al Hazm, he took it upon himself to find a ride for the both of us. A kind gesture like that made at least part of the day so much easier. Hussein had been working in Saudi

Arabia and was returning home to visit his family who lived about half-way between Kharab and Al Hazm.

Our new driver's name was Haadi. He owned a small well used (you might even say *beat up*) Toyota pick-up ... no, not a 4-wheel drive. Those little pick-up trucks had no problems traversing the flatter regions, whether or not there was any pavement. We had left the pavement behind long ago on the first leg of the trip, and we would encounter no pavement whatsoever on this second leg.

The cab of Haadi's truck was filled to capacity, with two male passengers sitting with him. But as was common practice all over the country, he was more than willing to stuff as many passengers as possible into the truck bed ... and that's where Hussein and I ended up, along with another man and a boy.

We were soon on our way once again along the unpaved desert road. The greenery was soon only a memory. The sun contributed to the desert atmosphere, mercilessly beating down on us, with temperatures reaching into the low 30's centigrade.

Haadi drove along at a fair clip. The landscape was relatively flat, but that was not to imply that it was void of potholes and bumps ... there were still plenty of those. As a result, the bouncing in the back of the pickup (with shocks that should have been replaced long ago) was constant. Unfortunately those little trucks didn't allow the possibility of standing up so as to absorb some of the shock with the legs, and so my behind was getting slightly tender.

We encountered another vehicle from time to time, but I was thankful there was very little traffic to worry about since Haadi didn't like to slow down ... not even when we he approached a blind turn in the dirt road where trees blocked his view. He merely leaned on the horn to give anybody nearby enough warning that he'd be coming around the corner, and he'd keep right on going.

There wasn't much to do while bouncing around in the back of the pickup besides hang on and watch the scenery go by. On both sides of us, mountains loomed in the distance. From time to time we would pass patches of vegetation (hence the blind corners). And where there's vegetation, there's always potential for some sort of wildlife, even if only birds. Once when Haadi honked his horn, a couple of camel heads suddenly popped up over the shrubbery with a look of bewilderment. Obviously we had rudely interrupted their meal. I'm sure I must have had quite a surprised look on my face as well. It made me laugh out loud. I needed that.

Unfortunately holding a conversation in the truck bed was almost impossible. The first obstacle was distance. Each of us sat in his own corner to allow for maximum opportunity to hold on to the sides of the truck. Secondly, the endless creaking of the truck mixed with the wind zipping past our heads didn't help. At times when I did attempt an exchange of a few words with Hussein, who was seated nearest to me, every statement was followed by an "excuse me."

At one point I leaned over towards Hussein and said loudly, "It sure would be nice to stretch my legs." And no sooner had the words crossed my lips, than the truck came to a stop.

"Well you got your wish," Hussein said with a smile.

The plentiful shady trees were very inviting. Without any hesitation, we all quickly jumped out and stretched. But I wanted more than a stretch, I wanted a walk, and so I started wandering a bit. When I eventually turned around, I noticed everyone else had busied themselves with gathering up dry branches which were scattered on the ground. Somehow I hadn't received word about this *group project*. I wasn't sure if I should feel obligated to participate or not, and so I just continued sauntering about within sight of the truck.

Now I was somewhat concerned about where all the gathered wood was being deposited ... namely, in the bed of the truck. That obviously meant there'd be even less room for the four *backseat* passengers. I mean, those little Toyota pickups really didn't have very much room in the back to begin with. But when it was time to move on, the four of us successfully managed to find our usual places in the four corners of the truck bed, encircling the wood pile which only required a little readjusting.

Soon after getting under way again, we encountered a flowing stream which we ended up crossing a number of times. Then we drove into some low-lying hills, and as we rounded one corner a village came into view. We had arrived at Waghara (meaning, *to be hot*). That seemed like an appropriate name since the tiny village was built right beside a hot spring, quite clearly the source of the stream we had been crossing.

Since the noise of the road trip had finally ceased, I was able to hear Hussein more clearly as he explained, "People come from all over to enjoy these hot springs."

"Do people just come for the day?" I enquired.

"No, some people come for longer. They can rent one of those houses," he said, pointing at a row of very simple one-level mud houses just off to the right of where Haadi had parked his truck.

Then it hit me ... "This is a *resort*," I said to myself.

The resort obviously wasn't built in a location that would attract a large international crowd ... although, there I was, a token Canadian ... probably the first non-Yemeni ever to set foot in Waghara.

We had been bouncing around in the back of Haadi's truck for about three hours by then, and we were all ready for a longer break. This was the perfect spot for such a reprieve ... a very peaceful setting.

I was also ready for lunch. In fact, I was famished. Thankfully Waghara boasted a small restaurant. I discreetly double checked my financial situation and calculated that I should be able to allow myself the cheapest thing on the menu.

Everyone from our truck, including me, trooped on over to the restaurant. Haadi talked briefly to an elderly man, and then turned to me and asked, "Butros, will you join us? We're going to eat in one of those small houses," pointing with his chin.

"Oh great. This is going to be embarrassing. What should I do?" I discussed with myself. "I can't join them, because if they order as a group, then I'll be expected to pay my portion no matter what they order, and I just can't afford it. But I'll seem rather snobbish if I don't join them."

Deciding not to give any reasons for my decision, I merely said, "Thank you, but I think I'll just eat right here in the restaurant if you don't mind."

Thankfully no one seemed offended. They put in their order while I found a place to sit down in the restaurant and waited for someone to serve me. There were actually tables and chairs in the restaurant, and I imagine my Yemeni companions concluded that I'd rather sit at a table than on the ground with them. I have to admit it was indeed a treat to experience the luxury of sitting on a chair.

The aforementioned old man, a mature woman, and a younger woman all worked there. As expected, it was the old man who approached me. I wondered what was going through his mind as he asked me in Arabic, "How can I serve you?" He had obviously just had the opportunity to observe me interacting with the others from the truck. Maybe he thought I was from Syria, which was a common mistake because of my *northern* accent (Yemenis usually just lumped Jordan and Syria together).

I responded, "What's on the menu?" I didn't think it appropriate to say, "What's the cheapest thing on your menu?"

There were no printed menus, and so the man quickly rattled off a list of things ... some of which I didn't know. I went for the *fetta* (bread soaked in oil and milk) and *hilbe* (a simple broth eaten with bread) ... definitely a poor man's meal. I'm quite sure my waiter wasn't expecting me to order that, but it was his duty to serve and he brought me what I ordered without trying to talk me into ordering anything else.

After the delicious meal (and it really was delicious), I ordered and enjoyed a relaxing cup of hot tea.

It wasn't until after I thanked the old man for the meal and paid him that he got brave enough to start up a conversation ... while the two women made sure their work brought them close enough to listen in. "Where are you from?" he asked.

"I'm German, but I carry a Canadian passport," was my answer.

After processing that bit of information, and seeing that I was open to satisfying his curiosity, he went on to ask, "So what are you doing here in Jawf?" And by then the women were no longer working, but were rather standing right beside the man listening intently as the conversation went on.

They were extremely friendly, and obviously intrigued with this foreigner who had unexpectedly appeared at their restaurant for a meal and a chat.

When they were finally forced to busy themselves with other customers, I made my exit and looked over at the others from our truck. Having finished their meal, one of them walked over to the cab of the truck, pulled out a couple of bundles, and then returned to the others. It was qat, and they started to chew. Obviously they weren't in a hurry to get under way any time soon. This was going to be a long rest.

As I leisurely wandered around, I encountered another old man who seemed anxious to share his wisdom with me ... although he did not have the gift of speaking slowly and clearly, and so many *excuse mes* were thrown in while we interacted. "These hot springs are very good for my health," he informed me.

"I'm sure they are," I agreed. I had no reason to think otherwise.

"My son doesn't think so," he went on. "But I finally convinced him to bring me here."

"Where is your son?" I inquired.

"He's over there," he answered, pointing to a small group of men sitting in the hot water chattering away. I guess whether or not the son believed the hot springs had the power to cure whatever ailed his father, since he had to bring his father anyway, he was going to enjoy himself.

"I wish you health and prosperity," I said.

By the time the men from our truck finished chewing, their qat, two hours had passed ... much longer than I had hoped for. I really wanted to get to my destination and didn't want this to turn into a two day trip. But they weren't through yet. Some of them decided to spend a bit of time in the hot springs.

I wanted to join in, but wasn't willing to go prancing about in my underwear, or go in with my clothes on. Guess I should have packed my bathing suit in my backpack! So I just continued to wait patiently. I was totally at their mercy.

24

Ghost and Clown

Hey, I had wished for a longer break, and my wish came true, I got a longer break ... over two hours worth, which, as I already pointed out, was much more than I had hoped for. Then it was into the back of the truck once again as we got under way for the final stretch of the trip, leaving behind the Waghara resort ... another one of those once in a lifetime experiences.

Soon after our departure, we hit a military check point. The soldier routinely approached the driver's window to start his inspection at the cab, and then he walked around to the back of the truck. His approach from the driver's side naturally forced him to notice the man and boy sitting at the very back of the truck bed first. Then a 90 degree turn of the head to the left brought Hussein into focus, and by then he was standing right next to me. I rather enjoyed the look of shock that appeared on his face when he finally caught sight of me sitting there looking up at him. Seeing a foreigner way off the beaten track was one thing, but to catch him sitting in such humble circumstances, crowded in the bed of a truck along with three Yemeni travelers in addition to a pile of firewood, just wasn't normal.

I merely smiled at him, and before he had the chance to say a word, I handed him a copy of my travel permission paper, and said, "This will explain what I'm doing here."

He was dumbstruck. He looked down at the paper, decided it looked official, and so waved us on. I sure broke up the routine of his otherwise dull day.

We were now driving along on pleasantly flat terrain, and so, in addition to less bouncing, we were making good time. I thought, "This is too good to be true," ... and it was ... for all of a sudden, without any warning, my eye caught sight of something out of the ordinary appearing off to my left. Something was working its way up the side of the truck. Then a quick turn of the head revealed the same thing happening on the other side ... and also at the back. I didn't think I had time to look overhead ... I had my back up against the truck cab. It was all happening so quick ... all within a matter of seconds.

154

A very powdery dust was about to envelope the truck, which obviously included those of us who were sitting in the bed of the truck. No doubt it would blind and choke me, unless I did something to prevent it. I couldn't thwart the enveloping part, but I could probably prevent the blinding and choking part ... at least temporarily, and only if I reacted fast. My fellow passengers also saw it coming, and we all reacted simultaneously, heads ducking down close to the chest, eyes closing, breath held, shirts brought up to cover mouths and noses. As for me, I had one more important item to protect from the onslaught. I had been holding my precious tape recorder in my hand which I had been using to verbalize some thoughts as we drove along, since writing was an impossible task with all the bouncing around. Well, somehow I even had sense enough to quickly tuck my tape recorder underneath my shirt.

I had never in all my years experienced anything like that before. It was another one of those bizarre unfolding dramas that didn't seem probable outside of a nightmare, novel, or movie.

Many thoughts swiftly flashed through my mind. And one very serious thought was, "How long will I have to hold my breath?" Taking a breath, no matter how small a breath, would surely result in choking, of that I was sure ... even though I'd be inhaling through my shirt. It was such a fine dust, it would go right through most any material no matter how tight a weave, and would instantly plug up the lungs.

I decided it was safe to uncover my head, slowly open my eyes to narrow slits, and take a breath after I felt the truck come to a stop, heard the driver's door open, and then heard Haadi's voice close beside me asking with some concern, "Are you all okay?"

Thankfully we had traversed the cursed plot of ground relatively quickly. From beginning to end the event probably only lasted a maximum of ten seconds, so I hadn't turned blue before getting the chance to take my first sought-after breath.

"Yes, we're okay, praise be to God," I heard Hussein say.

"Praise be to God ... Praise be to God ... Praise be to God," was then chorused by everyone.

I cleared my throat once or twice, and then added my "Praise be to God" ... and I meant it. But then a critical thought passed through my mind, "Haadi must have traveled on these roads numerous times. Wouldn't he have known about this powdery stuff? So why didn't he give us any warning, or at least slow down?!"

"Sorry," Haadi said, "we were talking and I didn't notice the powder before we drove into it." He seemed sincerely apologetic.

"Okay, I guess he's off the hook," I reasoned. "He obviously didn't do it on purpose."

I brushed some more of the dust from around my face and then open my eyes a little wider. Everyone in the back of the truck looked like ghosts, and I obviously looked the same. We were all totally (and I mean totally) caked from head to foot in fine powdery dust.

Now that the threat was over, everyone started to relax and talk all at once, while those of us in the back jumped out and dusted ourselves off as best we could. Soon laughter was added to the chatter once it was determined everyone was indeed doing fine.

But that incident put me on edge for the rest of the trip, my neck often craning as I attempted to look beyond the cab to spot any more dusty patches before we hit them. In fact we did pass through a few more patches of the powdery stuff, but they were much smaller, and thankfully didn't have anywhere near the same effect on us. Clearly Haadi was paying closer attention and slowed down each time he spotted one.

Our next stop was a depressing one. We had arrived at Hussein's village. My travel companion and I said our goodbyes, and then I watched as he crawled out of the back of the truck with his bag, brushed off some more of the dust, walked to the cab of the truck, paid Haadi, and then headed toward a house where relatives had obviously caught sight of him and were already coming out to welcome him home.

I was very sad to see him leave. Hussein was a kind, gentle, friendly man. I assumed it was due to how he was raised ... namely, in a kind, gentle, friendly setting. I had a desire to meet the rest of his family, but it wasn't to be.

As Haadi started to pull away, I watched from the back of the truck as Hussein started kissing and hugging his relatives who were clearly overjoyed at having their son, husband, and father, back home again. I had never even asked how long he had been away, or if he would be returning to Saudi Arabia to continue working. I also never found out the name of his village.

Later on, after the trip was over, I found out from Haadi that Hussein had paid my fare, and so I said to him, "If you ever encounter Hussein again, please thank him for me."

"I certainly will," he promised.

We moved on from Hussein's village, made one more stop to drop off the man and boy from the back of the truck, and eventually reached Muslaab, Haadi's village. The larger town of Al Hazm, where I had hoped to end up that day, was still about another hour's drive further east, but somehow I had a feeling that Haadi wasn't planning to drive me to my destination that evening.

Haadi stopped the truck between two mud houses, and everyone piled out. I must have looked a mess as I clambered out of the back of Haadi's truck. But of one thing I was sure, the dust wasn't going to help disguise my foreignness.

A crowd started to form around Haadi and the two men who had been riding in the cab of the truck with him. "Welcome home!" and "Praise be to God for your safe arrival!" were stated many times.

Of course, the greeters couldn't help but notice the foreigner who had ridden into town with them, and who had crawled out of the back of the truck all caked in dust.

One young boy came right up close to me and just stared. I concluded that he'd never seen a foreigner before (which was probably very true). But a little later Haadi pulled me aside and asked, "Do you know why the little boy was staring at you?"

"Probably because I'm a foreigner," I answered.

Haadi explained, "Yes, that's true ... but that's not the main reason. The boy asked me how you are able to walk."

"Pardon me," I said, "I don't understand what you mean."

"The boy has never in his life seen someone wearing pants," he clarified with a laugh.

As I pointed out in chapter 2, most Yemenis wore wrap-arounds or robes, and pretty well the only place I recall seeing pants worn was in the city. Well obviously the boy had never been to the city.

I was sure Haadi was laughing at the boy's reaction rather than at the way I was dressed, and yet I suddenly became somewhat self-conscious about my appearance. If I stood out so much to that boy, it meant many other Yemenis I had encountered during my travels would have thought the same thing, whether they'd seen pants before or not. It's just that it was never pointed out to me quite the way it was on that particular day. I suddenly felt like a circus clown.

25

Welcome or Not?

"Come on Butros, let's go," Haadi said.

"Where are we going?" I inquired, some hope arising at this unexpected turn of events. "Please let the answer be *To find you a ride to Al Hazm*," I found myself hoping, for that was the destination I had planned for that day.

"We're going to my house," he informed me.

I had thought we were already at Haadi's house, but I was clearly mistaken. He was merely dropping off his two traveling companions. So I followed him back to the truck. And this time I had the opportunity to sit in the cab with him.

We drove a little ways through the village, and then stopped in front of another two story mud house located in a more sparsely populated part of the town.

"This is Butros from Germany," he introduced me to a couple of men who had suddenly appeared ... a much smaller welcoming committee than I had witnessed at the previous stop in the village.

"Nice to meet you," I said to each one in turn.

One of those men turned out to be his elderly father. Haadi's father had a slight build, but when he shook my hand, he had the strong grip of a working man. His long loose-fitting light blue robe was well used, and clearly in need of a wash ... but who was I to talk. His head covering, wrapped around his hair, hung unintentionally loose on one side. A pair of well worn flip flops just barely kept his feet out of the dirt. He looked out at me through his cold vacant eyes set in a heavily wrinkled face, giving me the feeling he wasn't all that excited about my presence. Or maybe he was just staring at the way I was dressed too. Or maybe he had just had a bad day. Who knows.

That was okay since I wasn't planning on staying in their town anyway. As I already pointed out a couple of times, it was my intention to make it all the way to Al Hazm that day. And so Haadi's father wouldn't have to worry about me hanging around. I decided I better bring up the topic of moving on before it started to get too late to do so

... there were still a couple of hours of daylight left. So I said, "Haadi, can you tell me where to find a ride to Al Hazm?"

He looked at me as if I had just asked him a rather silly question. "Okay, so what did I say wrong?" went through my mind.

Then he said, "You won't be able to find another ride today."

"Why not?" I inquired.

"No more vehicles will be making the trip today," he said. "It'll be getting dark soon."

"Are you sure?" I prodded.

"Yes, I'm quite sure," he said confidently. "But don't worry. We'd like you to be our guest. You can spend the night right here. And then in the morning you'll be able to find a ride to Al Hazm."

It was the first indication I had been given that they wanted me to stay. Did they really want me to stay, or was Haadi just feeling obligated to invite me?

I looked over at his dad who was just standing there glaring at me. Okay, so maybe it was just my wrong interpretation, but he certainly didn't make me feel welcome. He didn't say anything to me at all, and he was the head of the household, so he was the one who should have extended the invitation. I thought to myself, "I really don't want to stay here."

But to Haadi (admittedly with some hesitation) I said, "Thank you very much. That's very generous of you." The *you* was said in the plural as I talked to and looked both at him and his father. Did I catch a glimmer of an attempted smile on his dad's face?

Haadi's dad shuffled off and disappeared. Then Haadi led me through a door which opened onto a courtyard where a number of sheep and one cow were hanging out. They were all contentedly nibbling away at a pile of hay, and they all glanced my way ... probably having a good chuckle at the funny clown wearing the ridiculous pants.

From the courtyard we entered another door which led into the house itself. Well, actually it led into a dark stairwell (hmmm, sound familiar?). It seemed especially dark since we had just come in out of the daylight, but my eyes adjusted quickly since light managed to sneak in from the door with wide spaces between the slats below. Since it was only two stories high, light also managed to flow in from the similarly constructed door located at the top of the stairs. So there was no need for me to stop and pull out my flashlight as we started climbing the stairs. But since it was far from being bright light, I still took slow cautious steps as I followed my host up the stairs of varied heights and lengths.

We ended up on the roof. The roof was flat with a low wall running all the way around the edge ... a pleasant place where families could relax and enjoy the cooler evenings.

Haadi excused himself, leaving me on the roof all on my own. Alone at last!

I was glad for a reprieve ... albeit short lived, since Haadi's younger brother soon showed up to keep me company. It's rude to leave your guests all alone for too long.

"Hello Butros," he said.

I had just met him downstairs upon my arrival, but I couldn't remember his name. "Could you tell me your name again?" I asked.

"I'm Muhammad," he said. He was a pleasant fellow and we talked for some time. And that's when I found out about the lack of education in *Muslaab-A*.

I started referring to the village where Haadi lived as *Muslaab-A*, because I found out something quite peculiar. The village was divided into two parts, with a definite plot of land between the two sections.

Muslaab-A had no electricity and no school. Muslaab-B had both a school and electricity. Not one of the men in Muslaab-A was educated, and none of the children were attending school, even though there was a school very close by in Muslaab-B. Muhammad told me that the children of Muslaab-A didn't have time to study. It made me wonder if some sort of hard feeling (or even a feud?) existed between the two sections of the village. I never got that clarified.

Haadi soon returned to the roof with the objective of leading us all down a level to their living room.

"Good evening Abu Haadi," I said as I entered the room, having spotted Haadi's dad sitting off to one side. *Abu Haadi* means *father of Haadi*. In Arab cultures it's very common and polite to refer to someone as "father of ..." followed by the name of his oldest son. So I would be referred to as *Abu Andrew* (*father of Andrew*) ... although at the time I wasn't married and so didn't have a son. And even though Andrew is my third child, since my first two children were girls, they don't count. Well, they obviously do to me, but in the Middle East only boys carry on the family line. So it's only when you have a boy that you can be called *father of ...* That's just the way it is.

"Good evening," Abu Haadi mumbled at me in a barely audible voice.

"Have a seat, Butros. Make yourself at home. Our house is your house," Haadi said.

I walked over to one of the well-worn mats furnishing the room, making sure to sit as far away from Abu Haadi as possible without trying to make it seem like that was my intention. He still made me nervous. He persisted with a look of suspicion on his face as he watched me enter and take a seat. He never said anything to me while I interacted with his sons. He would only ever converse with his sons.

As the sun started to set, and the light in the room started to fade, Muhammad walked over to a window ledge and lit a small oil lamp. As you may recall, they didn't have any electricity. The room never actually got *bright* with the light given off by the lamp, but it did allow us to at least see each other's faces.

After some time, Haadi stood up, left the room, and soon returned carrying a small basin, a bar of soap on a plate, and a jug of water. He put the basin and soap in front of me. I automatically pulled up my sleeves and reached out my hands over the basin. He slowly poured a little water over my hands to wet them, after which I picked up the soap, washed my hands, and then stretched out my arms again, hands over basin, while he poured some more water on them to rinse off the soap and grime.

Once every one had washed up, he left the room again, and this time when he returned he was carrying a single rather small looking metal bowl filled with *fetta* which he set down on the floor close to me. My initial assumption was that the contents of the bowl was intended for me, and that he would be bringing in three more bowls. But it was soon apparent that I was mistaken. All three of them suddenly scooted over closer to the bowl ... and to me. The bowl didn't look like it contained enough food for one of us to get full on, let alone four adult men. It was pretty obvious that this family lived and ate simply, and it looked as if I was going to be eating some of their meager supply of food. I felt guilty. But I certainly couldn't refuse their hospitality ... it would have been an insult. And so when Haadi invited me to indulge, I did.

All four of us began reaching into the bowl, using only our right hands, bringing hands from bowl to mouth, and thus started the process of emptying the bowl's contents.

Now by western standards that may not sound like the most sanitary way to eat, but it was quite customary all over the Middle East to eat group meals that way ... especially in rural areas.

The fetta was tasty, although it had a slightly different flavor from the fetta I had eaten earlier in the day at the restaurant. Here at Haadi's house it had more milk than oil in it.

Based on what I related to you about their situation, I made sure to eat very slowly. I took only small amounts at each reach to the bowl, showing delight while eating, and then finished eating before the others. I could have easily eaten four times as much as I did and still wouldn't have been full.

Of course, when Haadi noticed that I wasn't eating any more he reprimanded me, "Eat Butros, eat!"

"Thank you very much! It was delicious!" I replied.

"But you haven't eaten anything at all," Haadi argued in typical Arab style. "Take some more!"

To which I responded appropriately, "I ate lots, and I'm full. Praise be to God."

"Praise be to God," Haadi concluded the argument as he and his father and brother continued to finish off what was still in the bowl.

And when there was nothing visibly left, Abu Haadi took hold of the bowl, and started to run his fingers along the inside to get every last morsel ... which made me feel all the more like I had just eaten a portion of what was rightfully his.

I quickly tried to lay all those thoughts aside and did my best to relax as tea was brought in and we all sipped and talked a bit more. I really was grateful for their generosity and hospitality which they offered to this stranger.

Earlier on Haadi had informed me I would be sleeping in the living room, but when it was actually time to call it a day (which I wished would have been a lot sooner), I was escorted back up to the roof where Haadi and Muhammad set up four sleeping mats ... one for me, and the other three for Haadi, Muhammad and another brother who I had yet to meet.

I was glad we would be sleeping on the roof. I was afraid the other option might have involved sleeping in the same room with Abu Haadi, something I didn't wish to experience.

Before turning in, Ali and one of his brothers became very talkative. As exhausted as I was, we talked on into the night. They were curious about me ... where I came from, what I believed, etc, etc.

I must say I always found it much easier to *speak* Arabic when I was tired than I did trying to *listen* to others talking at me, especially when it was a different dialect from what I had learned. So I was quite content to do a lot of the talking. They appeared to understand me quite well. And the more we talked, the more accepted and unforeign I started to feel.

I hadn't wanted to stop in that village, and yet overall it really did turn out to be a positive encounter. Well, positive when I wasn't in the presence of Abu Haadi that is.

Eventually the opportunity came to lie down, and it wasn't long before my thoughts turned to dreams.

I didn't sleep through the night though ... I never did when I traveled. At one point, when I woke up to the heavy breathing of the three sleeping bodies nearby, I looked up into the sky, thoroughly enjoying the stars, the cool breeze, and being *alone* ... eventually drifting off again.

When the sun started to make its appearance on that side of the globe, and the sky started to turn from black to dark blue, that was the end of what little sleep I did manage to get.

Soon we were all sitting together eating breakfast ... feta again. But I was honestly thankful and enjoyed it. I also admittedly enjoyed it much more not having Abu Haadi sitting across from me.

After the good interaction the previous evening, I seriously considered staying a little longer in Muslaab-A. But I had informed them that I'd be leaving that morning ... and no one said, "Why don't you stay longer with us?" So I wondered if I would even be welcome to stay on.

In Yemeni households, as was the situation in Jordanian households, the father was the master of the house, and the children, no matter how old they were themselves, had no choice but to listen to him. I still didn't get the feeling that Abu Haadi was happy with my presence in his home. I assumed he allowed me to stay because of Haadi, and to display generosity, which in turn affects the honor of the family. So in the end I decided against finding out if I could stay longer.

Since I was going to travel on to Al Hazm, I hoped I could get off to an early start. But I was still at their mercy ... I needed their help to get to the right place to catch a ride.

Well, after breakfast, Haadi, his father and I climbed into the truck (in the cab for me again ... woohoo!), and then we drove for a few minutes to a field where his father quickly hopped out, walked away from the truck, and started working.

It seemed that most of the men in this part of Jawf province either grew crops and/or raised livestock. I noted cantaloupe, watermelon, a variety of vegetables and a type of plant that was fed to their sheep.

It was a bit awkward (yet again) because Haadi's father had walked off without saying anything to me. He didn't even give me the chance to say good bye to him, or thank you, or anything else. I was quite sure he knew it was my intention to leave the village. Or did he? Did he think he'd be seeing me again later that day?

While I was still processing, Haadi suddenly drove off and the two of us ended up at another field where, without any explanation, he jumped out and started working, leaving me sitting all on my own in the truck. I had assumed he would be taking me to a spot where I could find a ride to Al Hazm. So was that his way of trying to get me to stay another night at their house?

Hmmm ... I had to think this through. They hadn't invited me to stay longer, and Haadi knew I wanted to travel to Al Hazm, so why was I still hanging around? I wasn't sure how to deal with this rather awkward situation. I must have mis-communicated my intentions. Or was there something they wanted from me?

I had tried to pay for the ride the day before, and that's when I found out that my other Yemeni travel companion (Hussein) had already paid for me, and Haadi refused to take anything more from me. So I didn't think they wanted any money from me.

I finally decided to take a direct approach. I walked over to him and said, "Haadi ... I really don't want to be a bother, but I think I should try and find a ride to Al Hazm before it gets too late."

He responded, "Okay, I can take you to Muslaab where you'll be able to find a ride."

I was confused. I thought we were in *Muslaab*. So I concluded he was taking me to a more central part of the village ... like maybe a central market area. So we got back in his truck and he started to drive.

It was soon quite clear that we had left his village, and he kept right on driving. Eventually we arrived in another village which he told me was called *Maslab*. Okay, obviously I had misunderstood him. My ears just didn't catch the slight difference between *Muslaab* and *Maslab* in the middle of his rapid fire speech.

As I got out of the truck, I thanked Haadi over and over again for his hospitality and told him how much I enjoyed spending time with him and his family, and told him to greet them all for me again, and asked God to bless him and his family, etc, etc.

I didn't have to wait long to catch my next ride since I took the first ride that came along which happened to be going in the right direction. I was suddenly on my way to Suq Al-Athneyn. The word *suq* means market, and the word *al-athneyn* means *Monday* ... so I was on my way to *Monday market*.

26

The Last Stop

After arriving in Suq Al-Athneyn, I found out that finding a ride to Al Hazm wasn't quite as easy as I had been assured it would be. So, what else was new. But I finally did get a ride ... and it was once again in the bed of a small Toyota pick-up. So again, what else was new.

The driver took me all the way to just outside of Al Hazm. I was relieved to have arrived at my last stop for this first round of research trips to the four areas of focus. I would soon be heading home to Sana'a.

I didn't mind strolling the rest of the way into town ... "so I can demonstrate just how well I'm able to walk wearing *pants*," I said in an audible voice to myself ... the comment from the kid in Muslaab-A having popped back into my mind.

As I made my way towards the northern edge of the town, I was, of course, observed by many curious eyes. At that point I definitely wished I could have blended in, even just a little. But then again, I had to keep in mind that my foreignness usually served me well, attracting those who were inquisitive enough to get to know me and help me with my research.

As I neared the town, my ever roving eyes caught sight of a small store, and I headed straight for it.

"Peace be with you," I said as I entered the establishment.

"And with you be peace," replied the store tender with that familiar look of wonder showing on his face at my unexpected presence.

"I'd like to buy a cold bottle of water and a *kickers* chocolate bar please," I said.

I had a good laugh shortly after arriving in Sana'a. One day I entered a store to buy a chocolate bar. My eyes caught sight of a well known chocolate bar in the west, a *snickers* bar. I loved snickers bars (still do), but didn't expect to find such a treat sold in Yemen. I was quite sure such delicacies would cost a fortune, as most imported products did in Middle Eastern countries. Well, as I started to reach for the bar, I suddenly noticed something strange. The packaging did indeed look like a snickers wrapper, but the name was misspelled ... it was spelled *k-i-c-k-e-r-s*. Strange.

"Okay," I started to argue with myself, "do I chance it? If the name is spelled wrong, what might they have done with the recipe itself?"

"Why not give it a try," I answered myself. So, I went ahead and bought a kickers bar ... at what I considered a reasonable price, I should add. I unwrapped it. It looked just like a snickers bar should. And when I bit into it, it actually tasted good ... pretty much the same as a real snickers bar back home.

Of course, I did some research and found out that the name was not misspelled. The bar was merely a locally made copy of the western made bar, all except for the name which was altered slightly. Fascinating.

Anyway, back in Al Hazm ... the store owner fetched me a bottle of water out of the fridge and a kickers bar from off the shelf. As I paid, I was hoping the store owner would take an interest and start up a conversation with me. But no such luck.

So I took my *meal* and headed outside, and started to think about what my next move should be.

Well, what happened next wasn't quite what I had in mind, but it didn't really surprise me. Along came someone from security and asked to see my travel permission paper. Of course, I was always prepared ... and so I whipped out a copy of my *to whom it may concern* paper and handed it to him.

He looked it over, appeared satisfied, and then disappeared as quickly as he had appeared ... most likely returning to whatever he was doing prior to my arrival. Hmmm, even he didn't want to strike up a conversation.

So once again I decided to head for the nearest school. Al Hazm was the main town in that region, and so I assumed I would find a large school there. I was right, and had no problem locating it.

Just as anticipated, when I encountered the teachers, they were Egyptians. I received a warm "Welcome Butros, welcome" after introducing myself to them. Then as I went on to explain about my research, I was thrilled to find them supportive and encouraging.

A rapid progression of events followed. That very afternoon, after classes let out, one of the teachers introduced me to a number of friendly teenage students. And after only some very brief interaction, I was pleasantly surprised to hear one of them suggest, "Butros, why don't you come to my house."

"Thank you Ahmad, I'd like that," I responded. "When would be a good time?"

"My brother should be arriving soon to pick me up," he said. "He can give us both a ride."

I couldn't believe my good luck. And it wasn't long before his older brother showed up in a Toyota pickup.

What an unexpected surprise for him when his younger brother informed him, "Brother, I'd like you to meet Butros from Germany. I invited him to our house."

"Welcome," he said extending his hand to shake mine. He seemed quite pleased with the prospect of having me as a guest.

Soon all three of us were sitting in the cab of the truck for the short drive to their house. The introductions continued after our arrival, as I met a few more male members of their family. This was turning out so much better than anything I had dared to hope for.

I was led up a set of stairs, and we entered an ornately decorated sitting room (see photo below) where I was invited to take a seat. I walked over to the far end of the room and settled down on one of the comfortable mattresses with cushions that went all the way around the edge of the room in typical Yemeni style. I always considered it a great honor whenever I was given the opportunity to enter a Yemeni living room. It made me feel like a really special guest.

No sooner had I sat down, than they all disappeared. I'm sure I was soon the talk of the house ... and possibly the talk of the whole neighborhood. I was most likely the first foreign guest they ever had in their home. I sure wished I knew what they were all really thinking about me. I was certainly impressed by them. But alas, I knew I wouldn't be in Al Hazm long enough to get to know any of them very well.

My thoughts were soon interrupted by the opening of the door, and the rattling of glasses on a metal tray carried by one of my hosts. Entering the room with them were four more young men.

I quickly stood up for the introductions, during which I discovered none of them were family members.

Everyone took a seat, and the tea was poured. While we sipped our tea, and listened to music, I explained to them what I was doing in Yemen ... how I was studying and comparing various Arabic dialects. All the while a distracting swarm of flies constantly buzzed all around me (most likely because I hadn't had a bath for many a day).

Much to my delight, every one of those six young men showed an interest in what I shared with them. Not only that, but they were also very eager to help. I was pleasantly shocked by the overwhelming positive response.

The fast pace continued, and suddenly my tape recorder was all set up, the microphone pointed at the boldest of them, the one most willing to begin the recording session, and he told me his story ... "My friend was returning from Sana'a to Jawf with his truck full of goods. As he was driving along through the wadi, suddenly an unexpected flash flood turned the dry wadi into a raging river and carried away the truck and all of its contents. Some of the local residents saw what happened and managed to rescue the driver, but they had to abandon the truck. As for the goods, they were all hopelessly lost ..."

The story teller went on to say that later, when there was an opportunity to do so, they returned to recover the truck. Once again, it wasn't until after I played the story for these young men, and they explained certain words and phrases, that I fully understood the story. And once I did understand the content, it suddenly hit me, "The dry river beds I had been crossing and sometimes driving in as I traveled through Jawf province the past few days are not always dry." A downpour in another part of the country could cause havoc many miles away ... something I would actually experience firsthand in the not-too-distant future.

After the first story teller finished, two more of the young men also volunteered to tell me stories about similar incidents. I couldn't believe how much I was able to accomplish in the very short time I had been in Al Hazm.

If I would have stayed in Muslaab and tried to do the same thing, I'm quite sure I wouldn't have had the same kind of cooperation. I suppose education, bringing exposure to the rest of the world and fanning the curiosity of the youth, had a lot to do with it.

When we were done with the texts, along with the translation of other material into their dialect, the four additional fellows said their goodbyes and, along with my two hosts, started to file out. But just before making his exit, Ahmad turned back and informed me, "Butros, you will be having supper with us." Then suddenly they were all gone.

I wished the pesky flies would have left with them, but they insisted on hanging around to keep the poor foreigner company. I swatted away at them while I waited for my hosts to return.

It had been a long day ... a long day with very little nourishment. I wouldn't call the bottle of water and a kickers bar, which I had eaten so many hours earlier, much of a meal. So when my hosts reappeared carrying another tray, this time laden with rice and chicken, I was very grateful indeed. I hoped I didn't seem too eager, and I made sure not to eat too much, assuming the leftovers would be heading back to the women for their meal. Food never tasted better.

I continued to enjoy their company during and after the meal, but eventually decided it was time to move on. When I hinted to Ahmad that I should start making my way to the Egyptians' place, he quickly volunteered his brother to drive me. Earlier in the day the Egyptian teachers had indicated I would be more than welcome to spend the night at the school with them.

When we arrived at the school, I thanked them again for their hospitality and for the help with my research. As they drove off, as tired as I was, I knew I'd need to spend some time socializing with my next set of hosts. So I prepared myself mentally to change from dealing with the Jawfi dialect to hearing the Egyptian dialect again.

The Egyptians were clearly pleased to see me again. They had already finished their meal, but one of them still asked me, "Butros, what can we offer you to eat?"

"I already ate at Ahmad's house, thank you," I responded.

"Then would you like a cup of tea, Butros?" one of them asked. The kettle was already boiling.

"Yes, please." I responded.

They made typical Egyptian style tea ... strong and sweet. The tea is poured into a glass which has been prefilled to a quarter full with sugar (maybe only a slight exaggeration ... Egyptians typically love their tea very sweet). Time for a sugar and caffeine high.

For the next hours I sat and visited with the three Egyptians who lived at the school. I filled them in on my positive experience with Ahmad and his family and friends, and the progress I had made on my research. And, of course, I thanked them for the part they had played by introducing me to Ahmad.

I was so thankful when the time came to sleep. They brought out a mattress for me, I unrolled my sleeping bag, and then waited for my mind to switch off.

27

The Bad Shot

The next morning, after a pleasant relaxing breakfast with my Egyptian hosts, I informed them, "I need to head to Sana'a this morning."

It had been five long days (and five short restless nights) since I started on this trip ... I just started day six.

"Why do you have to leave us so soon?" they asked, clearly disappointed. "You just arrived yesterday."

"I have to continue with my research, but hope to return to Al Hazm in the future," I said.

They were happy to hear that I planned to return, and said, "Good, good. You're welcome to come and stay with us any time!"

"Thank you for your help and hospitality," I said as I packed my few belongings. "Can you tell me where I should go to catch a ride to Sana'a?"

"Yes, of course," one of them answered. "I'll take you to the best place to catch a ride." And off we went walking side by side through town still chatting.

As the Egyptian left me standing in a rather deserted spot at the south end of the town (for I needed to head south and then west to get to Sana'a), I suddenly felt lonely and forlorn. I didn't want him to leave me. I wanted him to stay until I found a ride. At that point I could tell I had no energy left to keep going.

But I did keep going. What helped was knowing I'd be sleeping in a bed in Sana'a that night ... at least that was the plan.

I deposited my backpack on a concrete step extending from the foundation of a deserted-looking building, and sat down next to it. Then I waited for a vehicle to come along and give me a ride.

It ended up being another long wait. Very few vehicles passed that way, and those that did weren't going my way. Not many pedestrians walked by either, but when they did, I was an unexpected target for their eyes.

Eventually another 4-wheel drive came along with two men sitting in the cab. I went through the routine of waving for them to stop, even though I wasn't optimistic about it resulting in a ride. They stopped.

I walked up to the driver and rattled off my usual phrases, "Peace be with you. I'm looking for a ride to Sana'a. Are you going that way?"

He replied, "We're not going to Sana'a," which was exactly what I expected to hear. So I was about ready to say "thank you anyway" and walk away ... but then he went on to say, "but we can take you to the main road that leads to Sana'a."

Without any hesitation, and with hope renewed, I said, "That would be great. Thank you very much." I was sure it would be easy enough to catch another ride once I arrived at the main road. It was the waiting in Al Hazm that seemed to be the problem. I didn't even bother asking how much he wanted for the ride. I could sort it out once we arrived at the drop off point.

I walked around to the passenger side, and the fellow sitting there hopped out, his eyes looking over this curious out-of-place sight. I just ignored *the look* and climbed in beside the driver, while the other guy reclaimed his window seat. The two of them were pleasant enough, and all the more so once we started conversing and they realized I could actually communicate quite well with them in Arabic.

We hadn't gone very far before the driver spotted and pointed his finger towards a man up ahead of us standing at the side of the road and said, "Hey, that's so-and-so." Then he leaned over with a smile on his face and talked past me saying something to the other fellow I didn't understand. The pedestrian was holding out his hand to indicate he was looking for a ride.

But instead of slowing down, as I had imagined he would, the driver unexpectedly sped up. And as he drew ever closer to the now somewhat puzzled pedestrian, he suddenly veered to the right so we were heading straight for him.

"He's going to run that man over!" I thought ... and started picturing in my mind a bloody motionless body plastered against the windshield of the truck. Was this going to turn into some sort of revenge killing? It was all happening so fast.

Well, it didn't take the victim long to realize that his life was in danger. And so in self defense, and much to my alarm, he quickly lifted his rifle, which had been dangling off his shoulder by a strap, and awkwardly raised it with no time to take careful aim.

"He's going to shoot at us!" I screamed in my mind. But there was no time for those words to come to my lips because it was all happening in a matter of seconds.

Sure enough, his rifle discharged a bullet, with the intent of hitting, possibly killing, the driver ... or at least one of the three individuals seated in the cab of the vehicle ... all three of them obviously co-conspirators in this plot to assassinate him. Little did he know that the person sitting in the middle was innocent!

At the very moment the shot went off, our driver quickly swerved to the left, away from the would be victim. He brought the truck to a complete stop and turned off the engine.

I didn't move. I didn't feel the bullet enter my body, but I still looked down to see if there was any blood. Then I looked over at the passenger to my right, and finally at the driver to the left. They were both okay too. In fact the driver was laughing. He was laughing! Suddenly it was all very clear to me ... it was a joke. The whole stupid incident was nothing more than a big fat joke! Wow, was I ever upset.

"Are you crazy!" I blurted out at the driver. I was furious, and I didn't care what he thought. I mean, he could have ended up with a dead foreigner on his hands, and he was just sitting there laughing. His companion started laughing too ... probably partly due to my reaction.

The driver jumped out of his truck ... still laughing.

By now I was looking back at the man who had shot at us, wondering if he was planning to shoot any more. I had forgotten all about him. But it was obvious that he had finally recognized the laughing driver and realized it had been done in jest.

My heart was still pounding away at twice its normal speed.

I could see that the almost-victim was distressed ... seemingly not upset with the driver, but rather with himself because he had taken a shot at us, and could have killed one of us.

"Just wait until he finds out that a foreigner is sitting in the front of the cab," I mumbled audibly in English, knowing no one present would understand me anyway. There were a few more choice things I wanted to say to the driver, but then decided it wouldn't be worth it.

The hunter and the prey greeted each other warmly ... the one smiling broadly, the other still deeply concerned but growing ever calmer as they interacted. They walked hand in hand to the front of the truck and kept talking as they proceeded to examine first the grill, then the body of the Landcruiser, to see if they could find a bullet hole anywhere.

I didn't even bother getting out of the truck. I wasn't even sure I could have stood up on my wobbly legs at that moment. And if I could have, I might have been tempted to just start walking the rest of the way to Sana'a.

The other passenger jumped out of the truck and stood with the other two, all three of them talking together. I started to calm down. "I guess no real harm was done," I said trying to calm myself even further.

The driver invited the man to hop into the bed of the truck, proudly got back behind the steering wheel himself, and started to drive. Then he turned to me, still with a big smile on his face, and asked, "How are you doing Butros?"

"I'm okay," I answered ... and it's true, I had gotten over the worst of my feelings. Then I added, "I still can't figure out why you did it," which made him laugh out loud again.

Then he and the fellow on my right talked some more about the incident. The extra passenger was soon dropped off at his destination, where I'm sure he related the whole encounter to his family and friends, including the part about the very pale foreigner he almost shot that day.

We moved on. We were driving through flat desert, nothing but hard-packed sand with tire tracks going off in every which direction ... no noticeable *road* that I could make out. Then ahead of us, in the middle of that desert, I noticed a mound off in the distance, and as we drew closer, I detected some structures on the mound and presumed we were going to pass another village.

"What's the name of that village?" I asked the driver.

"Those are just ruins," he informed me. "Nobody lives there now. It's called Baraqish."

I found out later that around 400 BC Baraqish functioned as the capital of the Minaean Kingdom and was called Yathul. It's located about 18 kilometers to the south of Al Hazm.

"Do you want to stop and see it?" he asked me.

"Sure, why not," I said. "Are we allowed to go inside?"

"We'll see what the guards say," he responded.

As we drove closer I caught sight of a guard post ... a small rickety shack with a couple of men who were probably in charge of making sure that none of the locals disturbed the site. The driver pulled over, and the three of us jumped out of the truck and approached the guards.

"Can we go inside?" The driver asked.

"Does he have permission to do so?" asked one of the guards looking over at me.

The driver looked at me, and I decided to try an experiment. I pulled out my *to whom it may concern* paper, showed it to the guard and said, "I'm doing research here in Yemen," not clarifying what kind of research.

The guard decided it looked official enough, and so said, "Sir, you're welcome to have a look around." I found out later that it wasn't an easy thing to get permission to see the sight, and here I just chanced upon the opportunity.

I assumed the two men with me would have never had the opportunity to enter that restricted area had I not been with them, and I didn't want to deny them the chance, so I asked them, "Do you want to join me?" And they did ... although they didn't really seem very interested and mostly just hung around smoking and talking.

I wandered past the impressive brown ruins of ancient buildings, towers and walls, wishing I had studied Sabaeic so I could have read the inscriptions etched into some of the city's walls. I only spent a brief time walking around before rejoining the other two fellows who were patiently waiting for me near the entrance. We thanked the guards and were on our way once again.

We eventually reached the main paved road leading west towards Sana'a, and turned onto it. Driving on the desert sand wasn't at all terrible ... I mean it was about a hundred times better than the bumps and curves of the mountain roads I had been on to the west of Sa'da.

But just getting onto a smooth road, a road I knew would lead me back to *civilization* ... well, it felt especially pleasant.

When we came to a military checkpoint, my *friends* (yes, I had gotten over the earlier stupid joke incident) informed me, "We're going to turn off the road at this point and keep heading south. You'll need to wait here with the guards until you can find a ride that will take you to Sana'a."

"Thank you very much for the ride," I said. "It was nice meeting you. How much do I owe you."

"Nothing," he said.

"That's not possible. I want to give you something for your trouble," I insisted as I pulled some money out of my pocket.

"God be with you," he replied as he reached over and gently pushed my hand away.

So I insisted no more, and thanked him and his friend again.

Of course, the checkpoint guards were watching and waiting, wondering what was about to take place as the driver and I got out of the truck. I followed the driver over to the guards who were standing next to a very simple shelter they used to protect themselves from the blazing sun. Nothing else was to be seen in any direction. I assumed they'd be replaced by other guards at some point, and I wondered if they had a two-way radio for communication in case of an emergency. I felt sorry for them.

The driver said to the guards, "This man needs to travel to Sana'a. Can you arrange a ride for him with one of the vehicles passing this way?"

"Who is he? Where did you pick him up?" one of them inquired.

"We brought him with us from Al Hazm," replied the driver.

"What was he doing out there?" he asked next.

"Why don't you ask him yourself. All we did was give him a ride," said the driver.

"Can he can speak any Arabic?" was the next question, as he looked over at me.

"Yes, I can speak Arabic," I jumped into the conversation. "And here's a copy of my permission papers. I'll tell you what I was doing in Al Hazm in just a minute. Can you arrange a ride for me?"

Relieved to hear me speaking Arabic, he answered, "Yes, we can do that," as he looked down at my travel document.

Then I turned to the driver and bid him a final farewell. He got back into his truck, and drove off into the desert on the south side of the road to who knows where ... I never did find out where he was from. I assume if I ever had the chance to wander through that part of Yemen again someday, stories would be circulating about *Butros*, the crazy foreigner with a Syrian accent.

I then turned my full attention to the guards and, taking advantage of my captive audience, started talking to them about my research while I began the wait for my next ride. I felt so much more relaxed knowing I would soon be on my way home.

Not many vehicles were passing that way, and so when the first few stopped and then drove off again without me, I started to wonder if the soldiers were really going to help find me a ride or not. It didn't seem like they were even asking any of the drivers to consider taking me along ... although I wasn't really close enough to actually hear what they were saying.

Eventually a very fancy looking car showed up. They were routinely waved over just like all the previous vehicles. And then it happened ... one of the soldiers called me over and told me to get in the front passenger seat of the black Mercedes Benz with tinted windows. That was definitely not the kind of vehicle I was expecting to get a ride in!

Hmmm, a Mercedes Benz indicated to me that most likely some very important people would be sitting in there ... people I couldn't see through the tinted windows. I was looking pretty scruffy at the time, carrying a backpack and wearing far-from-clean clothes. I wondered about getting into that fancy car. But I definitely didn't want to miss a chance at a ride, and definitely would enjoy sitting in that car rather than packed into the interior of an old crowded vehicle or in the bed of another pickup.

So I thanked the soldiers for their kind help, and headed over to the vehicle. I looked through the now-open passenger door and saw that the man sitting behind the steering wheel was a Yemeni. I spoke the greeting "Peace be with you" as I started to get in.

"And with you be peace," he responded.

"Are you sure it's okay to ride with you?" I asked him.

"Yes, of course," he said politely. "Please get in."

It was only as I was getting in and was about to sit on the leather seat which had been kept cool by the air conditioning (talk about luxury), that I happened to glance towards the back seat of the vehicle and noticed two passengers ... oriental men dressed in expensive suits. In comparison, I looked like someone who just spent six days traveling without a shave, a shower or a change of clothes (all very true) ... a total slob.

"These are important men," I thought, "and this Yemeni is their chauffer. I better at least show them some courtesy." So I spoke to them in English and said, "Thank you very much for allowing me to ride with you."

They both nodded their heads, but neither one of them said a single word to me. They did say a few things to each other in their own language though ... "hopefully nice things," I thought.

I sat down and closed the door. Then the Yemeni put the vehicle in gear and we were off.

I still couldn't tell if the men in the back were bothered by my presence in the vehicle or not. Their rather blank expressions didn't tell me anything. I tried once again to engage them in conversation, and then quickly realized that neither of them spoke any English whatsoever. So that was the end of the one-way conversation.

I turned my attention to the very pleasant driver instead and talked with him in Arabic, while the two back-seat passengers continued to chat away in their own language.

Oh what comfort! I felt so spoiled ... and I felt like I really deserved it!

I think the Yemeni enjoyed having someone to interact with. I had no idea how he ever communicated with his two passengers ... they never said anything to each other as long as I was in the vehicle.

We arrived in Sana'a, and when we reached a familiar part of the city, I requested that the driver let me out. I asked him if I owed them anything for the ride and he told me not to give it a second thought, pointing to the back seat with his eyes at the obviously well off men. So I thanked him and the other two men, who once again nodded at me, and then started to make my way to AIYS[25] where I planned to stay once again.

---

[25] AIYS stands for *American Institute for Yemeni Studies* in case you forgot.

28

The Guardhouse

I was exhausted after the past six days of having one adventure after another without any real breaks to speak of, except for the short rather sleepless nights. So it felt like such a relief to walk up to the AIYS compound gate and ring the bell. I was *home* at last!

The director came out to let me in.

"How was your trip," he inquired as we walked towards the building. "You've been away for quite some time."

"It was great, but it's good to be back," I responded. "I've just been on the road for six days straight in Jawf, and it sure would be nice to get a hot shower and some badly needed rest. Do you have a room available for me?"

Since I had planned to be away doing my research for a number of weeks, I certainly didn't want to be paying for a room at AIYS that I wasn't going to be occupying. And I didn't know when I'd be returning, so I couldn't very well make a reservation. Now I was definitely warned that there would be no guarantee of a place to stay at AIYS between my trips, but I just decided to take my chance. I mean, what was the likelihood they'd be all booked up?

"Sorry," he said, "but we don't have any spare beds right now."

That definitely was not what I wanted to hear ... and I'm sure he could see it on my face.

"Are you serious?" was all I could think to say.

"Sorry," he repeated very businesslike.

"I was warned. Thanks anyway," I said rather feebly and with regret that I hadn't made a reservation.

"Oh great, now what?" I said to myself. I sure was looking forward to getting some rest. But now, instead of resting, I needed to expend some more energy (which I really didn't have) trying to come up with an alternative place to stay.

When Dave was visiting me,[26] we had stayed with an American friend named Al for a few nights. At the time, Al had said if I ever

---

[26] See chapters 5 thru 9.

needed anything I shouldn't hesitate to give him a call. Well, I decided I definitely needed something.

So I dug out his phone number, called him, and explained my situation to him. Sure enough, he was true to his word, and invited me to spend a couple of nights at his place. What a relief! He even drove over to AIYS to pick me and my bags up. I had stored my computer and suitcases at AIYS.

While staying at Al's place, word quickly spread that I needed to find a more permanent living situation in Sana'a. Wout & Marina, a Dutch couple I had become acquainted with, heard of my need, and they phoned me at Al's.

"Peter, we know of a place we think might be ideal for you," Wout said in his very Dutch accent.

"That's great. Tell me about it," I replied.

Wout continued, "We're renting a large house, and just inside the back gate of our walled property there's a rather large guardhouse that's not being used at the moment. You're more than welcome to live in it if you'd like."

To be very honest, when I first heard the word *guardhouse*, I pictured some little shack. I mean, I had seen some guardhouses before, and they were usually nothing to boast about. But at the same time I was quite sure my friends wouldn't expect me to stay in some hovel, and he did describe it as *large*, so I agreed to have a look at it.

I went over to their house and they led me out into their spacious backyard. You can kind of make out the guardhouse just to the right of the green gate in the following photo. [27]

---

[27] Photo provided by Wout.

Approaching it, from the outside I was already impressed. On the inside, it was a pleasant little place ... very clean and well maintained. The main room was about 2½ by 6 meters. It was also fully furnished, with a bed, a desk and chair, curtains, etc. And there was even electricity.

Just to the left of the main entrance was a second door which led to another smaller room. Inside the small room was a table where I could picture myself throwing together some simple meals. There was also a shower (albeit no hot water) and a squat toilet (sorry, no photo of that).

Okay, so I probably wouldn't have considered raising a family in it, but really, what more could I ask for as a single guy. I would have privacy, and a place to call home. It was definitely as Wout had described it, an ideal place for me. I didn't have to be asked twice ... I accepted their offer, and immediately moved in.

To top it all off, they wouldn't even allow me to pay any rent.

Then soon after I settled in, they handed me a key to their house and insisted that I feel free to use their phone and their more luxurious bathroom with hot running water (oh yes!). And then there were the delicious home cooked meals thrown in from time to time.

So the guardhouse ended up being my home base in Sana'a. No more wondering about where I'd be staying between my remote adventures.

The guardhouse served a dual purpose ... first and foremost, it served as an office, and secondly, it was a refuge. Just because my first round of trips was over, that didn't mean I could just kick back and relax. I had made copious scribbly notes (and my kids know what those notes must have looked like) in a notepad during my travels (which I used to write this book). I needed to type up those notes on my computer and expand them while everything was still fresh in my memory.

I also had much preparation to do before heading out on my next round of trips. Namely, I needed to spend time putting together the test tapes I'd be using to test Yemenis' comprehension of the various stories.

I had to prepare four tapes for each district. One tape contained a story in their own dialect which was used to teach the testing method ... hence my search for a story teller so I could record a story from each area. In addition, I prepared three tapes to test the comprehension of a story in Modern Standard Arabic, a story in Cairene Egyptian Arabic, and a story in Palestinian Arabic ... stories I had recorded prior to my arrival in North Yemen. I had specific questions about the content of each story, and those questions needed to be translated and recorded in each local dialect. And that's why, in addition to finding a person to tell a story in each dialect area, I also had someone translate and record the questions for me.

Using two tape recorders I dubbed the tapes, each tape with a story and the questions for the given dialect, four tapes for each area, a total of sixteen tapes.

If you want to know more ... you already guessed it, get hold of a copy of my thesis. Or a second option is to read appendix 2 found at the end of this book, where I give you the same information as in my thesis, but in a more condensed form.

29

My Sister

I felt like I had made considerable progress on those first trips to Raazih, Munabbih, Barat and Al Hazm. But I had a problem ... let's refer to this problem as problem #1 ... and that obviously implies there will be a problem #2 (if not more) coming up.

So, problem #1 was, I needed to get a broad sampling of the population which should include the testing of females as well as males. In fact, I considered the testing of females essential since they were less educated. The problem was that females were off limits to all males except their closest male relatives. You may have already gathered that bit of information from what I've written in the prior chapters of this book.

The solution to problem #1 was obvious ... I needed to get a woman to travel with me to test the female population. Then I would, of course, focus on testing the male population myself. Easier said than done! Who could I get to help me?

But, as you were anticipating, if I could indeed solve the problem and get someone to help, then with the solution would come another problem ... problem #2. Namely, I was a single male, so traveling with a woman companion who was not my wife (and as you'll recall I was not married at the time) would look, um, how should I say it ... immoral in Yemeni society. That was a big problem.

Solution #2 ... I could try and find a brother and sister to work with me ... or a husband and wife. Maybe if I would have searched real hard, I could have arranged something like that.

But I didn't even start the search for a *couple* to help me because I thought of problem #3 first. Solution #2 would mean I'd end up being accompanied by *two people* out to those remote areas of the country. Well, the problem would be the same problem whether it was one or two people accompanying me ... namely, the areas for my research focus were off limits to all foreigners, me being an exception because of my open-ended travel permission paper. As you will have noted in chapter 15 (entitled *Chains*) my permission paper didn't even work for me all the time.

Okay, there was no way I would have been able to obtain permission papers for anyone else even if someone did end up offering to help me. It seemed like a rather hopeless situation, right? No way. Solution #3 came to mind, which I hoped would work.

I let word get out amongst a few trusted friends about my need for someone adventurous, someone who could speak Arabic well, and someone who could pass for my *sister*. Yes, we would need to tell a *little white lie* for the better good.

Hmmm ... and the complication of permission for her to go into those remote areas? Well, I just planned to deal with it when the need to do so arose. I calculated that the only real problem area would probably be Munabbih ... and that would end up being a problem whether I went alone or with someone else. Hmmm ... not sure if it was good logic or not, but I was desperate to have some help.

Sian came forward as the one who was willing, qualified and adventurous enough to help me out. She saw it not only as a way to help me, but also as an opportunity ... namely, she would get the chance to visit parts of the country she'd never get to see otherwise. Thank you Sian!

But one more problem existed, problem #4 ... something else I would just have to deal with later. Problem #4 was, Sian only had eight days available within which to help me. I realized we'd only be able to cover two of the four areas within the eight days based on my experience thus far with travel to those remote areas. I hoped we would *at least* be able to cover two areas during that limited amount of time. So I would still need to find someone else to help with the testing in the other two areas.

One step at a time, and hopefully no extra unexpected problems popping up!

30

Our Father

Sian, my new volunteer partner in the work (and new sister), and I drove from Sana'a to Sa'da together in her car, where we spent one night with friends ... me in Harry's mud house, and Sian with one of her friends. And then it was time to get to work on the next stage of my research ... the actual comprehension testing.

We started out early the next morning (it was Wednesday, March 25th), catching a local taxi (thankfully always easy to find) from Sa'da to Taalih[28] where we would search for our long-distance ride. I decided to hit all four areas in the same order as the first round of trips I had done on my own, and so our first destination was going to be Raazih.

As soon as the taxi dropped us off in Taalih, my eyes automatically started scanning our immediate surroundings to determine where I should begin my inquiries about getting a ride. The best sight I could have wished for was someone I already knew. And it was my lucky day ... I spotted and recognized Saalih, the same man who drove me from Nadhiir to Sa'da last time.

Saalih was standing next to his truck trying to round up passengers. When he caught sight of me and Sian heading his way, he broke into a big smile.

"Peace be with you," I said as I drew near to Saalih and held out my hand in friendship.

"And with you be peace," he replied taking my hand firmly in his.

"How are you my friend?" I asked him.

"Praise be to God," he said with enthusiasm, which carried over into the question, "Are you going to Raazih? Because if you are, I have room for you in my truck."

"Praise be to God. Yes, I want to go to Raazih ... and I'm bringing my sister with me this time," I replied.

"Welcome to both of you," he said sincerely.

I decided that Sian and I should travel in style and comfort, and so I offered to pay for the entire middle bench seat so we wouldn't get

---

[28] The large market town just to the west of Sa'da.

squashed like I had seen happen a number of times already. Saalih was definitely fine with that.

Saalih's truck filled up very quickly, and so we were on our way by 10:30 AM. That was a great way to start the trip. Everything was falling into place ... and I was glad for Sian's sake ... okay, admittedly for my sake too.

As we drove along, I started to think of something I hadn't thought of before ... potential problem #5. I was going to be telling people that Sian was my *sister* ... so in all likelihood someone was going to ask whether she was married, and if she was planning to get married. So what if someone asks about marrying her. It would be a very desirable match for a Yemeni, but one I was sure Sian wasn't looking for. "Okay, I'll just have to deal with that issue if it actually comes up," I said to myself. No need to bother Sian with those kinds of details. I didn't want to make her more nervous than she probably already was.

The trip was uneventful, and we arrived in Nadhiir by 5:30 PM. Sure, it was still a very long day of traveling, but it sure felt good to arrive during the daylight hours rather than like the first time when I arrived after 9 PM in total darkness.

Upon arrival, Sian and I headed straight for Faisel's store. Faisel was the very friendly fellow who told me a good story and helped me with the translation of materials on my first trip.[29] It was so good to see him again, and it was clear that he felt the same.

Now I have to admit that, besides wanting to see him again, I was really hoping he would invite us to stay as his guests in his house. Obviously, since Sian was with me, I couldn't even think of staying with Mansoor and Saari again in their little shack. I'm sure they would understand the circumstances dictating that decision. I needed to connect with a family this time.

It wasn't long before three other young men popped into Faisel's store. I recognized one of them right away ... his name was Ibrahiim. He was also in the truck with me and Saalih the previous month heading to Sa'da. "Hello Butros, how are you my friend? It's so good to see you again," he greeted me warmly. "We heard you were back in town."

News travels quickly in those small towns, and my last visit was most likely still fresh on everybody's mind.

"It's great to be back in Nadhiir and to see all of you," I replied.

---

[29] See chapter 12, *The Endless Story*.

"Let me introduce my cousins to you, Abd Al-Hafiid and Abd Ar-Rahmaan," said Ibrahiim.

After the welcomes and nice to meet yous and introducing my sister Sian to them, Faisel handed out some cold Canadas on the house while we chatted and a few other young members of the community came into the store to join in the fun.

Abd Ar-Rahmaan eventually said, "Welcome to Nadhiir, Butros and Sian. We're glad you came, and we would like to invite you to be guests in our home."

"Thank you," I replied, "but we really don't want to be any bother to you or your family."

"No bother at all," responded Ibrahiim. "We insist."

That was precisely the kind of development we were hoping for ... an invitation from a Yemeni family ... it didn't have to come from Faisel. I didn't think I needed to ask Sian what her opinion was on the matter, since in that setting it needed to be her big brother's decision anyway. So I responded, "God bless you. Thank you very much. We accept your kind invitation. Praise be to God."

Off we went to the Abu Taalib neighborhood, for the three cousins were all part of the Abu Taalib family. I found out that the Abu Taalibs settled in Raazih about 400 years previously when one of their ancestors was appointed a judge for that area. They originally came from a place close to Sana'a called Rauda (located on the way to the Sana'a International airport). The Abu Taalib family boasts a direct descent from the prophet Muhammad.

Clearly the Abu Taalib family was well off ... part of the upper class. It was an honor to be their guests, and I was sure we would be treated very well by our hosts.

To the best of my recollection, although not totally clear from the photos I took, four houses, all built very close to each other, belonged to the Abu Taalib family.

After arriving at the door of one of the houses, initially Abd Ar-Rahmaan went in on his own. First we heard some voices, and then some movement. He was most likely making certain the women would be out of sight while we made our entrance ... of course, me (a male) being the problem rather than Sian.

Segregation of the sexes was quite complete. I never once caught a glimpse of a woman the whole time we were staying with the Abu Taalibs. This proved again that the approach I chose was the right one, a woman needing to do the research with the women and a man doing the research with the men. Although, as Sian pointed out, a woman researcher had the advantage in that, if necessary, she could have tested both men and women, whereas a male researcher could only test men and was therefore much more limited.

Almost all females in Raazih wore a veil ... except for the young school children. I was informed the Raazih girls were the most expensive girls in Yemen because they were so pretty. Consequently they were kept hidden away and well protected. So for a male stranger to stay in one of their houses was rather unusual. But I'm sure it worked because I was a foreigner, and I was there with my *sister*.

When the coast was clear, Abd Ar-Rahmaan opened the door and invited the rest of us to enter the four-story house. "Oh great, another stairwell," I mumbled.

"What did you say?" asked Sian.

"Oh nothing," I responded, not wanting to get into the history of fumbling my way up dark Yemeni stairwells. At least this one wasn't as dark as past ones had been. I was sure Sian had many stairwell horror stories she could have shared with me as well. We started climbing the stairs.

As we approached the third floor landing, the stairwell grew much lighter. I also caught the whiff of a familiar aroma, that of hay mixed with animal hair and droppings. And sure enough, an open door on the landing revealed the source of the light as well as the smell, some goats hanging out in a bright sun-lit room. I turned and gave Sian a look of surprise, as we walked past and continued up one more flight of stairs. On the fourth floor we entered the formal sitting room where we were invited to have a seat and relax.

Although I wasn't going to be meeting any of the women of the house, Sian was determined to spend time with the female folk rather than with us men. It would definitely be more appropriate, and it was the reason she had accompanied me in the first place. "Oh Abd Ar-Rahmaan," she said, "would it be possible for me to meet the women of the house?"

He perceived that as a very normal request from a woman, and so responded with, "Of course. Let me first go and see if they're ready to receive you." So he got back to his feet and made his way out the door while the rest of us stayed put and chatted.

I was trying to imagine all the commotion taking place in the woman's section of the house after Abd Ar-Rahmaan announced to them, "The foreign woman wants to meet and spend time with you."

It wasn't long before he re-entered the room and said to Sian, "The women are ready to meet you. Come with me and I'll take you to their quarters."

"Good luck," I said to her in English as she stood up and followed Abd Ar-Rahmaan out of the room. Sian's experience was going to be so entirely different from my own during our stay in Nadhiir ... of that I was very certain.

When he returned after his now third ascent of the stairs in a very short period of time, Abd Ar-Rahmaan asked if I'd like to head up to the roof to have a look at the scenery before it started to get dark. I wouldn't pass up an opportunity like that ... and what a spectacular view it was.

Afterwards we ate and sat and talked the evening away ... the whole time me with the men and Sian with the women.

I found out that Abd Ar-Rahmaan was divorced from his first wife and was now married to Abd Al-Hafiid's sister. Marrying your first cousin was very acceptable, and in fact was usually preferred over marrying an *outsider*. I found the same to be true in Jordan when I was living there.

The sharing of information was mutual ... I discovered things about them and their family and they asked about mine, including what my father's name was. As I informed them that my dad's name was Wilhelm, I suddenly thought, "What if the women ask Sian what her father's name is." It would prove rather awkward, since obviously her father's name would need to match my father's name, which I was sure it wouldn't. Oh great, they would find out that she's not really my sister!

I never had the chance to talk privately with Sian that first evening. The next morning, after breakfast, we had a walking tour with Ibrahiim and Abd Ar-Rahmaan, strolling along the paths that ran between the fields. At one point the two of them wandered off to interact with someone, leaving Sian and me alone to talk amongst ourselves.

The topic of our fathers' names suddenly came back to mind. "Have the women asked you about your relatives?" I asked her.

"We've talked about numerous things, including relations," she responded.

"Did they by any chance ask you what your father's name was?" I prodded some more.

"Yes, they did," she said.

"Oh great, that's what I was afraid of," I bemoaned my oversight of preparation for such an event.

I suppose the men also asked you about your father?" she asked.

"They sure did," I replied.

"So what is your father's name by the way?" she inquired.

"It's Wilhelm ... although in Canada he usually went by William," I informed her.

Sian gave out an audible sigh, and then started to laugh as she said, "My father's name is Willem. So I think we're safe."

I started to laugh along with her. Ibrahiim and Abd Ar-Rahmaan walked up to us and must have wondered what was so funny. We obviously never told them.

We spent the next day, and the day after that, interacting with, and testing the comprehension of anyone we could find who would cooperate. And we were fairly successful. I, of course, always hoped to test more people, but I was always thankful for whatever cooperation we could get.

Sian had a harder time of it with the women than I did with the men. At one point she informed me, "The women are totally in awe whenever they listen to the tape recorder and hear voices coming from the machine. Then to actually listen to the tape and understand the material was quite a challenge for them. There's always lots of giggling taking place, and I'm not sure how reliable the testing results are going to be."

We spent the second and third nights in Ibrahiim's house. His house was actually connected to Abd Ar-Rahmaan's house. The Abu Taalib families treated us very well during our entire stay in the town ... we were really quite spoiled, and we couldn't help but feel like at some point we would need to do something in return. I was so glad it had turned out to be such a great trip ... especially for Sian's sake.

But the moment came, it seemed all too soon, that it was time to move on. It was hard to say goodbye and to express just how thankful we were for their hospitality. All we could do was state it over and over again to each and every one of them.

Abd Ar-Rahmaan made sure a ride with comfortable seats was arranged for us, and soon we were on our way back to Sa'da.

31

Man Versus Nature

Needing to get the most out of Sian's limited time meant the very next morning after our return from Raazih, Sian and I needed to head on to our next destination.

Let me tell you, this trip did not turn out like any of the other trips I had taken thus far ... although, as you've probably figured out by now, no trip was ever like any other trip. The only similarity between all of my trips was that the unexpected always happened.

On this trip I was returning to Munabbih. I was a little (actually quite) concerned, because on my first trip there, as you may recall, the Police Chief had specifically warned me not to bother coming back to Munabbih unless I had acquired special permission in writing (in addition to my *to whom it may concern* paper) from the authorities in Sa'da city allowing me to travel to that region.

Well, I hadn't done that. Why? Because I was afraid that dealing with the authorities would have taken up way too much time. I've had plenty of experience in various Middle Eastern countries (including North Yemen) dealing with bureaucracy, and I assumed (no, actually I was quite certain) it could take weeks of hearing someone tell me, "come back tomorrow" for the umpteenth time.

In addition, what if, after I did talk with the authorities, they flat out refused to give me permission to travel out to Munabbih ... what would I do then? I had already invested a considerable amount of time and energy gathering necessary materials for my research in Munabbih, and I sure didn't want to start all over again in another region. It would have been quite a setback, and I just couldn't take any chances of that happening. I just had to get to Munabbih to do the comprehension testing.

I reasoned that it would be much *safer* to head on out to Munabbih, and then if I was confronted by the Police Chief, which was very likely based on my first experience, then I would merely apologize to him once again. I mean, what was the worst thing he could do to me?

But, to complicate matters even more, I was not only going there again without the required *extra* permission, but I was also taking someone else along with me who had absolutely *no* permission whatsoever ... namely, my *sister*, Sian, who was going to do the comprehension testing with the women. I would just have to deal with all those *technicalities* when the time came. In the meantime, my mind was made up, we were heading to Munabbih.

I calculated, according to my previous experience, that our actual travel time should be approximately 3 ½ hours. Adding a couple of hours for ride searching, a 9 AM start should give us plenty of time to make the trip.

Once again we had no problem finding a ride from Sa'da to Taalih. But at 2 PM, with still no indication whatsoever that we were going to find a ride, I was about ready to give up for the day. It was almost too late to start on a long drive into the mountains. I sure didn't want to end up winding around those treacherous mountain roads in the dark yet another time. That was not what I considered an *adventure* ... it was more like challenging nature when nature had all the advantages on its side and wasn't planning to budge an inch to accommodate human efforts.

And yet something inside kept me trying just a little longer. I approached another man. "Excuse me sir, do you know of anybody who might be driving to Munabbih?" I inquired.

The man looked me over, probably in wonderment that a foreigner would even be asking about catching a ride out to Munabbih. But then, much to my surprise, he pointed towards a truck and said, "The driver of that truck will be heading to Munabbih. He should be returning any minute now."

As much as I wanted to hear it, his answer still took me by surprise. Suddenly there was a glimmer of hope. "Shukran" (*thank you*), I said to the man. "May God watch over you."

"Maybe this is it," I said to Sian, who was quite tired of all the hanging around.

The two of us walked over and loitered close to the Landcruiser, watching each person who went anywhere near it, ready to pounce and ask the all important question about whether he could fit two more people in for the ride.

Not much time passed (thankfully) before three men arrived on the scene, heading in the direction of the truck we were monitoring. One of them was carrying a jack-hammer on his shoulder which he carefully placed into the open bed of the truck.

"He we go," I said to Sian, as I set out and boldly approached the three of them, with Sian close behind me, and started the interaction with, "Peace be with you."

All three of them turned towards us simultaneously. Then one of them, quite obviously the more important of the three, took a step closer and replied, "And with you be peace," while the other two just looked on.

"Excuse me," I continued, now directing my speech to the one who had spoken, "I was told that you're planning to drive to Munabbih today, and I was wondering if you would be willing to give the two of us a ride."

The man replied, "Why do you want to go to Munabbih?" I was quite sure he would have known that foreigners weren't allowed to travel out to remote areas like Munabbih.

I informed him, "I study linguistics and I'm doing research on some Yemeni dialects through the Yemen Centre for Research and Studies and the University of Sana'a." Then I produced a copy of my *to whom it may concern* permission paper so he could have a look at it, as I added, "Munabbih is one of the dialects I've decided to include in my research."

The man seemed intrigued and decided to properly introduce himself. "It's nice to meet you. My name is Majhuud, and I live in Munabbih," he said.

Aha, so he wasn't merely driving out to Munabbih, he was actually a resident of the region. That was great news! And I sensed he was feeling somewhat honored that I would be showing such an interest in *his* particular dialect.

"My name is Butros, and this is my sister, Sian," I said ... and then decided to explain a little more, "She's helping me with my research. While I talk with the men, she will be interacting with the women."

"Nice to meet you both," he said ... and then asked, "Have you ever been to Munabbih before?"

"Yes, I visited Suq al Munabbih about a month ago to make some recordings," I informed him.

We continued to converse for a few more minutes, and by the way Majhuud interacted with me, it was quite clear he was well educated. He was also a very pleasant person. Later on I found out he was actually the *sheikh* (meaning, *tribal leader*) of one of the villages in Munabbih.

The whole time we talked, the other two men were watching and listening, clearly fascinated by the interaction going on between the two of us, and probably wondering if they would be taking us on as passengers.

My impression was that Majhuud didn't want to pass up the prospect of getting to know these foreigners ... most likely an opportunity that may never again come his way. The suspense ended when he decidedly informed us, "You're both welcome to ride with us to Munabbih."

Okay, confession time ... I didn't inform Majhuud about my encounter with the Police Chief during my last trip to Munabbih. If I had done so, he most likely would have thought twice about taking us along. Anyway, after the drive was over, I was sure he would carry on to his destination and never even find out about it. But little did I know how events would unfold on this trip.

Once Majhuud had made up his mind to take us along, he took full responsibility for us, and started to treat us as his personal guests ... really going out of his way to help us.

Since the cab would be full with him and his two companions, Sian and I would have to ride in the back where we were unprotected from the elements. And since it had been raining earlier on, Majhuud went right back into the market and bought a large plastic tarp which he threw into the bed of the truck for Sian and me to cover ourselves with if the rain started to pick up again.

And so by 3 PM, six hours from the time we had started that morning, we were finally on our way to Munabbih, sitting in the back of an older model 4-wheel drive Toyota Landcruiser with a cool drizzle descending upon us.

The start to the trip was easy as we headed along a smooth paved road. But that only lasted about ten minutes before we turned left, off onto a dirt road (the paved road continuing on to Baqiim) ... and so the bumps began.

When the rain started coming down a little harder, Majhuud pulled over, jumped out, came to the back of the truck, and helped us unfold the tarp. Although we never did end up covering ourselves with it since the rain suddenly stopped again.

As we started heading a little further into the mountains, it wasn't long before Majhuud noticed something and then pulled over beside another 4-wheel drive stopped at the side of the road. It was a Salown full of passengers ... all of them craning their necks to try and get a glimpse of the two *non-locals* who were sitting in the bed of Majhuud's truck.

Majhuud climbed out of his truck and started talking with the other driver, while both of them had their eyes focused on something just below us off to the left.

Sian and I were gazing in the same direction, and then I heard Sian say, "It sounds like they're talking about the river down there."

"I agree," I said with some concern. "From what I'm able to gather from their conversation, more water is flowing in the river than usual!"

Ending his interaction with the other driver, Majhuud came to inform us, "Some heavy rain has been falling in the mountains up ahead."

"So is there a problem?" I inquired.

"Do you see that river?" he asked. Well two days ago when I drove from Munabbih to Sa'da, the river didn't exist."

"You mean it was totally dry?" I asked incredulously.

"Yes, that's right," he confirmed before getting back into the driver's seat.

Sian and I just looked at each other and wondered what would be happening next. But we didn't have to wonder long. Both vehicles moved on a little further, with the river coming in and out of sight as we drove along.

We eventually arrived at a spot in the road where we had a great view of the river. In fact, the river was right in front of us, blocking our way. The only way forward was by traversing that watercourse.

Four motionless trucks were already at the crossing point ... and our two trucks made it six. And soon two more trucks pulled up behind us.

Sian asked, "You don't think they're seriously thinking of crossing the river do you?"

"I don't know for sure," I responded, "but it doesn't look like anyone is attempting to turn around."

We didn't have to wonder for long ... two of the trucks started across. Let the real adventure begin!

The swiftly moving river was about 12 meters across. "That's a lot of water," Sian remarked.

"Yeah, it sure is," I responded ... and the story I recorded in Al Hazm suddenly came to mind, about the truck that was carried away by a flash flood.

Sure enough, any sudden increase in water flow, or even one wrong move, could easily cause a truck to overturn and be carried off downstream. I was also told (thankfully later) that submerged boulders, carried along by the water, could do serious damage to the truck ... and most likely to its captive human audience.

The two trucks inched their way along while the rest of us, still on solid ground in the other six trucks, anxiously watched with vested interest, knowing we would very likely be making the same crossing all too soon. So those first two trucks were the guinea pigs, and if they didn't make it, then I assumed the rest of us would turn back.

What a quandary for my mind to deal with. Should I wish for both trucks to make it safely across so Majhuud would be encouraged to make the crossing and give us the same experience, or should I hope that they don't make it (you know, like get stuck, not drown!) so the rest of us wouldn't have to make the crossing and so remain safe?

The first truck slowly but surely made it all the way across and safely up onto the opposite bank. The second truck was close behind the first, but as it neared the bank it suddenly came to a complete halt ... it was stuck.

Okay, logic told me that it was going to be too chancy for the rest of the trucks to make the crossing. Why risk it? I was picturing myself in an immobilized truck in the middle of the river ... a situation I didn't want myself and Sian to be in.

The lodged truck rocked back and forth over some large rocks as the driver put it into reverse, then forward, then reverse, etc. I had this sick feeling it was going to turn over and get washed away. And who knows what was already happening to its undercarriage.

The driver's door opened. I wish I would have had a pair of binoculars or a camera with a telephoto lens to capture the expression that must have been on his face at the time, as he slowly crawled out onto the hood of his truck with a thick rope draped over his shoulder. He slowly made his way to the front bumper, carefully leaned over, and then tied one end of the rope securely onto the truck's undercarriage. Then he stood up on the hood and with all his might tossed the rope towards the shore. The driver of the other truck caught hold of the rope, tied it to the back of his truck, got back behind his steering wheel, and slowly drove forward until the rope was taut. The rope started to strain as the truck on the shore pulled the weight of the truck in the water, which after a few seconds began to dislodge, and soon was able, under its own power, to make it the rest of the way safely onto solid ground next to the first truck.

To me it was quite obvious what the solution to this river-crossing problem was ... "Turn around!" is what I wanted to shout. Hey, I was willing to wait another day if it meant being able to live to see another day.

But Sian and I just kept silent the whole time and watched (and took photos). Much to our ... let's see, what word should I use here, *fear*? *distress*? *horror*? ... not one of those vehicles made any attempt to turn around. I mean, this wasn't like some theme park, where if a ride goes wrong they shut it down. Those drivers were all going to keep moving along that road (or what used to be a road!) in spite of the obstacles ... including Majhuud in his truck. They had formed a caravan, and apparently the caravan was going to stick together.

32

The Long and
Winding Roads

The next two trucks made it across the river without incident. And then it was our turn. There's no point in going into more detail about my apprehension as the front wheels of Majhuud's truck entered the river.

I knew that this wasn't the first time most of these drivers (probably all of them) had to deal with nature's blows. These were tough surroundings to live in and to traverse, and yet these were also tough and determined people who managed to live and survive in that rugged environment. I had a great respect for them. And at that point in time our lives were literally in their hands.

Sian and I were standing in the back of the truck (you definitely don't sit in a truck bed at a time like this), holding on to the roll bar just behind the cab as Majhuud slowly and adeptly felt his way over the unseen and ever-changing terrain below the wheels of his Landcruiser. Up and down, side to side, back and forth ... not a single moment that we didn't need to keep hanging on, knuckles white from the strain. The last thing we wanted was the need to call out, "Man overboard!" (or *woman* as it could be).

We were quite sure the many eyes on both banks of the river were not merely watching Majhuud's truck, but were also focused on the two non-local passengers who were bravely sharing this experience with them ... all of them surely wondering why we were doing it.

As the back tires exited the water onto the bank, Sian turned to me and said with relief written all over her face, "We made it!"

"Al hamdu lilah" (meaning, *Praise be to God*), I responded in Arabic. Then I asked her, "Are you still glad you volunteered to come along on this trip?"

"I'll need to think about it," she said with a smile.

"Yeah, I guess she's doing okay," I thought.

The truck behind us also made it safely up the bank. Our two trucks stuck together throughout the rest of the trip.

All eight trucks were on their way again, only to be met by the same stubborn river once more! It meant a second crossing ... and then a third. We were just about to cross a fourth time when a truck pulled up on the other side of the river. The driver shouted something across to a couple of our drivers who had gotten out of our their trucks and were standing at the edge of the shore on our side.

I didn't catch what the guy was shouting, and neither did Majhuud at first. So he slid out of his truck and joined the other seven drivers on our side of the river as they had a huddle and discussed the news that had been shouted our way.

It was only when Majhuud returned to the truck that I had the chance to ask him, "What's wrong?"

"There's been a landslide up ahead," he said. "The road is completely impassable.

"Did he say a *landslide*!?" I thought. "Oh great! I hadn't even thought of that!"

"We'll have to turn around and head back the way we just came," continued Majhuud, interrupting my thoughts, before getting back in the cab.

"Did you catch that bit of news?" I asked Sian.

She nodded her head with a concerned look, not knowing what to say ... unsure whether she should be relieved or rather fearful of crossing the river another three times on the return.

I said to her, "Fine, I don't mind waiting another day or two to find another ride. Do you?"

"Sounds good to me," she replied.

I just assumed Majhuud and the other drivers had by now decided the trip was impossible and so would be returning to Taalih, the town where we started from.

I already had visions of sitting all dried off inside Harry's mud house with a nice hot cup of tea before turning in and sleeping the night away in a comfortable bed.

The caravan of trucks all turned around and started heading in the opposite direction. The first river crossing went well. But at the second crossing one of the trucks behind us ran into difficulties ... they got stuck right in the middle of the river! It was a Salown, and it was packed full with passengers.

Thankfully this time one of the trucks on the shore had a winch. The driver quickly turned his truck around, and then pulled up as close to the edge of the river as he deemed safe. He tied one end of a rope to the end of the winch cable and then threw the rope as hard as he could up stream so it would flow into the hands of the man lying on the hood of the wedged truck. They had success on the third try. Next, the man on the hood pulled the rope until he had the cable's hook in his hands which he securely fastened to the undercarriage.

They weren't going to chance pulling the truck that distance while all the passengers were still inside. They had to lighten its load. And so one by one those very unhappy (I could add a few more adjectives here I'm sure) passengers had to get out of the truck and, while hanging onto the cable so no one would accidentally get washed away downstream, they slowly and carefully waded to the bank through the waist deep water which was relentlessly rushing at them, bare feet feeling their way along the river bottom.

One of the passengers was a small child who was transported on the shoulders of one of the men. Another was the child's mother who was also aided, although didn't have the luxury of being carried.

Once everyone was standing safely on the shore (albeit dripping wet and shivering), the stuck truck, with driver behind the steering wheel, was slowly but surely winched out of the river.

I said rather selfishly to Sian, "That could have been us wading through those torrents."

"I've been thinking the same thing," she admitted.

The dislodged truck refilled with its now miserable wet passengers, and the caravan started moving forward once again, with one more crossing to go. The third crossing was made without incident.

Eventually we turned back onto the safety and luxury of the paved road. Was I ever glad to have that adventure behind us.

"Hey wait a minute, aren't we going the wrong way?" I asked Sian.

"I wasn't really paying attention, but I think you're right," she said.

Sure enough, instead of turning *right*, which would have taken us back to Taalih, one truck after another turned *left* and started driving further north along the road towards Baqiim. We weren't returning to the comforts of Sa'da city after all!

I wondered if I should start pounding on the roof of the truck cab and demand that they let us out ... but I didn't.

We drove on for about another fifteen minutes, and then turned west onto another dirt road just before reaching Baqiim ... or more accurately, onto another rock and mud road. "Okay, so we obviously weren't going to be looking for a hotel in Baqiim," I concluded.

Majhuud drove on. By then it was 6 PM, and it was almost dark. That was not a good sign! It was getting dark before we even made any real progress into those mountains.

Majhuud suddenly pulled over and waved down the truck that was following us. You know, I didn't even recall if some of the trucks we had been caravanning with had turned south on the Baqiim road, or whether there had been a fork in the dirt road we were presently on, or whether they just drove on ahead of us and we lost sight of them. Anyway, from that point in time just our two trucks stuck together.

Majhuud walked over to the other driver, exchanged a few words with him, and then returned to our truck and interacted with his two companions.

The two men proceeded to get out of the cab and started on their way towards the other truck while Majhuud came over to Sian and me and said, "Butros, you and your sister are going to ride in the cab with me."

I don't recall if we did the culturally appropriate thing and protested ... I rather doubt it. I do hope we didn't seem too anxious to accept the offer, but we both crawled over the side of the truck bed and got into the truck cab, me first, followed by Sian ... that was the more culturally appropriate seating arrangement ... it wasn't done so I'd be warmer sitting between two other bodies!

It sure was nice to be sitting in comfort, and where it was much warmer and drier. It also gave us the chance to interact with Majhuud and get to know him a bit better.

The other truck took the lead, and we followed, although eventually we lost sight of it.

"No problem," I thought. "I'm sure it would be hard to get lost with just the one road to follow.

But when he came to a fork in the road, Majhuud stopped the truck and sat deep in thought. It was quite apparent that he wasn't sure which way to go. He informed us, "I've only ever been on this particular road once before."

That was not what I wanted to hear. "Oh great," I thought, "here we go again. What next?!"

Road signs were non-existent on those mountain roads, so Majhuud chose a road and we carried on. I'm not sure if Yemenis had some kind of rhyme like "eenie meenie miney moe" to help them decide in such situations.

Thankfully we soon happened upon a small village. Majhuud spotted someone walking along, so he pulled over, hopped out, and asked for directions.

When he jumped back into the truck he informed us, "We need to turn around, return to the fork in the road, and then take the other road."

Nothing seemed to bother him. I mean, I don't remember him ever getting frustrated, or angry, or excited, or being apologetic about all the set-backs and potential danger (the same could not be said of me and Sian). Majhuud would merely state the facts as he saw them, and carry on. It was fascinating to watch him operate. He always seemed to be in control ... even when it was quite obvious he wasn't in control of what nature threw at him.

So once again we did some back tracking and were soon turning onto the correct road. The driver of the other truck had noticed our absence, and kindly waited for us. When he saw us approaching, he put his vehicle back in gear and we started to move on together again. There was a significant amount of comfort in having at least two vehicles sticking together ... just in case.

By 7:30 it was totally dark ... and I mean totally. The thick clouds kept us from even getting a glimpse of the stars. We slowly wound along the dirt road cut out of the side of the mountain ... a road just wide enough for our truck, with less than a meter to spare, before we'd be plummeting hundreds of meters to our muddy graves.

We were making very slow progress, going over some particularly rough terrain, when suddenly we came to a complete stop yet once again. What I had feared actually occurred ... a mudslide. Right in front of us stood a huge boulder completely blocking the road.

Only half an hour earlier we had passed a truck coming in the opposite direction on this very road, and the driver had told Majhuud the road was passable. That meant this mudslide had just happened very recently.

"The boulder could have rolled down the mountain while we were on that very section of the road!" I thought to myself ... but dared not say out loud to Sian. But from the look on her face, I was quite sure she was thinking the very same thing. I tried to keep my mind from dwelling on that thought.

By then I really had my doubts that we would be able to make it the rest of the way to Munabbih. But for Majhuud it seemed like just one more obstacle that needed to be dealt with. He merely turned to us and said rather casually, "We'll have to do a little more backtracking so we can get onto another road."

Having such a network of roads made total sense considering all the scattered villages I had seen from the airplane window a few months ago. "But do we have to travel on all of those roads in one day!?" I thought. "Couldn't we just find some house and beg to spend the night there?"

So how do you turn a truck around when the road isn't much wider than the vehicle itself? Well, as I already pointed out in a previous chapter, every so often a wider cut was made into the mountain to allow vehicles to pass each other. Thankfully we didn't have to back up too far in the blackness (obviously the headlights are set only in the front of a vehicle!) before we could turn around. Majhuud turned the vehicle very slowly and very carefully, and then waited while the other vehicle did the same. Then we both started driving forward again in the opposite direction. We had to backtrack a long way before we turned onto yet another road.

We drove on, and unceasingly on ... up, and ever further up ... around and around ... hour after hour.

It was 11 PM when we finally arrived in Suq al-Munabbih[30] ... but thankfully we did arrive! I was ready to drop. What should have been an enjoyable three and a half hour trip (for that's how long it had taken me the first time ... and what I had told Sian), turned into quite the adventure ... one which, by the way, I was determined never to repeat.

After everybody piled out of the two vehicles, Majhuud said, "You both must be very tired."

"A little," I said with a smile.

Not having planned to arrive so late in the day, I wasn't sure where Sian and I would be spending the night. The last time I was in the village I had spent a night in the prison and then two nights with the Egyptian school teachers. I knew Suq al-Munabbih had a hotel, and so I had already thought of that as an option. But it looked like Majhuud had a plan in mind ... and that didn't surprise me in the least. "Wait here for a minute," he said before disappearing into a building.

"If I remember correctly, I think this is the hotel," I said to Sian.

Majhuud soon exited with another man, and the two of them stood there having a discussion about Sian and me. Then the other man went back inside while Majhuud came over and informed us, "The owner of the hotel is going to prepare a room for you so you'll have a place to sleep tonight."

Okay, so that was indeed the hotel. "That's great," I said. "Thanks so much for arranging that."

"You're welcome," he replied.

"Oh, and before I forget, I want to pay you for the ride," I offered.

"I won't take anything from you," he said firmly. And I could tell that he meant it.

I didn't argue ... I was too tired to argue. Sian and I both merely said, "Thank you."

We picked up our bags and followed Majhuud inside the hotel where at the moment we found quite a commotion. The hotel owner was relocating some of his other guests ... namely, kicking them out of a small private room to accommodate us. I didn't even feel sorry for them. I just wanted to be in a horizontal position ... and soon I was.

---

[30] If you want a reminder of what Suq al-Munabbih looked like, refer back to the photo in chapter 1.

33

Onward and Upward

"Good morning. Welcome Butros, welcome!" said the restaurant worker as Sian and I walked in, remembering me from the interaction we'd had a month earlier.

"It's good to be back," I said. "We'd like to order some breakfast."

"Right away," he said.

After a simple but good breakfast, I suggested to Sian, "Let's head over to the school. I really should visit the two Egyptian teachers who work there."

As we walked through the town, I was recognized and greeted by a few of the southerners I had met last time.

"Peace be with you," I said as we approached Ibrahim and Hassan, my Egyptian friends. They were sitting on the front landing of the school, having just finished their own breakfast ... the dirty dishes still scattered in front of them.

"And with you be peace," they both replied with big smiles.

"Welcome! Welcome Butros!" said Ibrahim.

"Praise be to God for your safe arrival!" added Hassan.

"How are you? What's your news?" I asked them.

"Praise be to God," they both responded.

"I'd like you to meet my sister who joined me on this trip," I said looking over toward Sian. "This is Sian."

"Welcome Sian!" they said.

"Will you be staying here in Suq al-Munabbih again, Butros?" asked Ibrahim hoping for an affirmative answer.

"Not this time," I said, and felt bad when I saw the disappointment on their faces. "Someone invited us to visit their village, and so we're going to be staying with them."

That's right, we would be heading out that very morning with Majhuud to visit his village ... which we learned later was called Al-Haza. We had made the arrangement with Majhuud the day before while we were still on our way to Suq al-Munabbih. Mahamed (one of the two men who was traveling with Majhuud the day before) assured us that the trip to their village would only take about half an hour.

Now I was really expecting (and was somewhat nervous about ... actually *really* nervous about) that while we were hanging out at the school, someone would show up to summon us to see the Police Chief up at the castle-like prison. As I had *hinted* earlier, I didn't think he would be happy to see us, since I had not acquired the extra permission he insisted I get before coming to Munabbih again.

When no one showed up, I just assumed he must have been out of the village at the time, otherwise I was sure he would have heard about our presence.

Actually, my experience from the last trip indicated that he worked late into the evenings, and so probably wouldn't even show up at the office until later in the morning, or more likely early in the afternoon. So we must have arrived sometime after he finished work the day before, and then we'd be leaving for Al-Haza before he arrived for work that day. How convenient!

But I was quite sure the Police Chief would hear that we had passed through the village as soon as he arrived at work later in the day. And I was also sure he'd be informed that we had gone out to Majhuud's village. So he would be on the lookout for us when we came back through in a couple of days.

Well, why get all worked up about what may or may not happen in the future ... it's better to just live and deal with the issues in the present, right?

Majhuud eventually showed up at the school along with his same two companions of the day before, and that's when I learned something new about Majhuud.

"Peace be with you sir," said Ibrahim with great respect when he saw Majhuud walk up. It was obvious he knew Majhuud and was treating him as someone important.

"And with you be peace," he replied.

Hassan was in the school building when Majhuud arrived, but when he came out, you could see the surprise on his face when he saw who our host was. "Peace be with you sir," he said.

After a bit of conversation I suddenly realized Majhuud was their boss ... he was the district school director. I'm not sure how big of a district he was responsible for, but nevertheless, our host held a very important position.

Ibrahim and Hassan already had a high opinion of me just for being a Westerner, but now I was hob-nobbing with their boss!

Soon our promised half hour trip started to Majhuud's village. It was a cloudy day, but thankfully not a drop of rain fell. And so once again Sian and I rode in the bed of the truck ... which suited me fine because we would get a great view.

The scenery was spectacular!

I made a mental note that we passed through at least three villages along the way, and each time I hoped that we had arrived at our destination. But we just kept right on going. I say *at least* three villages because sometimes we passed some isolated houses and I wondered if they were part of some village ... maybe it was just that the whole village wasn't visible from the road.

Finally, after a *two hours* ride on one of the roughest roads I'd been on yet, we arrived at the end of the road. I should have known that Mahamed was talking Yemeni time ... a half hour indeed!

Yes, it was literally the *end of the road*. A dead end! There was nowhere else to drive except back in the same direction we had just come.

I looked at Sian in disbelief and said, "Where are we?"

To which she responded, "Obviously in the middle of nowhere."

I gave a feeble smile. My shock was not just that the road had ended, but that I didn't see a village at the end of the road. Not a single building.

Hold it ... maybe I was mistaken. Not too far back we had passed a few buildings (look to the right in the above photo ... I took that photo looking back in the direction we had just come), although it didn't look like a whole village to me ... and why would we have driven right past it if that was our destination?

I climbed out of the bed of the truck, still looking around me (360 degrees around me, as well as up and down) to be sure I wasn't missing something. Then I nonchalantly walked over to Majhuud, and calmly asked, "Where is your village?"

"It's up there," he answered, pointing straight up the side of the mountain right in front of us.

I looked in the direction his finger was pointing, but I couldn't make out anything that resembled buildings. All I saw was the side of the mountain. I asked myself, "What have I gotten us into this time?" I dared not ask Sian for any more of her thoughts.

Surprise, surprise! The half hour trip wasn't over yet. We still had to hike the rest of the way up to the village ... seemingly straight up the side of the mountain from what Majhuud's finger was indicating!

Majhuud, as calm and casual as ever, said, "We're planning to finish the road all the way up to the village so we won't have to hike up and down the mountain anymore."

"Now he tells me!" still keeping my thoughts to myself.

I'm assuming the purchase of the jack-hammer in Taalih was going to help the village accomplish the task. It was obvious that an enormous amount of work had already gone into getting the road cut to allow them to drive as far as we did.

And so we started the hike ... *onward and upward.* Majhuud, holding his flip flops in one hand and a package in the other, led the way barefoot. He was followed by his two companions, also barefoot ... one of them carrying packages while the other one balanced the jackhammer on one shoulder. Sian and I tried to keep up at the rear, each of us carrying a small backpack.

After half an hour of hiking up steep paths, we arrived at, no, not the village, but rather at the village school. The village itself was still a bit further up the mountain. Unbelievable! Talk about being isolated from the rest of the world.

At least we had arrived on some flat ground where we could stand erect without having to worry about losing our balance and tumbling back down the path. At that point I turned around and looked back at the way we had come ... the seemingly endless mountains between where we were standing at the time and Sa'da city where we had started. It was quite the spectacular view ... but at the same time it was admittedly somewhat frightening! We were indeed very very isolated.

While we were standing there, Majhuud called out, "Oh Khalid! Khalid, come on out!"

Evidently the village teacher was inside the school building and Majhuud wanted to introduce us to him. Out walked a tall young man ... and it was clear he wasn't from Egypt. Khalid was from Sudan, and was he ever surprised to see me and Sian.

"Hello Khalid, my name is Butros and I'm from Canada," I said to him as I reached out and shook his hand.

"Welcome," Khalid responded, still with a look of bewilderment.

"And this is my sister, Sian," I said.

"Welcome," he said again as he shook her hand.

Majhuud interrupted any further interaction by taking Khalid aside so he could talk to him in private. They exchanged a few words before Majhuud turned to us and said, "The three of us are going up to the village. I think it would be good if you and your sister stayed here at the school with Khalid for a while and rested, okay?"

"That's fine," I said, before looking over at Sian to make sure she was okay with that.

"That's fine with me too," she said.

"Good. We'll come back down to get you a little later," Majhuud added.

Majhuud must have observed that this trip had taken quite a toll on us ... and he was right. So they turned, walked the few remaining steps on the flat ground, and then started the next part of the ascent ... but at a much faster pace now that they didn't have to worry about the two clumsy foreigners who obviously didn't know how to maneuver very well on mountains.

I could tell Khalid was still trying to get his mind around the fact that he suddenly had two unexpected guests. That's not to imply he was frustrated ... in fact, it was quite clear he was very pleased.

34

Social Studies Lesson

I had no idea what Majhuud had said to Khalid, but it was evident that he must have designated him as a co-host ... and Khalid was a great host. He started by giving us a tour of the school facilities.

From the outside, the school was built like all the other buildings we had passed along the way ... made of local materials ... namely, stones of various shapes and sizes all stacked and carefully fitted together ... nothing fancy but very artistically done in my humble outsider opinion. I assume the locals just saw it as functional.

The school actually consisted of two buildings. Khalid led us into the larger one and announced, "This is my home." We found ourselves in a spacious room with rather simple sparse furnishings. Two foam mattresses were lying in the middle of the otherwise bare concrete floor, one of which must have served as his bed at night, and the rest of the time the two of them most likely functioned as *couches* for himself and his guests. A small corner of the room, just to the right of the entrance, was set aside as a kitchen where he had a one burner propane stove and a few pots, pans and dishes. A little further down the same wall stood a low table with some books spread out on top, and a suitcase underneath. An unscreened window (just an opening with no glass) was set in the wall to our left, overlooking the scenic mountain range we had just

215

finished traversing that day. The window's shutter was open at the time, allowing sun and fresh air to enter.

"Very nice," I said.

We walked the length of the room and Khalid opened a wooden door to reveal a second chamber which served as a storage room containing only a few scattered items here and there that I didn't really take the time to focus on.

We walked the length of his room once again, and then walked around the outside of the structure until we came upon the second smaller building set behind the first. "This is where I teach the students," he said as we entered. There was one fair size room with desks and chairs. He continued, "For now this is big enough. But once more students start to attend, then we'll need a second teacher and will use one of the rooms in the other building for a second classroom."

"How many students do you have?" I asked.

He answered, "I teach grades one through seven and I have twenty seven students."

Sian and I were impressed. "It sounds to me like education is really taking off in the Munabbih region," Sian said.

"Yes, mostly for the boys. I only have one girl student so far, and that's Majhuud's daughter," Khalid informed us.

It didn't surprise me that the district school director wanted to set a good example for the rest of the region by having his daughter attend.

Khalid led us back to his living quarters and said, "Please have a seat while I prepare some lunch for us."

"Don't go to any trouble for our sakes," I protested.

"I'm going to eat anyway, and I want you to join me," he said, making it clear that he didn't want an argument.

So Sian and I made ourselves comfortable on one of the foam mattresses, while Khalid prepared some food for the three of us. He was a very pleasant person, and it was relaxing as we chatted together and became acquainted with one another.

I think our visit turned out to be a real treat for him. I mean, he himself was a foreigner living far away from home, and so we immediately had something in common, in spite of our differences. What also helped was that my and Sian's Jordanian Arabic (yes, Sian had also studied in Jordan prior to moving to Yemen) was much closer to his dialect than the Yemeni dialect of Munabbih was ... actually closer than any dialect in Yemen was.

As the three of us sat and conversed, we started to get a good understanding of what life was like in Al-Haza. There was no electricity at the school, although the village itself enjoyed the luxury of a generator, which was only ever turned on in the evenings. Any fuel had to be hauled in from the outside, which meant they needed to use it sparingly. Of course, any other products they couldn't produce locally also needed to be brought in. All water had to be carried up from a spring located a little ways down the road we had driven in on. Not sure if they had a system to catch rain water. Anyway, life was definitely not easy in that remote place.

About half an hour after finishing lunch, the unexpected happened ... unexpected for Yemen that is. Two teenage girls suddenly showed up at the school. Word had obviously spread that Sheikh Majhuud had brought a couple of foreigners as guests to the village and that they were down at the school with the teacher, Khalid. And so the two girls, somewhere between the ages of 13 and 15, had hurried down to have a look at the strangers. Such a thing wouldn't have happened anywhere else in North Yemen I'm sure. At least the girls had brought three younger boys along with them.

Khalid invited them to come into the room and join us for some tea. They all trooped in, all eyes, of course, focused on Sian and me. Khalid told them to sit on the second mattress, and they did.

Initially the girls just talked with Khalid, while sending glances our way. The boys just sat and stared.

"Go ahead and talk with them," Khalid encouraged them. "They can speak Arabic."

It didn't look like they believed him, so Sian decided to break the ice and asked them, "What are your names?"

"My name is Fatima," one of them said. "And this is Khadija." Khadija just giggled at first, but then they both started to open up and interact with Sian, still giggling from time to time.

I'm sure it ended up being a rather enlightening Social Studies lesson for those Yemeni kids. We were the first non-Arabs ever to set foot in that village.[31] Many of the village residents had never been outside of the district of Munabbih, and in fact some of them had never even set foot outside of the surroundings of their own little isolated village. Imagine what a novelty it was to have us show up. I wonder if

---

[31] Khalid was from Khartoum and was an Arab.

we became part of their folklore, with stories still circulating today about Butros and Sian.

A rather scary thought at the time was, "How they view us is going to have a big impact on how they'll view the West from now on." What an overwhelming responsibility Sian and I had to give them a good impression.

I also entered into the conversation, but typically preferred to direct what I said to Khalid. I was too used to not making eye contact or interacting with any marriageable aged girls. In many parts of Yemen girls were already married off by the time they were 13 ... and definitely at least engaged by the age of 16. When I was visiting in the Hadhramaut region in later years, I heard that if a girl isn't spoken for by the time she's 16 then she's very unlikely to get married at all.

And so, there I was, a single man, with a couple of teenage girls hanging around. Well I didn't want to unknowingly get myself engaged ... something which almost happened once while living in Jordan ... I'll save that story for my next book.

I should also point out that it wasn't very easy to interact with those girls. We often had to get Khalid, who had been living in Al-Haza for a while, to interpret what they were saying because they were uneducated and just spoke rapidly in their local dialect, which Sian and I couldn't always follow very well.

After a while Majhuud showed up. He came to get Sian and me started on the next stage of this seemingly endless adventure. It was time for some more mountain climbing ... namely, going from the school up to the actual village.

What a climb it turned out to be! At times it felt like we were going straight up, as we followed an extremely steep path up the side of the mountain. I wished someone ahead of us would have tied a rope around my waist and theirs so I could be confident that I wouldn't fall too far if I lost my footing.

I did a little slipping and sliding a few times on the climb, but never did fall, and we eventually made it all the way up to another level of relatively flat ground where we encountered the first of many houses which formed the village Al-Haza.

As we made it past the first house we found ourselves on a small flat open patch of ground, kind of like an open public square, which allowed us a view of a number of other houses which were built on various levels ... about fifteen of them ... although later I discovered more houses off in different directions that I couldn't yet see from my current rather limited vantage point.

As you can see in the photo, the houses had the same stone construction as the school. Majhuud told us that some of the houses were over 200 years old. I couldn't help but wonder how those houses would endure an earthquake.

We marched on, maneuvering through the maze of narrow dirt walkways which led from one house to another, until we suddenly stopped at a door where Majhuud announced, "This is my house."

"Very nice, praise be to God," I said, followed by the blessing, "May God watch over you and your family."

Majhuud replied, "And may God watch over you both." Then he led us inside.

We started climbing some stairs, and soon reached the kitchen where Majhuud's wife was busy cooking. At first, all I could make out was her silhouette in the dimly lit smoke-filled kitchen. I could hardly breathe because of all the smoke ... there was no ventilation to speak of. I rather doubted her lungs could be doing very well. And no matter where we went in the house after that, we couldn't escape the smoky smell.

We continued the tour, walking past a number of other rooms in the house, none of which we were invited to enter, until we eventually arrived on the roof. The roof was a rather large flat open area with a low wall encircling it. Off to the left, a door led into another room ... or was it another house ... I couldn't tell, but would soon find out, as Majhuud was leading us in that direction.

Sian and I were ushered through the door into a large room. Without any warning, we suddenly found ourselves in the presence of six men.

They reclined on plush foam mattresses along two of the walls, talking and chewing qat. As we entered, all eyes immediately focused on the two of us.

Majhuud introduced us, "This is Butros and his sister Sian from Canada, and they are welcome and honored guests of Al-Haza."

"Welcome ... welcome," came the chorus of voices.

"This is ..." Majhuud repeated as he escorted us around the room introducing us to each one. We, in turn, shook hands and replied to each new introduction with the polite appropriate response.

Then Majhuud said to both Sian and I, "Please sit down here," pointing to an empty mattress near where we were standing, at which point Sian wisely spoke up, "Majhuud, would it be okay if I went and spent time with the women?"

"Yes, of course," Majhuud agreed without any hesitation. We had made it very clear right from the start that the main reason for Sian coming on the trip with me was for her to interact with the women. "Please come with me."

"See you later," I said to her in English as he led her off ... I assumed to another room somewhere in his house.

As for me, I sat down and proceeded to talk with a few of the men. Although it proved to be a bit of a challenge, since they weren't as capable of adjusting their vocabulary to make themselves understood as Majhuud was for this Jordanian Arabic speaker. The qat chewing didn't help either, since it affected their speech. In addition, I had to deal with the racket of the generator just outside Majhuud's house which kept the TV going in the corner. It was a real struggle to communicate with them. But once I was able to turn the conversation to my most comfortable topic, Arabic dialect differences, it helped immensely. I found that topic always went over well with any Arab in any country, and this was no exception.

When Majhuud returned, he headed straight for the TV, while saying something in rapid speech to everyone else that I didn't understand. He turned the channel selector and had a disappointed look on his face when he couldn't get any other channel to work. So he turned it back to the same channel that had been on, and then sat down beside me and said, "We can only get one channel here in our village, the channel from Saudi Arabia."

"So you can't get any Yemeni channels at all?" I inquired.

"No. That's why I purchased an antenna in Taalih and set it up on the roof. But it doesn't seem to make any difference for the reception."

I wondered why it had taken him so long to return after dropping off Sian ... he had been on the roof adjusting the new antenna. "That's too bad," I said, but knew what was coming next. Often when I traveled people would ask me about medicines or technical things just because I was an educated Westerner, and they assumed I would know about such things. Well, I managed to disappoint a lot of people.

"Do you know about setting up antennas?" he asked, just as I had predicted.

"I'm afraid not," I answered honestly.

The hours passed, and eventually Majhuud informed me, "I'm going to escort you back down to the school building."

"You must be kidding!" isn't what left my lips, but was definitely what was resonating through my brain. It was hard enough traversing that rugged terrain in the daylight, but having us do so in the dark was not what I considered an acceptable suggestion. I had just assumed we would be spending the night somewhere in the village, and that someone would be sent down to the school to pick up our belongings. I was apparently mistaken.

Khalid had come up to the village sometime after us, and so he would be descending as well. We left the meeting room after many "good nights" and "sleep wells" had been exchanged, and then we headed down some stairs and along a hallway. We stopped in front of a door where Majhuud entered and reappeared with Sian following behind.

"How are you doing Sian?" I asked.

"Fine," she lied. She looked exhausted.

"We're going to be hiking down to the school." I informed her.

"Yeah, that's what Majhuud told me," she said with some concern in her expression.

"Let's just go as slow as we need to, okay?" I tried to encourage her.

Need I point out that going down the mountain required much more caution and skill than going up did. I was convinced that the path had gotten much steeper over the past hours. I found myself often slipping and sliding on the rocks ... although at times I slid on the seat of my pants on purpose. I sure was glad we were accompanied (actually guided) by some of the locals, otherwise we would have never found our way. Even Khalid confessed that he wasn't able to find his way around at night. It was such a relief when we all arrived without incident.

Sian ended up sleeping in the storage room while Khalid and I slept in the main room.

The night was once again a welcome friend ... a time when I could close my eyes, and not have to interact with anyone for the next few hours.

35

Feasting and Dancing

After breakfast, Sian and I hung around the school waiting for Majhuud to arrive and escort us back up to the village. While we waited, we had the opportunity to observe the arrival of Khalid's students.

It was so amazing to watch those kids casually walk down the steep mountain side as if there was nothing to it. They made it look so effortless. I envied them. They all descended barefoot, some of them carrying flip-flops which they slipped on their feet once they hit the level ground. I was determined to try and conquer that mountain trail barefoot myself once Majhuud arrived.

While we observed the students, they were, of course, also observing us. By then every last one of them would have heard about us, and they were curious.

It was fun to see Khalid in action. He really cared about those kids. During our time in the village I heard that the students really liked having Khalid as their teacher. The same was stated whether Khalid[32] was present or not.

Majhuud finally showed up. So we excused ourselves from our audience and started to follow him back up the mountain. I did go

---

[32] Khalid is the tall person in the white shirt in the photo.

barefoot, and found that I was indeed able to maneuver much better, and therefore felt much safer.

We spent the whole morning and afternoon being entertained by the villagers, and we also did as much comprehension testing as possible ... once again Sian with the women, and me with the men. Majhuud had encouraged everyone to cooperate with us.

It wasn't until some point in the afternoon that Sian and I finally had the chance to see each other and debrief. "Testing the women here in Al-Haza is an impossible task," Sian pointed out in frustration.

"Why, did something happen?" I asked rather concerned.

"No, they're very nice, and they're more than willing to interact with me," she said. "But I'm having a very hard time understanding what the women are saying to me or to each other."

Poor Sian. Those women had been so isolated their whole lives, and I rather doubted that they ever had the opportunity to sit in front of the TV to familiarize themselves with other varieties of Arabic. They never had to adjust their language to accommodate anyone else. If only Sian had someone to translate for her. But alas, she was all on her own. "Sorry it's so frustrating," is all I could think to say.

"Frustrating is right," she continued ... "First of all, it takes a lot of effort just to try and get them to understand what I'm trying to do. None of them have ever even seen or heard a tape recorder before, and most of them aren't even interested in participating. And then when someone does agree to take the test, when I administer it, the women hardly ever understand the content. It's hardly worth the effort."

In response I said, "Hey, even if you don't get to test many women, what you just shared with me is very important information." I hoped that would at least encourage her a little, because what she shared with me really did indicate very clearly just how much effort it would take to educate rural Yemeni women using Modern Standard Arabic or another dialect like Egyptian. "Sian, just do what you can, and don't worry about the results," I added.

I mentioned earlier about how I tried to avoid female contact. Well, after having spent some more time in Al-Haza, I observed that men and women interacted with each other much more freely than in other parts of the country. In fact the women didn't even wear any kind of face coverings. I'm not sure I should even admit that I noticed, but most of the women in Al-Haza were very pretty.

So I managed to get over my fear, and actually talked with a number of the women. That's not to imply that I ever spent time *alone* with them ... there were always men around. I still made it a habit to interact as little as possible with them. I thought I better leave that job to Sian. Even when I did converse with them, I had the same problem Sian did, the Al-Haza women and I often misunderstood each other.

After Sian's and my brief reprieve, Majhuud showed up and informed us, "It's time to eat."

That sure sounded like a good idea to me.

We had been in Majhuud's house, and I just assumed we would be eating the meal there. But when we arrived at the front door, it was obvious we were going to exit, so I inquired, "Where are we going Majhuud?"

"We're all going to be eating at someone else's house," he told us ... at least that's all I can remember him telling us.

When we arrived at the other house, Sian once again asked to be taken to where the women were hanging out. The women would be in the kitchen cooking up a storm, and it would be a more relaxing atmosphere for her to interact with them, just spending time with them in their comfort zone ... definitely not trying to test anyone.

Once Sian was dropped off, Majhuud and I entered a large room where only a couple of men were present at the time, and they looked like they were making preparations.

They greeted us as we entered.

I looked around and thought, "I don't think this is going to be a simple ordinary everyday meal."

The two men were laying out plastic table cloths on the floor. That could only mean one thing based on similar past experiences ... namely, men would congregate around large platters of food placed in the middle of each table cloth. It looked to me like many people would be attending this meal. This was definitely not going to be a simple ordinary everyday meal!

So what was the occasion? Majhuud never told me more than that we were going to be eating a meal ... unless he said something and I missed it ... which was very likely.

Suddenly the guests (all men) started arriving ... and they arrived in droves ... streaming into the room.

"So what's the occasion?" I kept asking myself. I needed to know if there was something special I should be saying, but it was too late to ask

Majhuud, and so all I ever said was, "nice to meet you," over and over again.

The introductions and hand-shakings seemed endless. I didn't think that many men could be living in Al-Haza. I concluded that people must have been arriving from other neighboring villages as well. This was obviously an important occasion.

My fear in such situations was that I wouldn't recognize people I had already met before ... I had been meeting so many people during my stay in Al-Haza. I always tried my best to remember faces and names, but I was sure I would fail that evening. I just concluded they'd have to find it in their hearts to forgive me my failings, realizing I was new in the neighborhood. I mean, all *they* had to do was *meet the foreigner* ... I had to meet dozens of them!

We were all just milling around when suddenly several men trooped in, each carrying a large platter overflowing with mounds of steaming rice. It was time for the village women's culinary efforts to be displayed. One platter was carefully placed in the middle of each table cloth.

Following close behind the platter carriers, two more men carried a huge pot between them. It appeared they were struggling with the weight of its contents. The two of them went from platter to platter, stopping at each one so they could pull out and place a generous amount of goat meat on top of the rice. The parade continued as yet others entered bearing side dishes which were placed beside the larger platters. In typical generous Middle Eastern style, there was an abundance of food ... much more than could ever be consumed by those present.

"I sure wish I had my camera with me," I mumbled to myself.

The men were then invited to gather around the platters, and that's what they did ... I mean, that's what *we* did. Actually Majhuud came over to me at that moment and said, "Butros, come with me."

I gladly followed him to one of the platters. I was observing and making sure to follow his every move, although I found nothing unusual about the procedure. I mean, it wasn't really any different from other feasts I had attended in other Arab settings. The men naturally divided themselves into groups so there'd be roughly the same number around each platter.

But before anyone dug in, a few men entered, each carrying a jug of water, a bar of soap and a basin. It was time to wash up ... following the same procedure I've already described for you in chapter 25, entitled *Welcome or Not*.

After the "bismillah" (meaning, *In the name of God*) was uttered by someone at each platter, the feasting began. Right hands reach in, break off a small piece of meat which gets rolled into the middle of some rice, and then the mixture gets carried up to the mouth and the thumb flicks it in. The entire procedure is done with the one hand ... the right hand, which is considered the *clean hand*.

It was delicious!

I was doing a good job, but Majhuud, as my host, was concerned that I get my fair share, and so from time to time he would push another chunk of meat over towards me and say, "Eat Butros, eat."

To which I would reply, "Thank you Majhuud, I'm eating, I'm eating."

"Do you like it?" he inquired.

"Yes, it's delicious," I replied. "Praise be to God."

"Praise be to God," he said with a smile, satisfied I was indeed enjoying myself.

Once the men were finished eating, the remaining food was taken back to the women so they and the children could eat. Sian assured me afterwards that, as a female *guest*, she had received more than her fair share.

After the meal was over, and after another hand washing, Majhuud led me out of the room and we met up with Sian outside. Then the three of us rounded a corner and started a gradual descent along a narrow path which ran between houses in a part of the village we hadn't yet seen.

"Wow, this village is much bigger than I thought it was," I said to Sian.

"Listen, there's music playing," she commented.

Sure enough, I could make out the sound of a drum and a flute, both very skillfully played. Then as we turned another corner, we suddenly found ourselves approaching an open plot of ground set between yet more houses on three sides, and looking out towards the distant towering mountains on the fourth side. At one end of the town square we could make out the musicians who were accompanying two male singers. In the middle of the courtyard were some dancers. "Wow, it looks like a major event going on here," I said. By now I was convinced that we had been and were continuing to observe a local wedding.

Majhuud deposited Sian and I next to a stone wall where we had a good view of the activities going on in the town square, while he moved on to mingle with others. Locals were coming and going and stopping to chat with us and with each other. It was a very relaxing festive event being enjoyed by one and all, and we felt totally welcome. In fact, throughout the whole day everyone had been quite relaxed around us.

I could hear the generator start up somewhere off in the background, and then lights, which were strung up around the dance area, flickered on to fight off the darkness. In addition, many of the locals, who were scattered around the edges of the village square, lit kerosene lanterns.

When we first arrived on the scene, the dance which was going on had three participants, two men and one woman. Once again this demonstrated just how much more freedom the women had to interact with men ... although I never saw them touch each other during the dance.

The threesome dance started with the dancers weaving in and out and around each other. Then they started moving in a line circling around the dance floor. Sometimes one of them cut out of the line and went to the front. The dance continued for about five minutes or so, after which the music would pause, the dancers would make their exit allowing others to perform the same dance.

A second dance involved only men and, according to what a bystander told me, was performed at weddings. Finally some confirmation! This dance involved about ten men who formed a circle. As the circle turned, one side chanted something, and then the second side answered them. The dance went on for quite some time.

Some of the men were complaining, while explaining parts of the last dance to us, namely, that the piece of ground where the present event was taking place, was far too small. I could definitely see their point of view, especially considering the crowd that had gathered. Although somehow they seemed to manage pretty well with what they had.

In case you were wondering, Sian and I were not invited to join in the dancing ... at least not that I can remember.

The festivities continued for quite some time, but Majhuud, our ever perceptive host, eventually came up to us and asked, "Are you getting tired? Do you need some rest?" It was probably quite obvious that we were both exhausted after the day's events.

I turned to Sian, "Are you ready to go?"

"I think so," she responded.

Then I said to Majhuud, "It's been a very enjoyable time, thank you. But you're right, it might be good for us get some rest."

To tell you the truth, I was somewhat concerned that if I said we'd like to stay, then it could end up being many hours before we had another opportunity to leave. It was a good time for us non-participants to fade out of the scene. And so we never did find out how long the party continued, or how it ended.

Once again we trailed behind Majhuud ... but this time, instead of taking us down to the school, Majhuud took us to his house where he informed us we would be spending the night. Sian and I both already had our belongings waiting for us at the house.

We dropped Sian off first, and then Majhuud left me in another room all by myself ... such a luxury!

Without any hesitation, I unrolled my sleeping bag on top of the mattress and laid down for a well-deserved good night's rest.

But something was amiss. My arm started itching. I decided I must have been bitten by something while watching the dancing.

Then I suddenly felt something move *inside* my sleeping bag. I had memories of such movement. Then it came to me ... "Oh no ... fleas!" I said in an audible muffled voice.

I immediately unzipped my sleeping bag, and turned on my flashlight. But do you think I could find a single flea? No way! They were in survival mode. I didn't have this problem down at the school, and oh how I wished I was sleeping there again.

I was trying to come up with a solution, which brought to mind the possible reasons for the problem I was facing. So, if there are fleas, then that means animals carried those fleas to the room. So, what kind of animal could it possibly have been?

Two possibilities came to mind based on past encounters ... I recalled seeing the goats in a room on the third floor in Nadhiir, and then there were the rodents in the shack, also in Nadhiir. I never did find out the source, and it was definitely not something I felt I could ask my host about.

I hardly slept a wink the whole night because of those little critters. Most of the night was spent scratching and waiting for the sun to rise.

36

Guilty as Charged

After two *memorable* days (and nights) in Majhuud's village, it was time for us to start the long journey back to Sa'da.

Needless to say, I was exhausted, as I'm sure Sian was. I never found out if her room was flea-infested as well. But as happened on all my sleep-deprived trips (which so far applies to *all* of my trips), the adrenaline just kept flowing, and so somehow I managed to keep going.

Majhuud continued to treat us well, offering to drive us all the way back to Suq al-Munabbih. Actually, I didn't know how else we would have made our way there, since any traffic that far out would have to originate from his village ... unless someone from another village came for a visit ... and a number of guests very well could have spent the night in Al-Haza after the previous day's festivities.

Before we left, Majhuud pulled me aside and asked, "Do you think you could do me a favor?"

I couldn't imagine what it was he wanted to ask me to do for him, but I started to get a little nervous. I really owed him a lot considering how much he had done for us. It was a fact that throughout the Middle East if someone does you a favor, then it's expected you'll do something for them in return. While living in Jordan, the most common request was for help in obtaining a visa to Canada. I always made clear that it was a very difficult request to fulfill since I didn't have the proper *waasta* (meaning, *connections*). Would Majhuud ask me to help him get to Canada? I hoped not.

"What is it that you want me to do for you?" I asked calmly.

He held out his closed hand and then opened it to reveal a small piece of rock, and commented, "As you know, we've been clearing land in our village. In the process, we've come across some mineral deposits, and we're wondering what they are," and then he pointed at a gold-colored portion of the rock as he talked. "Do you think this could be gold?"

I took the rock from his hand, held it in my own, and examined it ... well, kind of *fake* examined it ... I really knew nothing at all about such things, and I answered honestly, "I'm not sure."

"Do you know anyone in Canada who could analyze it for me?" he asked next.

I was relieved. His request was not at all unreasonable. Taking a Yemeni rock to Canada was much easier than trying to find a way for a Yemeni person to get to Canada.

"Yes, I'm sure I could get someone to look at it for you," I responded, thinking of my geologist friend, Glen. When I was doing my undergrad degree, Glen had hired me one summer to work with a team doing land survey, which involved hiking through forests, flagging trees and taking soil samples, later to be analyzed in a lab to ascertain what the mineral content of a particular plot of land was.

"But how can I get the information to you once I find out if it's gold or not?" I inquired.

"I'll give you an address where you can write to me," he said.

So I pulled out my ever ready note pad and pen and wrote down the address as he told it to me. Then I wrapped the rock sample in a piece of paper and placed it safely in my backpack.

Just to let you know, once I arrived back in Canada I did indeed get the sample into Glen's hands, and he had a look at it. Unfortunately I had to write and inform Majhuud that it was not gold.

Too bad! I could just picture Majhuud living in a palace in Al-Haza with a helicopter landing pad so Glen and I could be flown in ... Glen working as the on-site geologist and me functioning as his translator. I guess it wasn't meant to be.

So back to our departure ... Sian and I said our goodbyes and thank yous to everyone in the village we could, and then started on our way. Of course, *starting* meant one more descent down the treacherous path leading to the school.

We paused at the school and said good bye to Khalid and the students before we continued our hike down to the beginning (or *end*, depending on your perspective) of the road where Majhuud's truck was still parked, exactly where he had left it two days earlier upon our arrival at Al-Haza.

This was yet another village with people who had a very significant impact on my life. They treated Sian and me with great respect as their honored guests. Sadly, they were people I would most likely never get the chance to see again. They are people the world would never even know existed. But you now know, because I've taken the time to write and tell you about them. They are people whose existence really matters.

Sian and I made ourselves comfortable in the cab of Majhuud's truck. No one else from the village accompanied us. And so we began the slow, bumpy, winding ride to Suq al-Munabbih.

My mind was not at peace. I knew a challenge still lay ahead of us ... most likely a *big* challenge. Namely, I would have to face the Police Chief. He surely would have heard about us entering his district, and heading out to Majhuud's village. That meant he'd have his men on the lookout for us. There was no other way out of the region ... we had to pass through Suq al-Munabbih. I would have to face him and his question, "Where is the paper from security that gives you permission to be out here in Munabbih?" asked with his ever so serious expression.

I would have to answer him honestly, "Sir, I didn't get the extra permission." I knew I was guilty of disobeying his authority, and that very well might be considered a threat. I wondered if this time I would end up *in* the prison as a prisoner instead of as a guest.

The only way to avoid facing the Police Chief, would be if Sian and I could immediately find a ride, as soon as we arrived in Suq al-Munabbih, and then depart before he even knew we had come out of Majhuud's village ... although I knew it was very unlikely.

But something else was haunting me ... I hadn't informed Majhuud about what the Police Chief had demanded of me. I sure hoped I wasn't going to get Majhuud into trouble. I would feel terrible if that happened, especially after everything he had done for us.

We pulled into Suq al-Munabbih, at which point we thanked Majhuud over and over again for his hospitality, emphasizing what a great memorable time we had.

Majhuud knew we needed to find a ride to Sa'da, and he promised he'd be asking around for us. I told him that we'd be waiting at the school.

"Praise be to God for your safe arrival!" our Egyptian friends greeted us. "Welcome! Welcome!" They were genuinely glad to see us again. Soon we were all sipping tea and chatting together. They were very interested in hearing all about our big adventure in Majhuud's village, something I was sure they would never get the opportunity to experience for themselves.

"Please, stay here with us tonight," Ibrahim offered.

"Thanks for the invitation, but we really need to return to Sa'da," I said, and then asked hopefully, "Have you heard of anyone who might be driving to Sa'da soon?"

"No, but we'll ask around for you," said Hassan.

But then the dreaded moment arrived. We had only just finished our tea when someone showed up at the school and informed us, "The Police Chief wants to see you right away." There was no chance of avoiding him now.

The Egyptians looked at me, and must have been thinking, "Not again!"

I really started regretting the plan of action I had decided on, because in spite of the fact that I didn't have the extra permission paper, I should have at least shown the Police Chief the proper respect due him by going immediately upon our arrival to report our presence to him. And so not only had I challenged his authority, but I may have insulted him as well ... not a good thing to do anywhere in the Middle East.

"Please come visit me in prison," I said to the Egyptians jokingly. "Can we leave our things here?"

"Yes, of course," replied Ibrahim.

Sian and I stood up and then started walking slowly along the path leading up to the prison. "Are you okay?" Sian asked me.

"I'm fine," I said in my typical stoic manner. But in reality there was a pounding in my chest, a dizziness in my head, and a sick feeling in my gut. Needless to say, it was not from the exertion of going up the incline, but rather from the fear quickly building up inside me. I was on the verge of panic.

I couldn't control it. I knew something dreadful was about to happen. I assumed the doom was only going to come down on me, and not on Sian. So after I was imprisoned she'd be able to inform the authorities back in Sa'da of my whereabouts ... not that anyone could do anything about it. As I pointed out earlier, the Yemeni government had no control over this part of the country ... but at least they would be informed of the missing foreigner, and so could start some sort of negotiations for my release.

A servant met us at the entrance, and he escorted us past the prisoners in chains on the bottom level. Sian had not seen this part of the village before. I observed them more closely this time, picturing myself sitting amongst them in the very near future ... wondering what it would feel like to be placed in irons, something that, before coming to

Munabbih, I assumed only happened in history past and in movies. "It sure would be a great opportunity to learn their dialect," I thought, trying to cheer myself up.

We climbed the stairs, reached the landing, and then as we stood outside the door of the Police Chief's office, I turned to Sian and said, "Just let me do all the talking."

"Sounds good to me," she responded.

I wasn't sure how much Sian noticed of the dread I was feeling. I was just hoping I wouldn't pass out.

The servant went in first to announce our arrival. Then he came back out and led us through the door. I went in first, followed by Sian.

The Police Chief was sitting in his place of authority, looking very stern ... his silent gaze only increasing the fear I was already feeling. I was sure he must have been able to see my heart pounding away at an ever increasing rate, and the beads of sweat on my forehead. Those are always telltale signs that you're guilty of something or other.

Then he asked me the dreaded question (thump, thump, thump went my heart) ... and I think he already knew the answer before I even opened my mouth, "Did you get the special permission to come out to Munabbih like I asked you to last time?"

It wasn't easy (thump, thump, thump), but I looked him straight in the eye as I answered, "No sir," with my uncontrollably shaky voice.

"So why did you come out here again?" he asked. Before I could answer he added, "And who is this person you brought along with you?" as he looked over and pointed at Sian. "I suppose she doesn't have permission to be out here either."

My eyes automatically followed the Police Chief's finger and looked at Sian. She didn't look him in the eye, didn't budge, didn't even look nervous. "Wow, she's doing well," I thought.

"No sir," I said again to the Police Chief. I thought I would just keep it brief and be very respectful of his authority. And don't think I didn't respect him. He was a very powerful man.

"So who is she?" He asked.

I replied to him with the same answer I'd been using all along, "She's my sister, and I brought her along so she could talk with the women in the village we visited."

His eyes were trying to read me, trying to penetrate my mind. It was obvious he was very suspicious of my motives for coming all the way out to Munabbih ... not once, but twice. He was trying to figure out what I was really involved in that would bring me out to such a remote area.

"Tell me about what you were doing in the village ... in Al-Haza," he finally demanded. He never raised his voice, never really showed any anger, just always let it be known that he was in charge.

I took a deep breath and proceeded to talk about my Arabic dialects research ... something I had already told him all about the last time I met with him. He listened carefully as I explained things to him, emphasizing the necessity of bringing along Sian to work with the women. I also explained that getting the extra permission he requested would have taken far too long because I only had a limited amount of time within which to carry out my research. I knew he himself would be very aware of how the system worked, and that what I said was true.

He never interrupted me once during my speech ... listening intently ... probably waiting for something contradictory to pop up in what I was telling him.

While I was still waxing eloquent, Majhuud was suddenly ushered into the room. He had gone to the school and was told we had been summoned by the Police Chief. He greeted the Police Chief, greeted us, took a seat, and then asked, "Is there a problem?"

Talking about my research had calmed me down significantly, but with Majhuud's presence in the room, I started to tense up again ... because now Majhuud was going to find out about a significant piece of information that I hadn't shared with him.

The Police Chief started to explain the situation to him. I was watching Majhuud as he did so, looking for a reaction. Majhuud just listened. If what he heard bothered him, he never showed it. He had every right to turn to me and say, "Why didn't you tell me all this?" But he didn't.

When the Police Chief had finished his exposition, he looked over at us, and then turned to Majhuud and asked, "Please tell me what they were doing in your village."

Majhuud and the Police Chief were both important men in that region, and they obviously knew each other well, and they showed each other respect. I knew the Police Chief would take seriously whatever Majhuud had to say. So our fate was now in his hands.

In his usual composed manner, Majhuud proceeded to fearlessly explain what we were doing for the last two days in Al-Haza ... namely, we were doing linguistic research ... and nothing more.

It was Majhuud's defense that finally satisfied the Police Chief. You can just imagine how relieved I was. I was so thankful Majhuud had still been in Suq al-Munabbih, or who knows what would have happened.

The Police Chief once again turned his penetrating gaze towards me and Sian. I was still anticipating some sort of consequence, or at least a lecture for my blatant disobedience. He merely said, with the use of imperatives, "Listen, and I'm talking very seriously. Do not come back to Munabbih again, and I mean never, unless you obtain permission from Sa'da security. Understood?"

What a relief! "Yes sir, I understand," I said very humbly.

Did I sense the hint of a smile? Then he added in a more friendly tone, "If you do get permission, then you're more than welcome."

"Thank you sir. I'm very sorry I caused you so much trouble," I said as Sian and I stood up to leave. "Thank you for your kindness, and may God keep you and prosper you."

"And thank you again, Sheikh Majhuud, for your hospitality over the past two days," I said.

Then to both of them we said, "Peace be with you," as Sian and I started heading towards the door.

"And with you be peace," they both replied.

Majhuud stayed in the office, and I couldn't help but wonder if we were still the subject of further discussions.

A servant met us at the landing and led us down the stairs, past the prisoners, and most importantly, outside of the prison. Sian and I, feeling more lighthearted, headed back to the school where we told the Egyptian teachers about what had just transpired.

They sure must have wondered about me, having the gall to come all the way out to the end of the earth, not once, but twice, and both times without the necessary permission to do so ... and getting away with it both times. They knew very well that they could never get away with such a thing themselves ... and why would they ever want to? Westerners sure are a strange breed.

Sian and I still had to wait for some time before a ride came along. While we were waiting, we looked up and, much to our delight, saw a rainbow.

Soon after that we were on our way to Sa'da ... with nothing unusual happening along the way. We left with many memories, with data collected, and ready for some needed relaxation.

37

Lost in the Desert

Just as I had expected, Sian's limited time to help me with my research was all used up on those first two trips ... the trips to Raazih and Munabbih. Not only was her time used up, but I assumed her energy was used up too. Those two trips had taken quite a bit out of both of us ... but much more for her, most of the time having to deal with uneducated women who spoke a very different Arabic dialect which they were unable to adjust to accommodate her. So, I was quite sure that, even if she did find the time, she wouldn't have wanted to go on any more adventures with me.

Then one day, not long after the Munabbih trip, there was a knock on my guardhouse door in Sana'a. "Peter', you've got a phone call," Wout informed me. So I followed my host inside his house and picked up the receiver, "Hello?"

The voice said, "Hi Butros, it's Sian. I'll have a free weekend at the beginning of May. Do you want me to help you some more with your research?"

"Do I?!" I said, astonished at my good luck. "You bet I do!"

I had a few decisions to make. Should I take Sian with me to Barat, which was a little more complicated to get to, or should she accompany me to Al Hazm, which was a somewhat more straight forward route? Considering the time element, I chose Al Hazm.

Next, I had to think about transportation. I didn't want to end up spending most of our precious hours waiting for rides, otherwise it wouldn't even be worth taking the trip in the first place. So we definitely couldn't depend on local transportation. That meant I'd need to rent a 4-wheeler.

"Jeff, is there a car rental place you could recommend to me?" I asked the director of the American Institute for Yemeni Studies the next time I paid the institute a visit.

"Our institute has a Toyota Landcruiser that members are allowed to rent," he informed me.

"You're kidding. I didn't know that," I said with renewed hope.

We talked through all the particulars. The cost to rent the Landcruiser was very reasonable, and it was in great shape, almost new. I immediately booked it for the May weekend.

Hey, I know what you must be thinking, and I was thinking the same thing at the time ... should I be taking a chance by driving out to a very remote and wild part of Yemen without a local in charge of getting me to my destination? Well, why not? I mean, what could go wrong?

Then came another twist to things ... Sian phoned again and asked, "Would you mind if someone else joined us on the up-coming trip?"

"Who did you have in mind?" I inquired with some hesitation in my voice.

"Karen would like to come along," she clarified.

Karen was a single American girl who worked with Sian. I guess word was getting around that I provided the best tours ever in North Yemen. I really couldn't see a problem with having another person along. I didn't have any problems with my permission paper the last time I went to Al Hazm, and so I expected I'd be able to talk my way through having two additional people with me ... I hoped.

"Sure, that sounds fine," I replied. "In fact, I think having Karen along would provide you with good company while we're in the village doing the testing."

"That's just what I was thinking," Sian admitted. "In fact, I could get her to handle the tape recorder while I deal with the women."

"Okay, go ahead and tell Karen she can come along," I said.

I would just stick with the line that Sian was my sister. And then expand it by saying that Karen was her friend. Now that part was very true!

On May 7th, the day of our departure, Sian and Karen both had to work, which meant we weren't able to start driving until early afternoon. A serious drawback to starting so late in the day, meant we would end up driving the last stretch to Al Hazm in the dark. And yet I wanted to make sure we arrived at our destination on Thursday so we would have more of the weekend to find people who would be willing to participate in the comprehension testing. We would only have Friday, which is the Muslim day of rest, and part of Saturday. The girls would have to be back at work on Sunday morning, which was the start of the work week in Yemen.

We drove through Sana'a itself to get onto the main highway which put us in a northeasterly direction. Then coming off the high mountain plateau where the city is situated, we slowly wound our way down the perilously steep mountainous terrain until we finally reached flat ground which put us in a more easterly direction, heading towards Marib.[33] We would end up driving about half way to Marib before turning off to start heading north towards Al Hazm.

While on the Marib highway, we were stopped at three military checkpoints. Each time I would produce a copy of my *to whom it may concern* paper, and not once did a guard ask for anything from either of the girls. They didn't even ask where we were going, most likely just assuming we were driving straight to Marib. So far so good.

"There are the green and yellow barrels marking our turn off," I informed the girls. "All we have to do now is follow the barrels, and they'll lead us all the way to Baraqish."[34]

35

It was quickly approaching sunset by the time we turned off the main road ... and it wasn't much longer before we were driving along in the dark.

"Sorry you can't see anything," I said to the girls, "but there really isn't anything to see anyway." And sure enough, it was nothing more than sand and rocks all the way to Baraqish. Up to that point in time, everything was going well ... *up to that point.*

---

[33] Historically, Marib was the capital of the Sabaean kingdom, which some scholars believe to be the ancient kingdom of Sheba mentioned in the Old Testament of the Bible (see 1 Kings chapter 10). Marib is located about 120 kilometers east of Sana'a.

[34] Baraqish is the very important and impressive historical site that I mentioned in chapter 27, *The bad shot.*

[35] Photo taken by Sian.

Once we reached Baraqish, we were on our own ... with no more barrels to guide us. I knew we needed to head further north and a little more to the east. And so with Baraqish as my starting point, and having studied a map, it was easy enough to point the truck in the proper direction.

When we started on our way that afternoon, I was quite confident I could get us to our destination ... no problem. But my confidence was quickly fading. When the guy who almost got me shot a month earlier was driving me out of the region, it seemed so straight forward, and for some reason I recalled a distinct path leading through the desert. But now that I was the one doing the driving I couldn't make out a path. And if I would have reread my notes,[36] I would have known better ... tire tracks went off in every which direction on the packed sand.

I just drove on, carrying us further and further out into the middle of that large flat unfamiliar uninviting desert. Eventually I had to admit to myself (I didn't dare say it out loud to the girls) that I had no idea where we were, or how much further we still had to go, or in what direction we should be going. We were lost in the desert ... lost in the middle of a desert *at night*. Although I'm not sure daylight would have helped me much, except there might have been other vehicles out during the daytime that I could have waved down and asked for directions.

I was afraid if we just carried on, then we might end up driving way too far off course and eventually run out of gas and have to start walking. Scenes from movies came to mind ... images of skeletons laying on the sand in the middle of a desert somewhere ... those fools who didn't know any better than to go wandering off into a desert.

I wasn't trained to figure out directions by looking at the stars. I didn't even have a compass! Yes, I felt very unprepared ... and I felt very very stupid.

I suddenly had memories of the time I was out in the middle of a forest and thought I knew the direction I needed to head, but ended up getting disoriented and lost. That was the summer I was working for my friend Glen, the geologist. Yup, this was the second time I managed to get myself lost in nature. At least the first time I could pull out a compass to help get me back on track.

I decided to drive on just a little further, and I was encouraged when we came across a dry river bed. I was sure it would lead us to some

---

[36] See chapter 27.

inhabitants somewhere, so I followed it. We drove along and crossed it a couple of times. There wasn't a house, or a tent, or a single human being anywhere to be seen.

I finally gave up. I admitted (to myself) that I wasn't able to get us out of this mess on my own. We were hopelessly lost.

Then to make matters worse, at one point, as we were maneuvering along through the river bed, I felt an uncomfortable sinking of the wheels. We had driven right into some soft sand. I'm sure glad I had a strong heart ... it was just pounding away in my chest. So, not only were we lost, but we were now stuck!

38

The Missing Village

There we were, sitting in the dark, stuck in the sand, and hopelessly lost in a desert. Wait a minute. I suddenly remembered I was driving a 4-wheel drive. 4-wheelers don't get stuck! I reached over and shifted the little lever into the 4-wheel drive position. Then I slowly took my foot off the clutch and the vehicle rolled forward a bit. Then I put it in reverse and tried it again, and sure enough we moved backwards. We weren't sunk yet (pun intended)! With all four wheels working together, they managed to get enough grip ... and before I knew it, we were free ... although still lost.

I drove the vehicle slowly out of the gully, and as we reached the higher level ground once again, suddenly, off in the distance, I saw something. "Hey, I see a set of headlights," I said to the girls.

"No, there are actually two sets of headlights," Sian pointed out.

Sure enough, two vehicles were driving through the desert. But they weren't coming our way ... they were slowly but surely veering off, turning away from us.

Hope replaced despair. "I'm going to follow them," I informed the girls.

My heart started pounding again as I quickly put the Landcruiser back into 2-wheel drive and started heading straight for those headlights ... well actually toward the taillights now that the vehicles had turned and were heading away from us. I was determined not to lose sight of them.

I kept accelerating, gearing up to the highest gear as we flew over the sand, following those Yemenis who had no idea they were in the process of rescuing three foreigners. I never took my eyes off those vehicles, and just hoped that some unexpected obstacle wasn't going to suddenly appear in front of us. That would have been a disaster considering the speed we were going.

As we drew ever closer to the other trucks, I started slowing down and kept my distance, but still kept following them, confident that they would eventually end up at some village somewhere (I no longer cared which village), and then we'd finally be able to ask someone for directions to Al Hazm. Somehow, though, I had the feeling they were heading in the very direction we wanted to go.

When we eventually hit a gravel road, I was pretty sure it was the road leading to Al Hazm. Sure enough, a few minutes later we drove past the spot where I had waited so long for a ride ... the ride that almost got me shot over a joke.[37]

But I didn't stop. We drove right on through Al Hazm and out the other end ... out the north end of the town. Our real destination was not Al Hazm itself, but rather Muslaab-A,[38] a less educated area. That's where I intended to do the comprehension testing. I already knew Haadi and his brothers, and I thought they might be willing to help me get cooperation from the local population.

Not far out of Al Hazm we hit a military check point. They stopped us, looked me over, and then glanced over at the two girls. Much to my surprise, they just waived us on. They didn't even ask to see any ID whatsoever. I found that very strange.

When the same thing happened at the next check point, I started to wonder. Obviously they were thinking that I was someone I was not. "I wonder who they think we are?" I asked the girls without really expecting an answer.

When we hit the next (which ended up being the last) check point, I decided to ask for some directions. I didn't have a map. I was just going by memory. Umm, okay, so my memory didn't work all that great between Baraqish and Al Hazm ... and it seemed to be failing me again. So I asked one of the guards (in Arabic, of course) the best way to get to Suq Al-Athneyn. I told him I was going there to visit a friend. Without any hesitation, the guard gave me directions ... with no questions asked.

Later, after our return to Sana'a, when I related my check point experiences to Jeff, the AIYS director, he said the guards at the check points must have assumed I was working with Hunt Oil Company. Hunt was working in the area at the time, and their employees drove vehicles which looked exactly like the one I was driving. So obviously the Hunt employees enjoyed a lot of freedom to move around ... and thanks to Hunt, so did I.

The dark drive continued, and we eventually arrived at Suq Al-Athneyn. It hadn't taken us long at all. Then we headed in the direction of Muslaab ... again, to the best of my recollection. I remembered

---

[37] See chapter 27, *The bad shot.*
[38] See chapter 24, *Ghost and Clown.*

leaving Muslaab on a gravel road heading east. So I found a gravel road and started heading west.

When we arrived at the end of the gravel road, I wasn't sure where to go next, so I just continued driving along the same road which was now dirt. Once again I had no idea where I was going.

We passed some fields and houses along the way. I needed to get some more directions, but didn't think I should just walk up to any house and knock and ask ... although that probably would have worked too. Eventually I noticed a few rifle-toting men coming out of a house. So I got up the nerve to pull over the truck. They automatically looked up, watching as I jumped out of the cab of the truck. I walked over and greeted them. They were surprised to find themselves face-to-face with a foreigner speaking to them in Arabic.

"Can you tell me how to get to Muslaab?" I asked.

"Yes ... in fact we can take you there," one of them answered with a very friendly tone to his voice. "Follow us."

"Thank you," I said.

They hopped into their truck and started to drive, while we drove along behind them. We hadn't gone very far before they pulled over in front of another house. All three of them hurried inside.

"Okay, so where are we?" I was wondering.

Suddenly two of them reappeared and, still carrying their rifles, approached our truck. "We'll take you where you want to go now," one of them informed me through my open window.

Hmmm, time to do a quick assessment of the situation. I had just assumed that the three men would continue driving in their truck and we would follow them in ours. I guess the third man owned the other truck and didn't want to get involved. The next thing I know these two guys are standing next to me with their rifles obviously expecting to ride with us. So should I be getting suspicious, or what? I sure hoped I wasn't taking a chance. But really, if they had wanted to steal anything from us they could have easily done so by now.

"Karen, why don't you get into the front seat beside Sian so these two guys can get into the back seat," I instructed her.

Once everyone was in their assigned seats, I put the vehicle back in gear and they proceeded to direct me.

When we arrived at Muslaab, the men told me to pull over in front of a school. So I assumed we were in Muslaab-B, because, as you may recall, Muslaab-A didn't have a school.

Our two guides and I jumped out of the truck, and walked up to the school. I noticed a Sudanese teacher sitting inside. I greeted him, introduced myself, and then asked him about the family where I had stayed when I came from Barat to Muslaab the first time. I mentioned Haadi by name, and described the house and the area. But, after listening very patiently, he informed me that I was in the wrong place.

Just to be sure, the kind man decided to take us to ask a couple of locals. Again, I described how I had stayed with Haadi in Muslaab. Neither of them could help me either.

My guides started to interact with the men as well, and in the end they all agreed that the village I was looking for was a place called Maslab and not Muslaab. So I thanked them for their help, and the two armed men got back into the truck with us and offered to lead us to Maslab. And to make things even more confusing, I found out there was also a place called Masluub in that region!

The dirt roads (no pavement to be found anywhere) were relatively flat, although from time to time a knoll would appear ... but they never really posed a problem. I merely drove up and over them, and we continued on our way. But on one occasion, as we reached the summit of one of those small hills, we were all suddenly jerked forward. I managed to bash my shoulder against the steering wheel (nothing serious), whereas everyone else seemed fine, just shaken. The front end of the truck had fallen into a crevice. All the locals would, of course, know about the gaping hole, and they'd just drive a little further to the right as they ascended the hill so as to avoid it. Why bother putting up a barrier to prevent non-locals from falling in! I was stuck for the second (and hopefully last) time that night.

I put the Toyota back into 4-wheel drive and then into reverse. The front right and back left wheels were the only ones still on solid ground, and thankfully they gripped, so that we were quickly on the level again. Then I cranked the wheel hard to the right and we drove on with no unusual noise resulting ... so it appeared the truck was still mechanically sound. At the time, I didn't even bother looking to see what damage was done to the vehicle, but later when I did look, the nice new Landcruiser had a slightly bent bumper.

When we arrived in Maslab, the presence of a school once again indicated that it wasn't the village I was looking for. Once again, if I would have had my notes with me, I would have realized right away that I had been in Maslab once before. That's where Haadi had taken me to find my ride to Al Hazm.[39]

By then I decided I had better just give up on my goal of finding that elusive village, and rather see if we could get some testing done in Maslab. I was quite certain Sian and Karen had had just about enough of this night traveling, and our guides had helped us about as much as I could expect them to.

So I drove up to the school, jumped out of the truck, and approached the three rather surprised Egyptian teachers who worked there.

"Peace be with you," I greeted them.

"And with you be peace," all three of them responded, waiting in anticipation to see what would come out of my mouth next.

In my Jordanian Arabic, I told them our story, concluding with, "and that's how we ended up here." I sure hoped that my sob story would earn us an invitation to stay with them.

The three of them looked at each other and then back at us again, and then one of them said, "Please Butros (for I had told them my name), why don't the three of you stay right here with us." Hopefully having two single women with me wasn't the deciding factor.

"No, we couldn't do that. We don't want to be any bother," I said, making sure not to sound too anxious to take them up on their invitation, but knowing very well they would say, "it's no bother at all."

And sure enough, out came those very words, the words of honor, "it's no bother at all."

Oh, how grateful I was to hear those words. "If you're really sure," I continued.

"Yes, yes, please stay here with us as our guests," they now insisted.

The sob story had worked. "Then we accept. We would be honored to be your guests," I ended the argument while it was still going in our favor. I could indeed say that with all sincerity, because we really were feeling like they meant it.

At that, I turned my attention back to our two Yemeni guides. "Thank you so much for your help," I said to them. "We're going to stay here in Maslab," telling them what they themselves had just heard with their own ears.

"You're most welcome. Do you need anything else?" asked one of them.

---

[39] See chapter 26, *The Last Stop*.

"May God keep you," I responded.

And with that they turned and started to walk away.

"Wait a second," I called after them, "do you want me to give you a ride somewhere?"

"No thank you," said one of them as they continued walking.

I had no idea where they lived, they didn't ask for a ride, I assumed they wouldn't have just walked away if they had a long ways to go. It was a mystery. They were kind, helpful, asked for nothing in return, and then just left.

39

The Drowsy Village

The three Egyptian teachers, Sa'iid, Yahya, and Abd Al-Mawjuud, treated us royally. They offered us their own room which was, as usual, attached right to the school ... originally built just to be another classroom. And with their room came their three mattresses ... all part of the package deal.

"At least the teachers working in Yemen never have much of a commute to get to work every morning," Sian commented as we started moving into our room.

"I'm not sure I'd want to live that close to work," Karen kept the humor going (Sian and Karen were both teachers).

The Egyptians stayed in another school room, which I never did get to see, and so had no idea what condition it was in, or what they ended up sleeping on. I assumed they had scrounged up a few more mattresses for themselves from somewhere.

Something I neglected to mention earlier was that we arrived in Maslab during the month of Ramadan ... the Muslim holy month which is dedicated to abstaining from any food and drink whatsoever throughout the daylight hours. If you're not familiar with Ramadan, sorry, but I'm not going to take the time to dwell on it here ... it's easy enough to find information on the internet. What I will tell you is that Ramadan was not the best time to be doing any kind of research.

I guess you want to know why, right? So that means I should tell you something more about Ramadan ... well, at least about how Ramadan affected segments of the North Yemen population. The adults, especially the men, usually stay up most of the night while it was dark so they can eat and drink, and then they end up sleeping much of the daylight hours away. Well that was one way to deal with the *fasting*.

So that meant we most likely wouldn't get much cooperation unless we could find people who would be willing to interact with us (and be tested) during the night hours.

This was something I was well aware of before we started on the trip. But since it was the only time Sian could accompany me, I had to take a chance that maybe, just maybe, we'd still get some cooperation.

Sian, Karen and I sat and visited with our Egyptian hosts on into the wee hours of the morning ... they were also functioning on Ramadan time. We shared their food, had tea, chatted ... it was relaxing and enjoyable. That was just what we needed to help us forget those awkward moments of being lost numerous times prior to our arrival in Maslab. We finally turned in at 3 AM!

In spite of the previous exhausting day, I still couldn't manage to sleep past 7 AM. I suppose the many cups of strong sweet tea didn't help. So I got up and, as quietly as possible, went outside to have a look around. You can make out the one-story school building where we were staying in the middle of the following photo[40] ... a couple of people are walking right in front of the school.

There was very little movement that early in the morning ... mostly just some smaller children who had probably slept through most of the night. When they woke they were in all probability shoved out the front door so they wouldn't disturb the drowsy parents who wanted to get some more sleep.

Since it was already light, according to Ramadan rules, there would be no breakfast that morning, or tea break, or lunch, or anything whatsoever ... neither food nor drink until the sun set.

Well, there were actually some exceptions to the fasting rules. For instance, sick people didn't have to fast, and nursing mothers were not expected to fast, and neither were very young children. And if you were traveling, you could make up for any missed fasting days at another

---

[40] All three photos in this chapter were taken by Sian.

time. But even if someone wasn't fasting, they were expected not to consume anything in public places. For instance, in Jordan with a five percent Christian population, even though they didn't fast, Christians still refrained from eating in public.

So Sian, Karen and I really could claim two of those exceptions ... first of all, we weren't Muslims, and secondly, we were on a trip. We had actually brought along a small stash of food, and therefore did have a little something to eat for breakfast in the privacy of our room so as not to offend anyone.

Wanting to make sure we kept our focus on the work we had come to do, my ears were wide open, tuned in for any sound of movement from the Egyptians. I was definitely hoping the teachers would help us make contact with the local population, which I assumed would start with the student body.

"I think I heard something outside," I informed the girls, just prior to popping my head out the door. Sure enough, the Egyptians were out and about.

The three of us made our exit so we could interact with them, and then *casually* bring up the subject of comprehension testing again. I say *again*, because we had already talked about it the evening before, but I just wanted to make sure it happened.

"Good morning friends," I greeted them.

"Good morning Butros," responded Yahya in a sleepy voice.

"Good morning to all of you," added Abd Al-Mawjuud. "How did you sleep?"

"Praise be to God. Very well, thank you," answered Sian.

"Thank you for letting us use your room. We were very comfortable. You are very generous," I added.

"You're welcome," said Yahya, pleased to hear that.

"When will your students arrive?" I inquired.

"The students should be arriving soon," replied Sa'iid who had just sauntered out to join the rest of us.

I decided to get right to the point, "What do you think, will we be able to interact with some of your students after classes are done?"

"Of course ... of course," said Yayha.

"We would prefer to get help from the older ones," I clarified.

"Sure, I'll talk with them about it," Yahya said. "I'm the one who teaches all the oldest students."

It wasn't much longer before the students started arriving. But little did they know that their teachers were going to turn it into a show-and-tell day ... the teachers having miraculously produced three Westerners for them to meet.

Sian and Karen and I were sitting outside as the students started to arrive, and we were definitely spotted and gawked at. A lot of whispering was going on as they entered their classrooms.

The teachers were in their respective classrooms for only a few moments before Yahya suddenly reappeared and said, "Butros, please come in ... what I mean is, all three of you should come in."

That was rather unexpected. I thought they'd go through their teaching routine for a few hours before introducing us to any of the students.

"Okay, here we go," I said to the girls, who also thought this was rather sudden.

We walked towards Yahya, not quite knowing what to expect. Then Yahya had the three of us parade into his classroom and stand in front while he introduced us and told the students why we were in Maslab. It was a fairly accurate introduction, although I didn't like the part where he used the word *testing* when explaining what we wanted to do. The word *test* always puts fear in the heart of any student. I would have to correct that once I started to *test* the students' comprehension of the texts.

I was surprised that Yahya's class (and the other classes as well) were mixed, boys and girls together ... although all the girls sat at the very back of the classroom. Quite a number of girls were in attendance, making up roughly twenty percent of the overall student body. So there appeared to be a fair amount of variation from one part of the country to the next as to how education was handled, and how the genders were mixed or kept separate.

We weren't asked to say anything at that point. Once he was done introducing us, Yahya indicated we were free to go, so we made our exit. We would have to wait (I didn't know for how long), but I was encouraged, feeling sure we would get some cooperation.

The three of us loitered around the school, at times listening in on what was going on inside the classrooms, and for a time just sitting and chatting ... but all the time waiting for the go ahead from Yahya.

Usually during Ramadan, work hours and school hours are significantly reduced, and so after just a couple of hours of waiting, suddenly the schoolrooms started emptying out.

Most of the younger students bolted off, whereas the older students hung around, some of them watching us from a distance, and others coming up and freely mingling with us.

Yahya came out, and after interacting with a few of the students, called us over and said, "These are the older boys and girls who will help you. Butros, why don't you use my classroom. Sian and Karen can use the classroom next door, okay?"

"That sounds great," I responded.

And so we set up our tape recorders and got started. I had success testing one of the 13 year old boys while Sian tested a teenage girl. But when I started the process with a second boy, he became so nervous that I didn't even bother to finish testing him. I just barely had the chance to thank him for a job well done before he dashed out the door.

After that, I had no more cooperation from the boys ... the rest of them had all disappeared. Sian managed to test a second girl, but that was it for her too. It was very discouraging.

"Well, I really can't blame them," I said to Sian and Karen as they came out of their classroom.

"I guess that's not the way they wanted to spend the free part of their Ramadan," Karen said.

Most likely the kids all headed home to get naps since even they usually stayed up pretty late.

The whole village was for the most part non-functional, and stayed that way until mid-afternoon. And that included the Egyptians who had disappeared into their room while we were doing the testing ... which is how the rest of the students managed to get away ... the teachers weren't around to keep them corralled and cooperative.

"So what do you say we snooze while the rest of the village snoozes," I suggested.

"Agreed," both Karen and Sian chimed.

A short nap can do wonders for morale. We all felt refreshed, and so did the rest of the village ... but that didn't mean any of them got excited about being tested. We did manage to get a little more cooperation ... emphasis on the word *little*. By the end of the day Sian had tested a total of three females and I had done four males ... far far short of what I had hoped for, but better than nothing.

We spent another evening into the early morning hours interacting with the Egyptians. I found out something astonishing during the course of our conversation ...

"Are you serious," I said incredulously.

"Yes," Yahya insisted.

"You mean the Ministry of Education really makes the teachers change schools every year?" I asked, repeating what Sa'iid just told me, wanting to make sure that I had understood him correctly.

"That's right," he said.

"Doesn't that make it hard for you? I mean having to move, and get resettled?" I dug deeper.

"It's okay, as long as we end up moving to a better location, which is often what happens for teachers who have been in the country longer," said Yahya.

I had to admit that his last statement made sense from their perspective of moving up the scale, and yet I thought about the many different dialects and customs throughout North Yemen, which sometimes differed greatly from one district to another, and how hard it would be for the Egyptians to adjust.

Well, as I said, my research goal was to put them out of a job, pushing for the need to have more Yemeni teachers replacing the Egyptians.

After another night in the school, we left late the next morning since the girls needed to return to Sana'a. The weekend was over. The drive back was uneventful ... never even lost my way once.

40

The Adrenaline Wanes

At 4:30 AM I was already standing at the bus station in Sana'a, with ticket in hand, waiting to catch one of the big fancy buses to Sa'da city. I wouldn't actually be going all the way to Sa'da. I would be getting off at the bus stop in the town of Al Harf, which was located about two thirds of the way to Sa'da ... just over a 100 kilometer drive. Based on what I heard, and from what I saw on a map, it should be a much more straight forward way to get to Barat than the last time when I set out from Sa'da city.[41]

It was just three days since Sian, Karen and I had returned from the drowsy village of Maslab. My time in North Yemen was quickly drawing to a close. My flight to Canada was booked for May 25th ... less than two weeks away.

I was feeling burned out from all the traveling I had done thus far. I definitely had no desire to take any more trips to outlying parts of North Yemen. And yet I wanted to complete my research ... and that meant taking this one last trip to Barat in order to do the comprehension testing. Not that my research would be *complete*, since I wouldn't have Sian with me to test the women.

In addition to my lack of energy and enthusiasm, I felt lonely. It was nice to have company on my past three trips. And now I was all on my own again. On top of all that, it was still the month of Ramadan.

The bus left at 5 AM ... right on time. And three hours later I was stepping off the bus in Al Harf. Then came the unpredictable part, namely, finding a ride to my destination, which was the town of Kharab located within the Barat region. As you may recall, I had passed through Kharab on my last trip into Barat[42] ... the expected *wasteland* that wasn't.

Because of Ramadan, most people, having stayed up during most of the night hours, were probably still in bed at 8 AM when I showed up ...

---

[41] See chapter 19, *The Exchange.*
[42] See chapter 23, *The Resort.*

and would most likely be in bed for some hours yet to come. Al Harf had the look of a ghost town.

"Hello Butros," said a voice from behind me.

I turned around and saw the man from the local store who I had interacted with a number of times over the past hours. "Hello Muhammad. What's your news?" I asked.

"There's a man driving to Kharab and I told him you needed a ride," he said.

"That's great news. Thanks for remembering me," I said.

"No problem," he replied as the two of us walked to his store.

I took a quick glance at my watch. It was 2 PM. The driver was friendly, and my despondency started to dissipate.

The dirt and rock road was actually fairly flat most of the way to Kharab ... meaning, not too hilly ... but not meaning *smooth* by any means. One and a half hours later we were pulling into Kharab. It was definitely a shorter and easier ride than it had been from Sa'da city.

I was immediately on the lookout for ways to make contacts in the town. This time the place that stood out to me first was the hospital, and that's where I headed.

"Hello, is anybody here," I called out to an open door.

I could hear some movement inside, and then some voices, one male and one female. They weren't speaking a Yemeni dialect, of that I was sure.

A man appeared at the opening and looked out.

"Peace be with you," I said to the astonished man. I could tell right away that he was Sudanese.

"And with you be peace," he replied.

"My name is Butros ..." I went on, introducing myself, and telling him briefly why I was in Kharab.

"Welcome Butros. My name is Ali and I work here at the hospital," he said.

I was very pleased to bump into a friendly man. I found out that he was a male nurse. He and his wife and their three young children lived right at the hospital.

"Butros, where are you going to stay while you're here in Kharab?" he eventually asked. It was a question I truly enjoyed hearing.

"I'm not sure yet," I responded. "I assume there's a hotel here in Kharab. Can you tell me where it is?"

"No, you can't stay in the hotel," he scolded me for even thinking such a thought. "I want you to stay here with us as our guest."

Nothing would have suited me better, although I still went through the not wanting to be a bother argument routine, knowing just when to stop so I actually could stay with them.

And so the hospital ended up being my home away from home while seeking to make Yemeni contacts to do the testing.

I even had a roommate. "Omar, I'd like you to meet Butros," Ali said to Omar when he arrived at the hospital after his day's work was finished."

Omar was from Somalia. He taught English at the local school, but lived at the hospital. Wow, an English teacher to interact with, that was great. It was a relaxing evening ... good company, good food, no pressure. Just what I needed.

"I think I can do this after all," I encouraged myself. I was back in *work mode* with some regained optimism.

A good night's sleep also helped. Then after breakfast I accompanied Omar to the local school where he introduced me to some of the other teachers ... Sudanese, Somalis, and, of course, Egyptians.

The school in Kharab went up to the first secondary level. I was informed that none of the Kharab girls attended school. Once again the school ended up being a good place to find subjects for the comprehension testing, but it was not limited to the school.

I spent two full days (and three nights) in Kharab. And as I predicted, the testing was limited because of a lack of cooperation during Ramadan. But I persisted enough to find at least seven local males of varying ages who were willing to be tested.

Much time was spent socializing with my hosts who were very gracious, not only providing me with a place to sleep but also feeding me a number of meals.

Departure, travel and arrival in Sana'a were all thankfully rather uneventful.

41

The End

At last all of my travels within the rugged, remote, spectacularly scenic parts of North Yemen came to a close. I hadn't accomplished as much as I had hoped to, and yet there were definite limits to how much I could physically, mentally and emotionally handle ... and believe me, I had definitely reached (and had gone somewhat beyond) my limit.

Something that amazed me was that during my four months spent in North Yemen, in situations where I was often exhausted, stressed, not always in the cleanest environments, and eating whatever was offered to me, I never once got sick.

And if you hadn't noticed during the reading of this book, I want to point out something I already mentioned in the second chapter, and that is, in general, Yemenis are a great bunch of people. Having rubbed shoulders with dozens and dozens of Yemenis under many different circumstances, I was never attacked (intentionally that is ... the rifle shot in Jawf was not specifically intended for me) or threatened physically or verbally or even accused of anything (to my face that is ... and the Police Chief in Munabbih was just doing his job). I was always treated with respect and honor (okay, so maybe a couple of drivers had been rather obnoxious, but they acted that way with Yemenis as well).

Departure day was approaching quickly. The final days were spent writing up notes, getting paperwork in order so I could officially leave the country as planned, and saying many good byes and thank yous.

As I sat at the airport on that final day, with seat assigned, bags checked, having cleared through security and passport control, I had mixed feelings about having reached *the end* of my time in this country which had made quite an impact on me ... sad, because I really enjoyed the country and its people and I would miss them ... numb, because I was burned out ... happy, because I needed a break ... defeated, because I should have given myself more time to do the research ... apprehensive, because of what lay ahead (to be clarified after a few lines) ... and I could go on, but will spare you.

It was 5 AM. I would be flying out on the Lufthansa flight, departure at 7:05.

So here's the apprehensive part ... I had a teaching job lined up at a Canadian University for the summer, and then I'd be heading to the University of Texas in Arlington to finish up my MA in Linguistics, part of which would consist of writing my MA Thesis based on my North Yemen research.

If you'd like to have a look at my thesis, it's called *Communication Among Arabic Varieties: Comprehension Testing in the Yemen Arab Republic.* You can find a copy of it on my website ... petertwele.com.

42

Epilogue

Many historic events have taken place in Yemen since I was there 25 years ago.

Almost exactly three years after my departure, on May 22, 1990, North Yemen and South Yemen became one Yemen known as the *Republic of Yemen*. Four years later (in 1994), a four month civil war broke out between the former North and South Yemens, the south seeking separation. They didn't succeed ... they were defeated. Then another uprising of the South against the North occurred in 2007 with demands for equal treatment, claiming that the northern part of the country was economically privileged. The southern separatists continue their struggle to this day.

That's what's been happening in the south of the country. In chapter 4 (entitled *Base Two*) I mentioned what was happening in the north. In June 2004, an Imam started an insurgency against the government in the Sa'da province which turned into a violent conflict. A ceasefire in June 2007, was followed by a peace agreement in February 2008, but the tensions have continued as each side of the conflict accuses the other side of failing to implement aspects of the peace agreement.

Of course, in recent years the Islamic militant organization Al Qaeda shifted many of its operations from Afghanistan and Pakistan to Yemen, which forced the Yemeni government to put many of its resources into dealing with that threat.

And then to top it all off, the latest development was the *Arab Spring* (sometimes referred to as the *Arab Awakening*) ... an uprising consisting of mass protests calling for President Ali Abdullah Saleh to resign from his 30 year rule ... which he did in November 2011. His departure was meant to pave the way for political reforms.

But the tensions have increased throughout the country, with drastic effects on the population. According to media, nearly half the population is undernourished, and almost half a million people have been displaced from their homes as a result of the ongoing fighting.

During my time of research in 1987, I made it a policy never to discuss politics, and I never took sides. I just focused on the people and my sociolinguistic research. I obviously knew about the tensions, and I hinted at them in some of my chapters. I found kind people both in the areas where the government had control, and in the areas the government didn't control. It always pains me to see people suffer as differences develop into violence. And it pains me even more to think that many of the people I encountered during those months of research may have been displaced from their homes, or worse yet, killed.

I have been to Yemen a number of times since those memorable four months ... with visits to Sana'a, Ta'izz, Aden and Hadhramaut ... but never again to Sa'da or Jawf. I'll have to save some of my other experiences for another book.

Appendix 1

A Linguist's Nightmare

I mentioned in chapter 2 that my goal in going to North Yemen was to carry out sociolinguistic research. Sociolinguistics has to do with the study of the effect of society on the way language is used.

In this appendix I'm going to give you a little background information ... and it all starts with some pre-Yemen research and preparation.

In the spring of 1984, at the University of Texas in Arlington (UTA), where I was working on my MA in Linguistics, I was taking a class called *Language Use in Multilingual Societies*. I decided to write my term paper on *diglossia*.

Diglossia refers to a situation in which a community uses two languages (or dialects) on a regular basis. The community naturally speaks one of the two languages for all informal daily communication ... like interaction at home, or with friends, or in the market place, etc. What's important to note is that this language has a *low* value within that society.

The second language has a *high* value within the society, and is used for all written communication, and is usually only ever *spoken* (though it sounds quite stilted) in formal situations, like education, political speeches, religious sermons, etc.

Arabic happened to be an excellent example of diglossia, and it grabbed my attention (and obviously never let go). So I wrote a research project for my class entitled *Arabic Diglossia: Even More Complex Than It Sounds* (1984).

Arabic has had a long history, both as a written (high) language and as a spoken (low) language, and over time both the high and low languages evolved. The high variety is referred to as *Classical Arabic*. Classical Arabic is the language of the Quran and other ancient writings.

Then there's *Modern Standard Arabic* (MSA) ... and, as its name indicates, MSA is a modernized form of Classical Arabic which was developed to meet the needs of present-day society ... well, at least the needs of the educated segment of society. MSA serves as the literary standard throughout the Middle East and all across North Africa. It's also one of the official six languages of the United Nations. All printed material (with rare exceptions) in the Arab World (books, newspapers, magazines, official documents, and even reading primers for small children) is written in MSA.

Then there are the various (no, not just one) low varieties of the Arabic language ... the mother tongue which is learned naturally from birth. The low variety differs from one Arab country to another, and even from one region to another within the same Arab country.

I'll just briefly mention another Arabic variety which falls somewhere between the high and the low varieties, commonly referred to as *Educated Spoken Arabic* (ESA) ... something that highly educated people, like university teachers, would use with each other ... and is still considered a *high* variety. ESA uses some aspects of low Arabic and some aspects of high Arabic.

And so there exists this vast continuum of high and low Arabic varieties all being referred to as *Arabic*. Yikes! Let me put all this into a simple (but far from complete) chart for you.

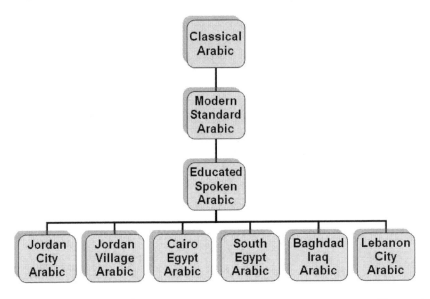

The above chart takes you from the highest Arabic variety (Classical Arabic) down a vertical continuum to the lowest Arabic varieties, of which I've only listed a representative few.

The low varieties form a horizontal continuum with varying degrees of differences. The more geographically close the dialects are, the closer they are to each other in form and comprehension. And so, of course, the opposite is also true ... namely, the more geographically distant the dialects are, the more different they will be.

So when someone from the Middle East or North Africa tells you that they speak *Arabic*, they're making a reference to their particular variety of low Arabic which may vary quite a bit from another variety of low Arabic. In fact, sometimes the difference between two varieties of low Arabic can be so great that when speakers of those two varieties happen to meet and try to *speak Arabic* together, they really can't understand each other very well at all. That would definitely be the case between a speaker of any variety of Moroccan Arabic attempting to communicate with a speaker of any variety of Jordanian Arabic. In that type of situation what they would do is move up (or at least attempt to move up) a language level and incorporate some of the high Modern Standard Arabic language ... that is, of course, if they are educated enough to do so.

As a result of my research paper, I decided some more investigation into Arabic diglossia would be a worthwhile project, something I could use to write my Master's thesis.

So I went straight to North Yemen to do research, right? Wrong! The truth is, I had no thoughts at all about going to North Yemen until a much later date. Initially, I just wanted to head somewhere to learn *Arabic*, and decided studying Modern Standard Arabic at the University of Jordan in the Hashemite Kingdom of Jordan would be a good place to do just that. At the same time, I would learn the Jordanian city low Arabic variety on my own by interacting with people on the street.

It turned out to be quite a challenge. I moved from a theoretical knowledge about diglossia, to getting hit right between the eyes with the reality of it.

My goal was to learn one (emphasis on *one*) low Arabic variety ... namely, the Jordanian city dialect (dialect = low variety). But what I hadn't planned for was the fact that people from other dialect areas were living and working within the dialect area where I was living and learning. The result was that I was never in a *pure* Jordanian city dialect situation. I found myself having to interact with Jordanians who spoke numerous countryside dialects. Then there were the hundreds of thousands of Egyptians who worked in Jordan, and they spoke a whole different set of dialects again!

So, in reality, I was trying to sort out and learn numerous Arabic varieties all at the same time ... trying hard (and it was hard) to keep them all sorted in my mind.

So, to summarize, there is no such thing as *one Arabic language* ... but rather there are literally hundreds of varieties of *Arabic*.

Well, thankfully I only had to deal with a few of the hundreds of varieties. But those *few* made my first six months of language learning in Jordan a linguist's nightmare! And yet, as the days, weeks, months and years rolled by, somehow it all slowly (emphasis on *slowly*) got sorted out in my head, and amazingly I started to get better and better at speaking and reading and writing in *Arabic* ... not fluently, but definitely satisfactorily.

And then I decided to carry out research in North Yemen. So, of course, when I arrived there, I had to start dealing with a whole new set of low Arabic varieties, all of them very different from what I had gotten accustomed to in Jordan ... another real brain stretcher! Thankfully enough similarities existed to allow me to get across things I needed to say ... well, most of the time.

Am I boring you? Or have I whet your appetite, and now you're just dying to know more about my actual research ... like what I actually did? Well, you can read all about it in my MA thesis entitled *Communication Among Arabic Varieties: Comprehension Testing in the Yemen Arab Republic* (1988). But in case you don't have the time ... or, more realistically, aren't able to find a copy of my thesis (it was never a best seller by the way, so you won't find it in your local bookstore or library ... but it is now available on my website, petertwele.com), I'll tell you very briefly what it was all about in Appendix 2 ... that is, if you're interested. And if you are, then go ahead and turn the page.

Appendix 2

The Test

North Yemen had a linguistic problem in 1987. The issue was that Yemenis had to learn to handle, what I refer to as, *imposed varieties* of Arabic on a daily basis. I use the word *imposed* because none of the varieties I'll be discussing were the mother tongue of any Yemenis.

First of all, North Yemen deals with the issue of diglossia (as explained in appendix 1), just like the rest of the Arabic speaking world. So that means Modern Standard Arabic (MSA), the high variety, is sanctioned for education, religious purposes, and most formal situations. Back in the 1980's a large portion of the population was uneducated, and any Yemeni who wanted to get an education needed to learn MSA.

Secondly, at the time, low varieties of Egyptian Arabic were being used throughout the education system in North Yemen. Many Egyptian teachers were employed because of a lack of trained Yemenis to fill the need for teachers. The Egyptian teachers were supposed to be using MSA as they taught the Yemeni students, but the fact was they often mixed in far too much of their own low varieties of Arabic when teaching (I can say that based on personal observation).

North Yemen also hired teachers from other Arabic-speaking countries ... Sudanese, Syrians, Jordanians, Palestinians, etc. So for Yemenis to further themselves in education they had to learn to adapt to the use of MSA. In addition, many had to learn to understand another low variety if their teacher happened to be a non-Yemeni.

I believe communication in the classroom was hindered by the immediate use of MSA, and it would be better for students to start their education with the use of the local low variety, and then slowly transition into the use of MSA. I also believe effective communication was even further hindered by the use of other low Arabic varieties (like Egyptian) in the education system.

The purpose of my study was to investigate, by the use of testing, how well rural Yemeni Arabic speakers were able to understand the *imposed* Arabic varieties.

I just focused on testing Yemeni comprehension of three of the imposed varieties ... (1) Modern Standard Arabic, (2) Cairene Egyptian Arabic, and (3) Palestinian Arabic.

I had recorded a short story from each of those three imposed varieties before my arrival in North Yemen. I had also formulated ten to twelve questions based on the content of each story, and those questions were to be used to test a Yemeni's comprehension of the stories.

As you will have noted while reading about my travels, on my preliminary trip to each of the four chosen areas I was always desperate to find someone who could tell me a local story and also someone to translate some other material for me.

Well the *other material* consisted of the questions based on the content of each of the three above mentioned foreign stories. Those questions needed to be translated into each of the four Yemeni dialects, and then recorded. During my second trip when I did the comprehension testing, those questions were played to each person being tested, and since they were always in the local dialect, they were easily understood.

As for the purpose of the local story, it was used to produce a *hometown test*. The hometown test was the first story that each subject listened to. It was nothing more than a training tool I used to teach each person how the testing worked based on a story they were guaranteed to understand 100%. It gave each subject the opportunity to take a test without the added obstacle of dialect differences to overcome.

After recording an adequate story, I then transcribed it while playing back the tape section by section. At the same time I inquired about any grammatical structures or lexical items I didn't understand.

Next, I developed questions based on the hometown story and recorded those questions in that local dialect as well. So in the end I had four tests for each dialect area.

So the first trip to each area was to collect stories and get the questions translated, while the second trip was to conduct comprehension testing. And that's when Sian joined me so she could administer the tests with Yemeni women while I tested the men.

Each test contained a story in its entirety which was played to the subject without interruption. That allowed the subject to become acquainted with the story. The tape was then stopped and the subject was told that the entire text would be played a second time through, section by section, with questions inserted. At the end of each question the recorder was stopped allowing the subject time to answer. The response was ticked off on a sheet of paper as correct or incorrect, and then the text continued. With the inserted questions, the subject only had to concentrate on one small section at a time, namely, the statement before the question which contained the word or phrase that directly answered the question. This way a subject was not tested on his or her memory, but rather on comprehension. The questions were placed where natural breaks occurred in the text (as nearly as possible) to minimize the disruption of the text. Questions were evenly dispersed throughout the body of the text in order to avoid a cluster around one portion of the text.

Headphones were used during the testing, which kept down distractions and prevented bystanders (potential subjects) from hearing the text and questions.

What follows is the Cairene text, translated into English, with brackets {} where the ten questions were inserted. The actual questions follow the text.

> One day my uncle brought a groom to my sister from Jordan {1}. Of course, the father agreed since the groom made clear that it was not going to cost the family anything except the marriage {2}. We requested that we see our sister once every year and the man agreed {3}. But after he left, five years passed and her first trip was in the fifth year {4}. During those five years we saw strange things from this man. Almost every year he sent a telegram from Jordan, "Come get your girl" {5}. There were always conflicts between them because of their customs in Jordan where all of them live in one house; every brother, he and his wife, lives on his own floor, though they always gather on the ground floor with the mother, and there they eat breakfast, lunch and supper {6}.
>
> The man had two old, unmarried sisters who were always jealous of my sister {7}. They always made problems and conflicts for her. And, of course, the man worked from eight in the morning until five in the evening, and she stayed in the house where there were always conflicts. As soon as he arrived they said, "The girl did so-and-so"; awful things which she really didn't do. He was disinterested about the conflicts between them. And, of course, my sister was always mad at him, and once she left the house walking because he was hitting her {8}.

Every year he sent us a telegram, "Come get her," and my mother went {9}. Afterwards things were better and they said they would not quarrel again, and then she returned. We lived in this situation about nine years until his mother died. After that, life improved in the house {10}. The mother and sisters were the cause of the conflicts. After his mother died the man stayed in his apartment and he received his food there, and they never gathered in the mother's apartment again.

1. What did his uncle bring from Jordan?
2. Why did the father agree with the marriage?
3. What did the family request from the groom?
4. How many years passed before the girl returned to visit her family?
5. What did the telegraph say which the man sent every year from Jordan?
6. Where did the man and his brothers and their wives and his sisters eat?
7. How did the two sisters feel toward the girl?
8. Why did the girl leave the house?
9. Who traveled from Egypt to Jordan when they received the telegraph?
10. What happened in the house after the man's mother died?
11. Where did the man stay and eat after his mother died?

Appendix 3

To whom it may concern

During my time in North Yemen *To whom it may concern* became a very important phrase for me. It was my *To whom it may concern* official government approved document (copy shown here)[43] issued to me, with

the all important official rubber stamps, that allowed me the freedom to move around in North Yemen, nearly unrestricted ... and this in a country which, at the time, put very heavy restrictions on any foreigner movement within its borders. I was only able to get to the remote parts

---

[43] Certain numbers have been purposefully whited out.

of the country with the use of my *To whom it may concern* letter. Translated, here's what the document says ...

> To whom it may concern:
> The researcher / Peter Twele
> Citizenship / Canadian
> Carrying the passport number: ********
> One of the researchers registered under the supervision of the center [YCRS][44] and who carries out studies comparing between dialects in a few Arab countries (Jordan – Morocco[45] – Egypt – Yemen).
> Therefore the center [YCRS] requests facilitation of his important work in the research and [requests] the offering of necessary support in adherence to the sponsorship system in the Yemen Arab Republic.
> [signed] Yemen Centre for Research and Studies

Without that document, I would never have had the adventures I've told you about in this book. So I thought it important to inform you about how I managed to qualify for such a letter.

Back in the 1980's quite a few expatriates were working in North Yemen. As you will have noted, there were Egyptian teachers galore, as well as teachers from a number of other countries ... many of whom I ran into in the villages I visited. Many others came from various countries in the West and in the East to work at a variety of other jobs as well. Then there were the tourists ... although North Yemen was nowhere near as popular as other touristy spots in the Middle East. And one other very important (and not uncommon) expatriate category was researchers ... the category I fell under. The government handled each expatriate category in a special way.

When I did my two week long exploratory trip, someone told me about the American Institute for Yemeni Studies (AIYS) and that they backed researchers. So I went to the AIYS office and met with Paul, the Resident Director at the time. He explained that to do research in North Yemen I would have to work through the Yemen Centre for Research and Studies (YCRS). I would need to start the application process by writing a research proposal which I would present to AIYS. Then AIYS would represent me and present my proposal to YCRS. Next, YCRS

---

[44] Bracketed materials are mine. YCRS is explained below.
[45] I'm not sure how they came up with Morocco.

would present my application to the department of North Yemen Security and wait for their response. Whew! I was told it would take about two months before YCRS would get a response from Security.

So I went ahead and made my initial application. In the meantime Jeff took over as the Resident Director of AIYS, and one day he wrote me a letter. The first sentence was rather discouraging ... it read, "There was an entirely unanticipated problem with your proposal."

"So that's the end of my research in Yemen," I thought to myself. "Should I even bother reading on?" Of course I did. I was curious to know why they were rejecting me ... okay, not rejecting *me*, but rather rejecting my research proposal.

So I started from the beginning of the letter, and this time read it right through to the end ...

> "There was an entirely unanticipated problem with your proposal. The na'ib ra'is [*representative of the director*] of the Yemen Centre [*YCRS*] was at first inclined to reject it, on the grounds that there already are three linguists doing research on dialects in Yemen; there apparently is, though we had not known it, a rule that only three projects may be approved on a particular topic. However, he was at last convinced that your proposed project was substantially different from studies on phonology, and that, moreover, your findings might contribute to future literacy programs in Yemen."

What a relief! And not only was my proposal accepted, but YCRS thought my research may even prove useful to the country's education system! Whether or not it actually did make a difference, I have no idea. Probably not. It most likely just ended up on a shelf somewhere.

The necessary papers were eventually sent to me in Jordan, which I presented to the North Yemen embassy. And soon my entry visa was in my hands.

But the entry visa merely allowed me to enter the country. Once I was in the country I still had to apply for and obtain a residence visa in order to remain in North Yemen. That involved getting an official paper from YCRS and then taking the paper to the building where they took care of visas for foreigners. I eventually obtained a six-month residence visa ... of course, only after running around to a number of different offices.

Okay, so far I was relating to AIYS and YCRS. But in addition, YCRS assigned me to a supervisor at the University of Sana'a. I reported to him as my research progressed. He, in turn, reported about my research to YCRS ... essentially just verifying that I was accomplishing my stated goals. My reports for him were rather short and routine. He was helpful but far too busy to really get involved much.

As I already said, just because someone managed to gain entry into the country didn't give him free access to all parts of the country. On the contrary, foreigners were very restricted in their movements. As a tourist, you needed an official permission paper from the General Tourism Corporation located at Tahrir square (translated, *Liberation Square*) just to be able to set foot outside of Sana'a itself. By the way, *Liberation Square* was the main square in Sana'a, the main site of the Yemen Arab Spring protests.

I received such a tourist permission paper on my exploratory trip. You walk in, you tell the man in charge where in Yemen you want to go, he writes down those specific places (unless they happen to be restricted areas, then they're off limits), he puts the official rubber stamp on the paper, and you're all set to go and see some rather impressive sites in North Yemen. And as you must have gathered from chapter 2 (*City of Wonders*), just a walk through certain parts of Sana'a itself can provide you with some amazing sites to look over.

Anyway, specific areas in the country were designated as *tourist areas*, and usually there was no problem getting permission to go to those places. But some areas were completely off limits to foreigners unless special written permission was acquired. If you ended up on your way to one of those off-limits areas you'd be turned away ... as I was once when I tried to visit a port in the coastal city of Hodeidah on my exploratory trip six months earlier.

As I understood it, tourists were limited to where they could go for their own protection, since in many parts of North Yemen the government did not have full control. They didn't want tourists getting themselves into trouble.

In recent years you may have heard about tourists who had been taken captive by some tribe. The tribal leaders would use them as pawns to try and force some issue or complaint they had with the government. Typically everything gets resolved without force being used or the foreigners being hurt ... let's see, I think I'm starting to ramble ...

As noted above, it was YCRS that wrote the *to whom it may concern* document for me, allowing me the freedom to travel to the remote areas where I wanted to concentrate my research. I made dozens of copies of this paper so I could present a copy to the guards I'd encounter at military checkpoints, and to any officials I happened to run into in the regions where I travelled.

"Why make dozens of copies of the *to whom it may concern* paper," you ask? Well, as I traveled around the country, I was guaranteed to run into military checkpoints along the way. Military checkpoints were everywhere ... located on all main roads going in and out of the capital, and at the entrance to all large towns. Checkpoints were also often found along the roads in between. All vehicles were stopped and checked. The soldier would look over all the passengers, and if there was a foreigner in the vehicle, then the soldier would ask for a copy of their travel permission paper. A typical scenario went like this ...

"Who's the foreigner in your car?" the soldier asks the driver.

(Now how could they tell I was a foreigner? Must have been my accent that gave me away.)

"He's from Canada," the driver responds ... at which point I'm sure the soldier is picturing a bottle of Canada Dry cola.

The driver usually would have asked me for a copy of the permission paper just before getting to the checkpoint.

"Let's see his paper," the guard demands.

The driver hands him the paper.

The guard looks at it. Often the guards were illiterate, and so what they were looking for was the photo of the foreigner on the paper as well as the official looking government rubber stamp of approval (see the scan of my paper above), and then they'd be satisfied.

I was told by other expats that it was safer just to hand the soldier a copy of the travel paper and not say a thing to him, and then he usually wouldn't ask any questions. He wouldn't expect the foreigner to be able to speak or understand Arabic anyway, and so they would feel awkward trying to interact with them.

"Okay, go ahead," the guard says to the driver, with another quick glance at me.

And off we went, leaving the paper with the soldier. Typically the soldier would just keep the paper. So that's why any official document used for getting around the country needed to be photocopied before leaving Sana'a.

I had heard of other travelers who hadn't made copies of their travel papers and it made for an argument at every checkpoint along the way to try and get their paper back from the guard. Obviously they would need it at the next checkpoint. No, there were no photocopiers at the checkpoints ... and anyways, there was no electricity!

On the road from Sana'a to Sa'da in the north there were at least three checkpoints, so I always carried between 15 to 20 copies on any given trip. The soldiers and officials never asked to see my passport, and I was warned not even to offer it to them, just in case they decided to hang on to it.

It was my *To whom it may concern* official document that allowed me the freedom to travel wherever I needed to go ... well, kind of.

About The Author

Peter Twele (MA in Linguistics) first moved to the Middle East in 1984, where he resided and traveled extensively for over 11 years. After studying Arabic for a number of years, he then worked and did research through a number of institutions in the Middle East, including the Phonetics Research Center at the University of Jordan, the American Center of Oriental Research, the American Institute for Yemeni Studies, and the Yemen Centre for Research and Studies. He has also taught in the Linguistics programs at both Trinity Western University in Langley, BC, and at the University of Texas in Arlington. To this day he continues with his desire to build bridges of understanding between the West and the Middle East ... mostly by trying to help Westerners understand and appreciate Middle East cultures. Visit his website at petertwele.com.

Made in the USA
San Bernardino, CA
13 April 2016